Strategy for creation

Strategy for creation

T Murakami and T Nishiwaki et al
Nomura Research Institute

WOODHEAD PUBLISHING LIMITED

Cambridge, England

Published by Woodhead Publishing Ltd,
Abington Hall, Abington, Cambridge, CB1 6AH, England

First published 1991
© Woodhead Publishing Ltd

British Library Cataloguing in Publication Data
A catalogue record for this book is available from the British Library

ISBN 1 85573 061 8

Translated by James Koetting, designed by Andrew Jones (text) and
Chris Feely (cover), typeset by BookEns Ltd, Baldock, Herts and printed
by Billings, Worcester.

Contents

Foreword   vii
Preface   ix
Introduction   xi

I   The dawn of the age of creation   1

1   *Creation intensification in companies - progression from the ages of industry and information*   *3*

Next-generation industrial structure and creative corporate activities   3
Internationalization and creation intensification   16
Mature industrialization, information intensification and implications for creation intensification   22
Changing value systems and creation intensification   25

2   *Creation intensification in society - images of the creation society*   *30*

Images of the creation society   30
The rise of creation industry   34

3   *Corporate response to the age of creation - strategy for creation*   *41*

The dawning of the age of creation and creative corporate activities   41
The need for strategy for creation   45

II Process of creation   47

4 *Process of creation in research and development*   49

Creativity in research and devcelopment 49
Case study of research and development 56
Method of and management for creation in research and development 61

5 *Process of creation in product development*   65

Creativity in product development 65
Case study of product development 69
Method of and management for creation in product development 88

6 *Process of creation in system development*   91

Creativity in system development 91
Case study of system development 96
Method of and management for creation in system development 105

7 *Process of creation in business development*   110

Creativity in business development 110
Case study in business development 113
Method of and management for creation in business development 127

III Strategy for creation   129

8 *Method of creation*   131

Method progression 131
Method of creation and application levels 135
Scheme of conception support system 137

9 *Management for creation*   147

Evolution of management 147
Management for creation 152
Comparison of leading Japanese and US companies 185
Toward 'creagement' 194

Appendix 197
Index 199

Foreword
By Robert Heller

In the post-war period the Japanese have shown a remarkable ability to succeed in one phase of economic development while already planning for the next phase. That's what strategy means; what the Japanese economy at large has achieved (moving the emphasis, for example, from shipbuilding and steel to motor vehicles and consumer electronics and then to financial products and advanced electronics). This has by definition been mirrored at the level of the firm.

The best Japanese companies have not only adapted to the new built-in obsolescence, which results from the rapid global evolution of technology and market development, but have helped create the latter processes by their swift exploitation of the new. Typically, they are no longer satisfied with the management approach that has brought more than four decades of unmatched success. While still challenging the US strongly for leadership in the information age, Japan is seeking to set the pace in a coming era when creativity may well be the decisive force in world markets.

To put the issue in practical terms, Japanese manufacturing strategy has been founded on low cost and high quality. As the West comes much nearer to the best standards on both counts, competitive edge will depend increasingly upon external and internal creativity: internal, to find radically new means of managing, making and serving: external, to find new products and processes to win customer preference. As this study shows, this new, intense creative effort must have profound results for management at all levels.

New answers must be found to the basic questions of how people are organized, how they are rewarded and how they work together. The general thrust of the answers is already plain. People will work more in free-standing but networked groups and less inside formal, fixed hierarchies: rewards will be linked less to seniority and budgeted financial performance and more to strategic and innovative contributions that achieve longer-term competitive gains. The networks of groups of individuals will be complemented by computerized information networks that allow rapid exchange of data and ideas and their successful translation into effective, well-implemented, consensus-driven plans.

In real life, such perfect patterns are seldom achieved. But already, in the real world, people are working more in groups, rewards are flowing more to creators, networks are burgeoning and creativity is being managed positively and successfully. One of the major end-century realizations is that creation is as susceptible to organized thought as any other work: the paradox being that managing creativity requires creative management, 'creagement', coined by the authors.

The concept is an extremely elegant one. The study has identified four aspects of 'creagement', each opened by four keys. Each of the resulting sixteen categories of 'management know-how' demands careful study. However it is the dynamic thrust of the study which Japan's competitors will have to understand fully and the deep cultural roots from which it has originated. Even the word 'creation' in Japanese breaks down into two parts meaning 'first make'. Creative management is about being first, not necessarily into the market of the technology, but into its most successful manifestation.

The study is full of similar insights: the acronym FINDS for the 'development of what is truly needed', for example, standing for 'fulfilment, intelligence, nourishment, discovery and sensibility'. This particular section, on product development, is central to the age of creativity and strongly illustrates its meaning with case histories like those of Sony's lightweight Handycam video camera and Asahi Super Dry beer. The cases show in the 'hard' terms of development, manufacture and marketing how the 'soft' disciplines of creativity achieve vital commercial breakthroughs.

The greatest challenge, though, is to break through in the arena of management itself, creating new systems, new approaches to business development and new methods of creation, realizing that it is management that will achieve the same effect as the great new product, the one that utterly changes a market. In all these areas, the cases present a detailed study of the new initiatives that are already opening up new horizons. Much of this 'creagement' process springs from the latest knowledge of how the human brain works, both in isolation and in interaction: that knowledge is a most powerful tool.

Will it be used most effectively by the West or the East? The result is a foregone conclusion if only the latter recognizes the coming phase of economic development and acts accordingly. This study offers Western managers a unique insight into the Japanese strategic mind as the new era unfolds, an age that will be created by managers who have mastered the highly manageable business of creativity itself.

Preface

While the tone of the Japanese economy is expected to remain favourable for the time being, the long-term outlook is not entirely devoid of factors of instability. Causes for concern include the worsening of global environmental problems, the prospect of a new energy crisis, exacerbated economic friction, and political instability in certain developing countries. And with the advent of the 21st century, Japan's society will begin to age at an unprecedented rate as the share of its total membership occupied by youth shrinks dramatically.

The prosperity currently enjoyed by Japan is the culmination of 46 years of postwar economic achievement. As the beneficiaries of this achievement, we must not be content to rest on our laurels, basking in this prosperity. Instead, we must find a way to use it to improve the international economic framework encompassing Japan and other countries, which is now under increasing strain, and to lay the foundation for its continuation into the 21st century.

With an awareness of this need, Nomura Research Institute, (NRI) formed a unit known as the Megatheme Projection Committee (chairman: Teruyasu Murakami, leader: Takashi Nishiwaki) for comprehensive research in this direction. A full list of members of the committee can be found in the appendix. The studies were conducted by a project team composed of members representing each department of research and consulting division. NRI's systems-related divisions and its offices in foreign countries also participated in this study.

The research identified 'strategy for creation' as the most important megatheme for Japanese companies in preparation for the 'age of creation' anticipated on the heels of the 'age of information'. Conventionally, creativity has been regarded by companies as a concern primarily in research and development, and as not amenable to management. The current project, however, rests on the assumption that corporate creativity is manageable, and pursues both the type of management needed to create an atmosphere conducive to creativity and the advisable method of creation in companies.

We are convinced that the findings will be of great interest for managers considering a shift from 'efficiency' to 'creation' as the bottom line of management of strategy, organizations, personnel, and information, as well as for all personnel involved in creative work such as business planning, research and development, and development of products, systems, and business. We hope to articulate this theme further in the future, and welcome your comments and suggestions.

NRI is deeply indebted to the members of the Japanese and US companies who co-operated with the interviews and questionnaire surveys implemented during the course of this research.

Seiji Oba
Executive Director, Research and Consulting Division
Nomura Research Institute

Introduction

Times are changing more rapidly than ever before. Companies are both products of their times and able to change the times through innovation. Corporate innovation is a function of strategy and management. Only companies with a strategy and management adapted to the times will be able to survive, grow, and advance. Like all living beings, companies inhabit a world of 'survival of the fittest'.

The transition from hunting and gathering to agricultural cultivation took place around 3000 BC. In the ensuing 'age of agriculture', management pursued the optimal 'co-work merit', i.e. optimal systems of co-work in step with seasonal or other natural changes.

The industrial revolution in the late 18th century ushered in a new 'age of industry', where great value was attached to material output. Management pursued the optimal 'scale merit', i.e. economy of scale, through divisions of labour and schemes of specialization and standardization on massive scales entailing close co-ordination of hundreds or even thousands of workers.

In the late 20th century, the invention of the computer and advances in communications are spawning a new age stressing the value of information – the 'age of information'. Groups endeavour to broaden the scope of their activities by expanding their range of customers, technologies, or territory through intensified collection, processing, and editing of information. Management pursues the optimal 'scope merit' through clarification and delegation of group responsibility and authority.

It is thought that the 21st century will see the dawn of a new age, the 'age of creation', in which the top priority will be creation of new value. Today, consumer needs are becoming increasingly sophisticated, individualized, and diverse. These constantly shifting needs are generating a corresponding need for management capable of creating new value to accommodate them. At the same time, ideas of what constitutes a good job are also undergoing great change. More and more, people are looking for employment in which they can feel a sense of self-fulfilment and the joy accompanying creation.

Major changes are also on the horizon on the corporate level. To date, Japanese companies have made inroads into the world market by improving technologies, products, systems and business imported from the West and introducing these improved versions with the backing of superior productivity and quality control. For the future, however, Japanese companies will themselves have to generate new concepts in technologies, products, systems, and business as assets to be shared with the international community in order to contribute to the advancement of that community in the economic, social, and cultural spheres. This implies the need for evolution into a 'creation society', a society in which the members are able to exercise their creative potential to the fullest.

With the approach of the 21st century, all companies, and particularly those in Japan, must erect systems of management in which the central concern is not 'the operation' or 'information', but 'creation'.

This book presents the results of a project of research concerning the advisable method of and management for creation in companies. The research was based on a case study of Japanese and US companies and a questionnaire survey with executives in charge of business planning at companies in both countries concerning the process of creation in research and development and development of products, systems, and business. In addition and, not directly linked to the main body of text, this book also presents various research work related to aspects of creativity from such wide ranging and diverse fields as psychology, cybernetics and cerebral physiology, (distinguishable in the text with an open book symbol).

On the subject of the method of creation, four points are to be made. First, a distinction should be drawn between individual, group and corporate creation. Individual creation refers to the activity of an individual working alone. The addition of the element of synergy, i.e. the joint activity of individuals, results in group creation. And the linkage of group creation to the actual corporate technologies, products, systems and business is what is meant by corporate creation. Of these three, group and corporate creation are regarded as manageable, and should be made subjects of management.

Second, the process of creation can be divided into four stages: 'hypothesis construction', 'dissimilation', 'concept creation', and 'chain of empathy'. While each of these four stages requires corresponding acts of human intellect, particularly important are ideation and conception.

Third is the IGKP model. Group creation takes place in an atmosphere of organizational and individual idea generators (IG), idea killers (IK), and idea promoters (IP). It is imperative to reinforce the growth of IGs and IPs and to retard that of IKs in order to prepare an environment in which IGs are in a position of strength relative to IKs.

The fourth concerns the 'conceptor' (conception support system). This system would be designed to support those intellectual acts that spark creation, i.e. ideation and conception. The report profiles the conceptor and its basic functions while stressing the need for its further research and development.

Adaption to the age of creation calls for management to re-orient around creation companies that have been oriented around industrialization or information.

We call this kind of management 'creagement'. 'Creagement' pursues the optimal 'network merit', i.e. the stimulation of the individual's motivation to realize his or her fullest creative potential and the induction of empathy toward the creative output on the organizational level. It is management of strategy, organizations, personnel and information that is geared for creation.

The report also proposes four keys for creagement for the four aspects of management (strategy, organization, personnel and information): 'creativisionary strategy', 'organization conducive to individual creation', 'creation-rewarding personnel management' and 'creation-oriented information management'. Since each of the four stages of creation apply in each of these four aspects, there is a total of 16 categories of management know-how in creagement.

The wellspring of creativisionary strategy is a vision that will motivate all employees to actualize their potential fully in order to attain it. Its four categories of know-how are 'practical vision of creation intensification', 'managerial shake-up design', 'trial orientation' and 'empathy integration'.

The organization conducive to individual creation links individual creators in loose-knit networks. Its four categories of know-how are 'hypothesis-generating organization', 'dissent-inducing organization', 'toleration of stand-outs' and 'empathy interface'.

Creation-rewarding personnel management accords high ratings and generous treatment to creators. Its four categories of know-how are 'enthusiasm-oriented management', 'portfolio personnel management', 'optimal IGKP arrangement', and 'empathetic personnel exchange'.

Creation-oriented information management encourages the clash and interplay of hypotheses and counterhypotheses that gives rise to creation. Its four categories of know-how are 'sharing of customer information', 'stress on free discussion', 'hypothesis refinement' and 'empathetic communication'.

The 1990s may be viewed as a period of transition to the creation society. For advancement in the 1990s and assurance of prosperity in the next century, companies will have to put creagement into practice by applying these tools – the method of creation and this body of management know-how for creation.

I

The dawn of the age of creation

1

Creation intensification in companies - progression from the ages of industry and information

Next-generation industrial structure and creative corporate activities

In Japan, the expansion of business around a booming domestic demand has led companies to adopt an aggressive stance in management supported by favourable performances in their main lines. At the same time, the same companies are taking vigorous action aimed at the creation of new business in preparation for the new age.

In November 1989, NRI conducted a questionnaire entitled 'Strategy for Creation' with executives in charge of business planning at the top 1,000 Japanese companies (in terms of corporate income). Properly completed questionnaires were retrieved from 217 of these companies. The questionnaire was designed to obtain an image of the structure of Japanese industry in the coming age. It contained a list of 100 next-generation fields of industry in ten segments, i.e. resources, materials, devices and components, machinery, equipment, production facilities, software, personal durable consumer goods, industrial durable consumer goods and services. The respondents were asked to indicate which of these fields their respective companies will have entered by the year 2010. 'Entry' referred to either production and sales of goods or supply of related services, as opposed to activities at the phase of research and development (R&D) or formulation of business concepts.

The food, steel and construction industries

The findings provided a general image of the new fields that are the targets of entry from 21 existing industries. A 21 × 100 matrix of the results is presented in Table 1.I.

Table 1.I Image of the next-generation industrial structure

	Resources						Materials											Devices and components							
	Manganese nodules	Cobalt-rich crust	Rare earth	Microbes	Animal/plant tissue	Seeds	Fine ceramics	New glass	New carbon	New metal materials	Materials using aerospace metals	Composite ceramic materials	Composite metal materials	Composite resin materials	Super engineering plastics	Superconductive materials	Implant-safe materials	Biochips	Optoelectronic devices	Josephson devices	Super lattice devices	2D circuit devices	Molecular devices	Micro-mechanical devices	Super LSI recording media
1 Food and marine products				●		▷						▷		◁	▷		◁		▷					▷	
2 Textiles				▷	▷									○			◁		◁						
3 Paper and pulp				◁	◁	◁	◁							○	◁		◁		▷					◁	
4 Chemicals			●	▷	●		◁		●	●	●	▷	●			●							●		●
5 Pharmaceuticals																	●								

6 Mining and oil			Δ	○	Δ	○			Δ					Δ	Δ		Δ	Δ							
7 Glass and cement							○	○	Δ			○				Δ			Δ						Δ
8 Steel			▽				Δ			Δ	Δ	▽	○			Δ	▽								
9 Non-ferrous metals										▽	▽		Δ	▽		Δ			Δ			▽		▽	
10 General machinery										▽															
11 Electrical machinery							▽					▽				▽		▽	Δ	●		●	●	Δ	▽
12 Transportation machinery							●					▽							▽						
13 Other manufacturing							▽	●				▽	▽	▽											
14 Construction																									
15 Electricity and gas									●							●									
16 Distribution																									
17 Financing																									
18 Real estate						Δ																			
19 Transportation																									
20 Information and communications																									
21 Other services																									
Share of total number of respondents occupied by those indicating entry	1	1	4	9	6	7	17	6	7	8	6	16	9	16	7	10	12	6	13	3	3	4	3	10	7

Note: Based on the responses to the question, 'Which of the new fields do you think your company will have entered by the year 2010 ('entry' meaning production and sales of goods or supply of services)?'
Share of total number of respondents occupied by those indicating entry: ○ 70% Δ 50–69% ▽ 30–49% ● 20–29%
Source) NRI questionnaire 'Strategy for Creation'. November 1989

Table 1.1 cont'd

Category	Technology	1 Food and marine products	2 Textiles	3 Paper and pulp	4 Chemicals
Machinery	Computer integrated manufacturing (CIM)	▷	◁		
	Point of sale manufacturing	▷	◁		●
	Robots for work under extreme conditions				
	Superconductive motors				●
	Atomic/molecular ion beam machine tools	▷			
	Atomic/molecular configuration machine tools				
Equipment	Equipment applying bioreactors	▷	▷	◁	○
	Equipment applying gene recombination	▷	▷		◁
	Equipment applying tissue culture	◁	◁	○	◁
	Equipment applying cell fusion	▷	◁		▷
	Super separation	▷			●
	Superconduction generators				
	Superconduction power storage systems		◁		
	Nuclear fusion generators				
Production facilities	Production in space				
	Undersea production				
	Marine ranching				
	Underground production				
	Unmanned botanical factories	●	◁		▷
Software	Expert systems	▷			
	AI				●
	Neural networks				
	Fuzzy logic				●
	Fractal systems				
	Neurocomputers				
	Biocomputers			◁	
	Sensibility-type computers				
	Optocomputers	▷	◁		

5	Pharmaceuticals
6	Mining and oil
7	Glass and cement
8	Steel
9	Non-ferrous metals
10	General machinery
11	Electrical machinery
12	Transportation machinery
13	Other manufacturing
14	Construction
15	Electricity and gas
16	Distribution
17	Financing
18	Real estate
19	Transportation
20	Information and communications
21	Other services

Share of total number of respondents occupied by those indicating entry:

6, 3, 3, 4, 2, 13, 5, 19, 14, 13, 7, 8, 3, 5, 1, 5, 5, 4, 13, 18, 12, 18, 2, 4, 8, 13, 11, 19

Table 1.1 cont'd

	Personal durable consumer goods														Industrial durable consumer goods											
	Housework robots	Digital VCRs	Home holography	Artificial organs	Home automation systems	Automatic kitchens	Nurse robots	Home diagnostic systems	Home security systems	Intelligent computer aided instruction	Colour motion-video videophones	Machine translation	Central systems for comfortable environments	Relaxation systems	Linear motor cars	Space planes	Hypersonic transport	Commuter air transport	New energy automobiles	Superconductivity-powered ships	Super heat pumps	Prefabricated satellite offices	Development of deep-earth space	Development of floating cities	Development of space stations	Development of undersea cities
1 Food and marine products																										
2 Textiles																										
3 Paper and pulp			△																							
4 Chemicals				△									△													

5 Pharmaceuticals				Δ			●	○																		
6 Mining and oil													○						Δ							
7 Glass and cement																										
8 Steel																										
9 Non-ferrous metals													∇										∇			
10 General machinery	∇						∇																			
11 Electrical machinery	∇	●	●		∇	●		∇	∇	●	∇		∇	●												
12 Transportation machinery																			●							
13 Other manufacturing					∇				∇																	
14 Construction					∇				∇				Δ	●								●	○	○		Δ
15 Electricity and gas	●							●	●	●			Δ				●		●		Δ		Δ			
16 Distribution																										
17 Financing																										
18 Real estate					Δ			Δ	Δ				Δ	Δ								Δ	Δ	Δ		Δ
19 Transportation															∇			∇								
20 Information and communications									Δ		Δ	Δ										Δ				
21 Other services									●																	
Share of total number of respondents occupied by those indicating entry	6	4	4	6	12	4	6	10	14	4	6	3	12	6	6	2	2	5	4	1	4	4	13	11	4	6

Table 1.I cont'd

Services	Design	R&D support/execution	Intellectual property rights services	Acceptance of invention consignments	Product development support/execution	R&D personnel dispatch	Training in specialized fields	Home shopping	Home banking	Information security services	Total physical distribution control services	High-tech maintenance services	Video production	Development of art environments	Engineering	Leasing	M&A services	Venture capital	Financial planning	Consulting	System integration	Share of industry occupied by existing business as of 2010
1 Food and marine products	▷	▷				▷		▷			◁		◁		▷					▷		61
2 Textiles	◁						◁				▷											68
3 Paper and pulp	▷				◁						○										◁	70
4 Chemicals	▷	●	●				●								▷					●		51

5 Pharmaceuticals																				●		46
6 Mining and oil					△										△	△		△		△		70
7 Glass and cement		△													△							50
8 Steel		▽	▽	▽	▽	▽	▽				▽				△	▽						53
9 Non-ferrous metals		▽													▽						▽	57
10 General machinery										▽		▽			▽						▽	47
11 Electrical machinery	●	●	●		▽		▽					▽	●		△	▽				●	▽	46
12 Transportation machinery															●							68
13 Other manufacturing	▽	●			▽						▽				▽	▽						53
14 Construction	●	▽										●			▽	●			●	▽		54
15 Electricity and gas		●						●							△	●				●		63
16 Distribution	▽				▽		▽	△			▽					△				▽		53
17 Financing						●	●		▽	●						▽	△	△	△	△		74
18 Real estate								△		△	△	△				△		△	△			70
19 Transportation						●		△			△				●	▽						71
20 Information and communications			△					○	△	△										△	△	80
21 Other services					●	●		●			▽		●			△	▽	●		△	▽	59
Share of total number of respondents occupied by those indicating entry	17	18	13	4	18	15	17	19	16	12	20	9	8	6	23	30	17	19	23	36	16	

The results for the food industry are shown in Fig. 1.1. As of the year 2010, it is estimated that new fields will form roughly 39% of the food industry. Basically, this industry is anticipated to expand its current borders and to be transformed into a total bioindustry. It is thought that items such as seeds and microbes will join minerals and energy sources on the list of vital resources for next-generation industry. As such, by the year 2010, the food industry is expected to encompass equipment generating new production processes such as bioreactor processes, tissue culture, cell fusion and gene recombination from these bioresources, and include related production facilities such as fully auto-mated botanical factories.

At the same time, it could generate services that make use of its store of accumulated know-how, e.g. total physical distribution control and engineering.

By the year 2010, new fields are expected to account for 4.7% of the total sales in the steel industry. There are three prospective orientations of evolution for the steel industry and its entrants, Fig. 1.2.

Entry by 50–70% of respondents	Entry by 30–50% of respondents	Entry by 20–30% of respondents
Tissue culture	Seeds Bioreactors Gene recombination Cell fusion	Microbes Unmanned botanical factories
	Total physical distribution control services, engineering	

Source: NRI questionnaire 'Strategy for Creation', November 1989

1.1 New fields in the food industry – 2010.

Entry by 50-70% of respondents	Entry by 30-50% of respondents	
Composite metal materials New metal materials Superconductive materials Aerospace metal materials	Composite ceramic materials Implant-safe materials Tissue culture Marine ranching	R&D support/execution Intellectual property rights services Acceptance of invention consignments Product development support/execution R&D personnel dispatch Training in specialized fields
Engineering	Total physical distribution control services, leasing	

Source: NRI questionnaire 'Strategy for Creation', November 1989

1.2 New fields in the steel industry – 2010.

1 Emergence as total materials manufacturers

The steel industry developed in response to needs for a commodity that was the lifeblood of industry as a whole. Entrants pursuing this orientation would transcend the conventional boundaries of the steel industry by supplying all materials needed by next-generation industry, from ceramic composites and superconductive materials to materials for implants and tissue culture.

2 Entry into engineering, total distribution control services and leasing business through diversion of know-how acquired to date, as was envisioned for the food industry

3 Evolution into an industry offering comprehensive support for corporate activities aimed at the creation of new technologies and products

In this orientation, the industry would support research and development and product development as well as operate services in invention consignment and intellectual property rights, and would consequently be included in the overall creation industry as defined later in this book. It is interesting that the steel industry is evolving simultaneously into a comprehensive materials industry and a comprehensive creation industry.

In the past, the steel industry was one of the trunk industries by which the power of a nation was measured. The questionnaire findings suggest that the industry will also attempt to assimilate those fields which will be at the core of the industrial structure during the 'age of creation'.

There are also three prospective orientations for the evolution of the construction industry, Fig. 1.3.

1 Expansion of the frontier of construction

Efforts to make space deep underground, on the sea, or under the seas usable for human production activities or habitation properly fall in the sphere of the construction industry.

Entry by 50–70% of respondents	Entry by 30–50% of respondents	Entry by 20–30% of respondents
Development of deep-earth space, floating cities, undersea cities, underground production, robots for work under extreme conditions	HA systems Home security systems	Relaxation systems Prefabricated satellite offices
	R&D support/execution Engineering Consulting	Design Leasing Financial planning High–tech maintenance

Source: NRI questionnaire 'Strategy for Creation', November 1989

1.3 New fields in the construction industry – 2010.

2 Entry into the interiors of homes and offices

In the case of homes, the subject would be home automation systems and relaxation systems. For offices, a major field would be provision of satellite offices, which are expected to spread rapidly in the coming years, in prefabricated form.

3 Establishment of the design, leasing, maintenance and engineering functions at the heart of the industry's ability to co-ordinate large-scale projects as independent industries in themselves

In this case, the construction industry would evolve into a project co-ordination industry resting on integrated control of these independent industries.

As compared with the manufacturing industries, the service industries generally do not exhibit a strong inclination to develop new types of business. Although new fields are anticipated to account for 31% of the total sales in the manufacturing sector by the year 2000, Fig. 1.4, the corresponding figure for the service sector is only 23%. While belonging to the service sector, the questionnaire indicated that the construction industry together with the distribution industry is hoping to attain a corresponding figure of 30%, on a par with that for the manufacturing sector, and consequently must be termed highly inclined toward the creation of new business.

Next-generation fields

The list of 100 next-generation fields in the questionnaire can be found in Table 1.I and include: 1) fields such as fine ceramics and design, in which specialized firms

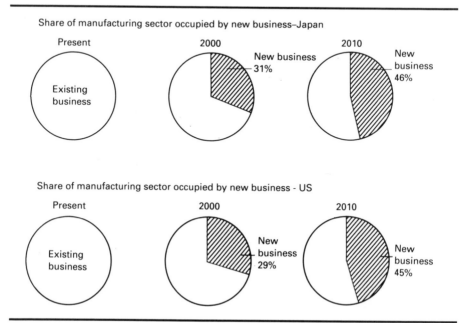

Source: NRI questionnaire 'Strategy for Creation in Japan and the United States', November 1989

1.4 Future composition of the manufacturing sector in Japan and the US.

are already active and which are anticipated to assume increasing importance and to emerge as fully-fledged industries in their own right by the year 2010; 2) fields such as home-use holography, space station development and atomic configuration machine tools, which are still at the stage of research and development (R&D) and in which the journey from the establishment of the technology to commercialization of products will be a long one; and 3) fields such as acceptance of invention consignments and intellectual property rights services, for which virtually all companies currently lack the resources required for commercial business.

The 100 fields are all highly futuristic in nature. Nevertheless, the questionnaire found that, for every field, at least one respondent was interested in achieving entry by the year 2010.

Today, when there is so much discussion of the 'softening' of industry and rise of the sectors of services and information, the manufacturing sector as a whole appears to have receded from the leading edge of change in the industrial structure. The results of the questionnaire do however foreshadow a stream of innovation in the world of manufacturing as well with the approach of the 21st century. The forces or vehicles of this innovation are superconductive materials and implant-safe materials in the segment of materials; biochips, super LSI recording media, and micro-mechanical devices in the segment of devices and components; new machine tools capable of processing on the molecular or even atomic level; new production systems for a leap from flexible manufacturing systems (FMS) to POS manufacturing based on computer integrated manufacturing (CIM) and new processes such as bioreactor processes, cell fusion, super separation, and production in space. This innovation could spawn new durable consumer goods for personal and industrial use that would be as important as automobiles and TVs/VCRs are today and open up whole new markets. The chain reaction set off by such developments could upgrade the overall industrial level and trigger a shift to a next-generation industrial structure exhibiting a new balance on this higher level, Fig. 1.5.

Various companies have already begun approaching the creation of entirely new fields through R&D programmes and efforts to acquire business resources which they now lack.

The process of transition to the next-generation industrial structure will obviously call for a vigorous creation of new business in existing industries. But it will also require the creation of a new identity for the existing industries themselves, as described for the food, steel and construction industries.

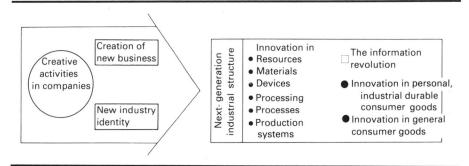

1.5 Corporate creative activities and next-generation industrial structure.

In a sense, this creation of new identities has already begun for a wide range of industries; it can be traced to the surge of restructuring and diversification in industry in the late 1980s. In short, the acceleration of creative activities is underway not only on the level of individual companies but also industrywide.

Internationalization and creation intensification

Early in the postwar period, Japanese industry began to import product concepts and technological 'seeds' in fields that had been established in the West during the early 20th century or immediately after World War II, such as automobiles, TV, refrigerators, synthetic textiles and plastics.

It then built its own industries in these fields through vigorous investment to expand productive capacities and cultivation of a homogeneous, disciplined work force. Backed by high productivity, superior quality control and price competitiveness, the output was then re-injected into the world market. This process eventually led to the outbreak of trade friction with Western countries, Fig. 1.6.

During the 1970s and 1980s, each time Japanese industry confronted an outbreak of trade friction in a given field, it responded by shifting its emphasis to another. As a result, the identity of the mainstay Japanese product field in foreign markets changed in succession from steel to shipping, automobiles and consumer electrical or electronic products. Simultaneously, the scope of friction broadened as Japan's economic relationship with the US and Western Europe matured. Once confined to the sector of trade, it gradually spread to technology and investment as well.

Today, the Japanese economy continues to turn in a favourable performance against the background of major change in the international political framework set in motion by reform in the Soviet Union and Eastern Europe and of restructuring in the global market as exemplified by the coming unification of the EC market and the deepening ties between the US and Canada.

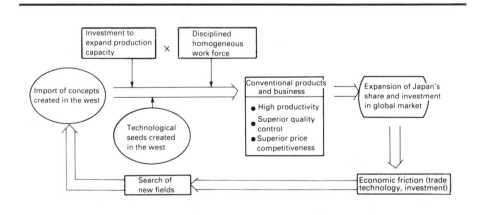

1.6 Cycle of internalization of the Japanese economy.

Having already become one of the world's leading net creditors and having overtaken the US in terms of national income per capita of population, Japan would appear ready to function as the engine for the world economy. Japanese companies imitated Western products and business concepts at such a breakneck pace that it is now becoming difficult for them to find additional concepts in the West to imitate. They are now finding themselves on the threshold of an entirely new phase in which they will be called upon to create models for the rest of the world, like the automobiles and TVs created by US and European companies during the first half of the 20th century.

At any rate, it is certain that they will no longer be able to continue in the cycle of generation of a domestic market, expansion of export, and ex post facto response to economic friction that has characterized their behaviour thus far.

What has been raised as a solution to the impasse is a switch from export to domestic demand as the main force behind the Japanese economy. Great success is now being achieved along this line due to the sustained expansion of domestic trade accompanied by increased import of manufactured goods and by an influx of foreign capital. However, progress along this line could also eventually come to an end if it rests solely upon an expansion of the domestic demand around conventional goods. As it is one of prosperity, the present time must be used to achieve a breakthrough that will assure prosperity into the next generation.

The breakthrough required is a fundamental change in the aforementioned cycle of the internationalization of the Japanese economy that will prolong the viability of the 'domestic demand' line. Such change cannot be affected if Japanese companies continue to enter business or product fields after those fields have entered the growth phase. Instead, they will have to create new fields of products and business, playing the leading role in nurturing them into the growth phase, Fig. 1.7.

The implication is that Japanese companies must resolutely invest in the very act of the corporate equivalents of creation, i.e. R&D and the succeeding development of products, systems and business. The kind of labour required will

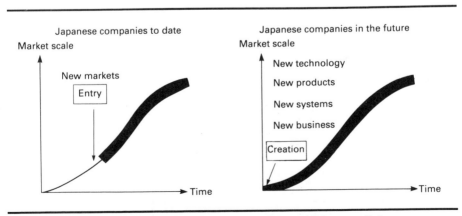

1.7 Japanese corporate entry into new markets; to date and future prediction.

not be the disciplined but homogeneous work force of the past, but a pool of diverse, thoughtful personnel whose energies will be harnessed to create innovative product and business concepts lacking Western parallels as well as the related technological 'seeds' and system concepts. Figure 1.8 shows the cycle of creation intensification.

The pattern would no longer be wholesale import of technology and product concepts established in the West to form the basis of new business, but initiation of the product and business life cycle; the creation and implanting of the underlying concepts. This more circuitous route would in effect prolong the viability of the 'domestic demand' line now taking root.

In working to establish new-concept products and business, Japanese industry would have to retain the strengths it has traditionally derived from its relentless pursuit of efficiency: high productivity, superior quality control and price competitiveness. The emphasis upon creation must not be construed as a de-emphasis of efficiency; levels of efficiency would have to be upgraded.

If successful in this transformation, Japanese companies would generate new fields of demand not present in other advanced industrialized countries or NIES and transplant them to foreign markets. The new concepts and 'seeds' of related technologies and systems would consequently take on the nature of public international assets. At present, in the context of relations between advanced countries and developing countries, such assets generally consist of military hardware, international currency and investment/aid. By contrast, the products of this creation would constitute international assets mainly in the context of relations between countries with high-tech industries and those with conventional industries.The results of such committed research in basic areas of science and technology would prove to be of great importance for the advancement of global industry and society.

New concepts must not only be created, but also used to galvanize industrial activities in other countries. This would entail an active promotion of their transfer to foreign countries. The globalised system of Japanese industry and its international networks of information and communications would serve as the infrastructure of this promotion.

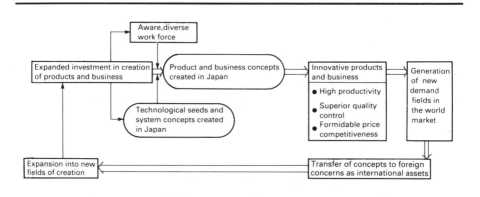

1.8 Cycle of creation intensification.

This new role for Japanese companies is shown with reference to their relationship with Western counterparts in Fig. 1.9. In simple terms, the relationship with the West during the 1980s was one-way on both sides – export of manufactured goods from Japan to the West and of research seeds from the West to Japan. The right side shows the kind of relationship that should be targeted for the 21st century. It is one of mutual exchange in both marketing and manufacturing. It is also one of mutual reciprocity not only on the level of material goods, but also with regard to intellectual products such as research and development results. At the same time, the relationship between Japan and developing countries in the 21st century should resemble that between the West and Japan in the 1980s.

The key to effecting this switch from the cycle of internationalization to one of creation is priority allocation of business resources to the creation of technologies, products, systems and businesses without parallel in the West. This implies a corresponding switch to the value and role of creative activities as the subjects of greatest emphasis in management, and the according precedence in allocation of resources to the creation of the required theories, ideas, concepts and know-how as well as to their translation into products and business. Moreover, this reordering of priorities would have to spread throughout all sectors of industry. As the prospective successor to those of industrialization and information intensification, this trend is called 'creation intensification'. Ultimately, creation intensification would transform not only companies, but also the educational system, information infrastructure and other elements of the overall social system. Figure 1.10(a) presents a simplified diagram of corporate activities in terms of function. The mainstream flow of functions is input of raw materials, manufacture of products and distribution of the output for sales to consumers. There are also sidestream functions for control of this flow and for planning and development of new products and services. The watchword in flow management is efficiency.

With the progress of creation intensification, this basic mainstream would have to be joined by another, accorded equal importance, for the creation of new products and business, Fig. 1.10(b). The new mainstream would consist of the functions of R&D, product development, system development and business

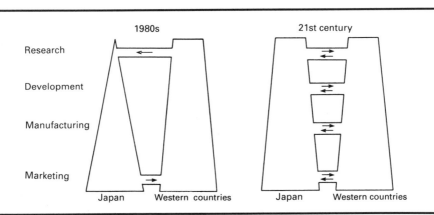

1.9 Role of Japanese companies.

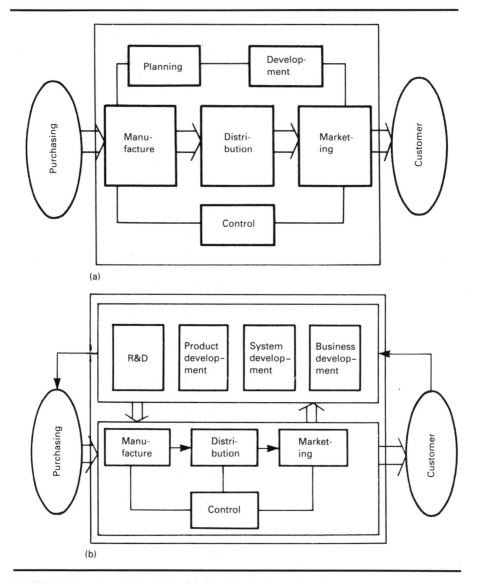

1.10(a) Basic corporate functions; (b) Creation-intense company.

development, and the watchword would be creation. The corresponding divisions would have to be targeted for priority commitments of personnel, material, financial and information resources. Finally, the two mainstreams would have to be managed in a co-ordinated fashion that maintains a close-knit relationship between them.

Reordering of priorities in the allocation of resources appears most clearly in the case of the interdivisional allocation of personnel resources. As shown in Fig. 1.11, in pattern A, which prevailed from the early postwar period to the period of high-level economic growth, allocation stressed manufacturing as companies rushed to produce any items in their field which were selling well at the time. In pattern B, which set in during the 1970s as the demand began to slump under the influence of the oil crises, more stress was put on marketing than

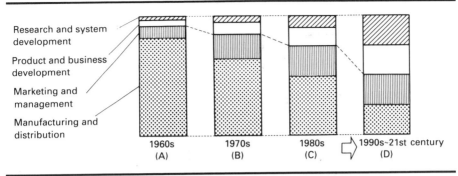

Research and system development

Product and business development

Marketing and management

Manufacturing and distribution

1960s (A) 1970s (B) 1980s (C) 1990s~21st century (D)

1.11 Changes in the allocation of personnel resources with the rise of creation intensification.

on manufacturing. The great strides in technology development and rise in the importance of information and communications during the 1980s stimulated a shift to pattern C, characterized by a rise in the relative importance of research and development and further reinforcement of marketing divisions. The movement toward creation intensification surfaces in the form of a bolstering of personnel resource allocation for R&D, product development, and business development. In addition, the trend of information intensification is transforming systems into effective tools for the creation of new business. This stimulates increased allocation emphasis on the development of systems that do not merely serve to rationalize work but systems that are linked to the development of entirely new business.

At the same time, the productivity of manufacturing divisions is dramatically improving in the process of transition to the next-generation industrial structure induced by innovation in production systems, processes and processing technology. For this reason, it should become possible for such divisions to post a higher productivity on a smaller allocation of personnel resources.

The culmination of this change would be an allocation of personnel resources on divisions involved in creation on a par with that on the efficiency-oriented divisions of manufacturing, distribution, marketing and control.

This personnel allocation with a view to creation intensification is already taking shape among certain progressive companies, for example, the long-term personnel allocation plans of a materials manufacturer shown in Fig. 1.12. The

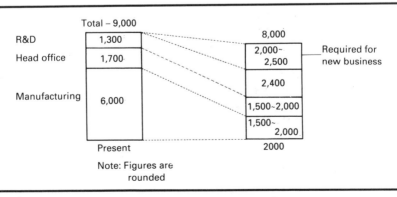

1.12 Allocation of personnel resources at a materials manufacturer.

plans call for a reduction in the number of employees engaged in manufacturing to 1,500 – 2,000, (one-third of the current number of 6,000), by the year 2000 through ambitious programmes of technological innovation and rationalization. Meanwhile, the R&D corps is to be expanded by more than 1,000, and an additional 2,000 – 2,500 personnel committed to the generation of new business or construction of a new business base. As a result the company is hoping to boost its sales and earnings far above the current level, while reducing its total number of employees from 9,000 to 8,000.

Mature industrialization, information intensification and implications for creation intensification

Figure 1.13(a) shows the typical phases of the product life cycle. A product is injected into the market, experiences growth which peaks and then recedes, and finally disappears from the market as a new product takes its place. The trend of sales basically traces a bell curve.

With profits, the basic pattern has been deficit during the injection phase, surplus during the growth phase, peak during the mature phase and recession during the sunset phase. However, this pattern has been changing in recent years. The gigantic proportions attained by many major companies are in effect freeing them from constraints of industrial classifications and enabling them to enter product and business fields in many different industries.

This trend has been given added impetus by de-regulation and the campaigns of business diversification deployed around the same time. It is now possible for a host of companies from different industries to descend upon a particular product field once it enters the growth phase and shows clear promise. The upshot of this rush is excessive competition that drastically erodes profits.

In response, pioneering companies involved in the creation of the underlying product concepts would attempt to reap the highest possible profits as early as possible in the product life cycle. The pattern of profits would therefore change to that shown in Fig. 1.13(b). Here, profits peak in the growth phase

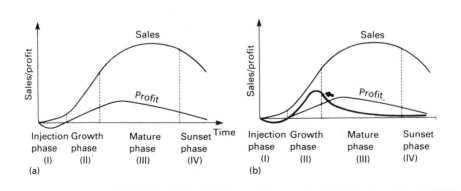

1.13 Product life: (a) Typical cycle; (b) Cycle in a mature phase of industrialization.

and taper off in the mature phase. In such cases, latecomers would face a dwindling chance of success, and could even suffer fatal losses in the tough competition.

In a status of mature industrialization like that characterizing Japan, virtually all major companies have the capability, albeit to varying degrees, to enter new fields of business as they emerge. In today's Japan, this is in fact occurring in the fields of semiconductors, optoelectronics, biotechnology, artificial intelligence and resort development. The aforementioned shift of the peak profit to the earlier part of the product life cycle could consequently be regarded as already underway. If so, high level profits from new business and products are now in the process of being confined to the circle of pioneering companies and capability for creation is already coming to the fore as an actual corporate need.

The life cycle theory has, of course, also been applied to companies them-selves. One example is the '30 year life expectancy' theory, which posits that a company producing a single product (e.g. steel) can continue to grow for an average of only 30 years, after which it is certain to decline. However if the company develops a new, equally successful product at the 30 year mark, when the growth of its former mainstay has peaked, how many more years of growth could the company look forward to? As shown in Fig. 1.14(a), where the curve of overall (corporate) growth is represented as the sum of the curves for the two products, the answer is 'none'; injection of the new mainstay at the 30 year mark would already be too late to enable the company to achieve further growth. Instead, the company's result would stay on the same plateau for another 30 years and then gradually decline over the subsequent 30 years. What if the new product is injected at the 15 year mark, when the first product is experiencing steep growth? In this case, the company could extend its period of growth by 7.5 years to 37.5 years, but its subsequent record would decline at an even steeper rate than that in the first case, Fig. 1.14(b).

While simplistic, this model illustrates how difficult it is for management to maintain growth constantly, however slight. Preparations for the start of develop-ment of the next mainstay must be launched at almost the same time as the initia-tion of business around the first mainstay, and this cycle must be compressed as far as possible. The assembly of ever more significant, innovative creation from the stock of creation that preceded it is becoming a prerequisite for sustained growth over the long term.

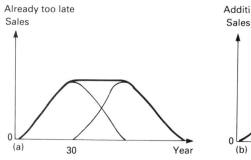
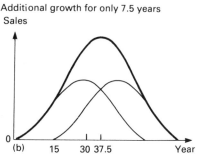

1.14 Injection of successor to mainstay product: (a) After it has peaked; (b) In the 15th year.

The trend of information intensification, which began to accelerate during the 1980s, is also exerting a great effect on the product life cycle. Information intensification has meant a sharp increase in the amount of information presented through mass media about products. This increase is, in effect, compressing the time lag between progressive and conservative consumers in the aspect of purchase of new products. At the same time, the establishment of multimodel, short run production systems and improvement of inventory control capabilities are acting to increase the absolute number of products on the market. The combined effect is a dramatic rise in the total quantity of informational stimulus to which consumers are exposed. By the same token, this has made any single stimulus short-lived, Fig. 1.15.

In addition, the development of point of sale (POS) and other customer information systems has enabled suppliers to ascertain the trends in customer needs rapidly and in great detail. This has made it possible for them to speed up the cycle of new product development and to discontinue products that are not selling well.

A similar effect has been induced by the accelerated pace of technological innovation in such areas as semiconductors. The rising speeds of information processing are shortening the time requirement for the development of new products mounted with microchips. In addition, the increasing speed of information propagation across national borders is boosting the speed of product penetration in the global market.

In short, information intensification is hastening product diffusion in a variety of ways. It consequently has the effect of shortening product life cycles, Fig. 1.16. For the companies supplying them, this amounts to a need to create new products and business at a more frequent rate than before if they are to continue growing.

As agents of great improvement in productivity, industrialization may be regarded as having operated mainly in the divisions of product manufacture and distribution, and 'information intensification' in divisions further downstream, marketing and control. If plotted on the same chart, creation intensification

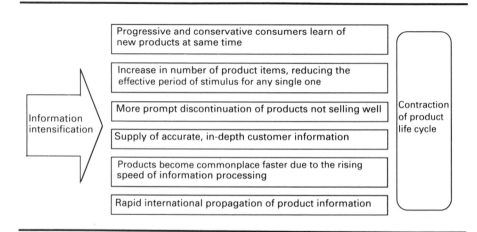

1.15 Contraction of life cycle due to information intensification.

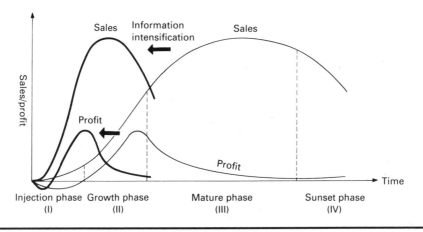

1.16 Contraction of product life cycle due to information intensification.

would represent a return to divisions further upstream, its productivity-improving effect occurring mainly in research and development, and development of products, systems and business.

As noted above, the contracting effect of information intensification on product life cycles is compelling managers to develop new products and business and place them on commercial footing at a higher speed than ever before. Moreover, in the current environment of mature industrialization, the second or third company to enter a new field of business can no longer expect to secure a feasible level of profits, which will increasingly fall to the 'pioneer' that originally opened it up, as shown at the beginning of this section.

The above considerations suggest that the maturation of industrialization and the progress of information intensification are pressing companies to promote creation intensification, which can consequently be termed the next 'big wave' following in the wake of information intensification, Fig. 1.17.

Changing value systems and creation intensification

It has already been a long time since observers began to point out fundamental changes in and diversification of the values held by Japanese consumers. The changes are clearly in evidence in Fig. 1.18(a), which shows the shift from material affluence to non-material affluence as the top priority in consumer lifestyles. In the late 1970s, the trends for both priorities intersected, spurring the discussion of 'diversifying values' noted above. With the start of the 1980s, however, the shift became obvious as the percentage of questionnaire respondents attaching top priority to non-material affluence passed 50 and that of those circling material affluence dipped close to 30.

Naturally, these changes are reflected in patterns of consumption, Fig. 1.18(b). In Maslow's five ranks of human desire, agriculture satisfies the most primary – survival. Through its mechanism of mass production and mass consumption,

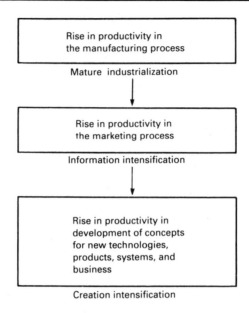

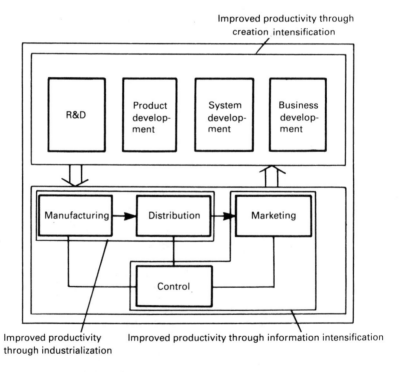

1.17 Improved productivity through industrialization, information intensification and creation intensification.

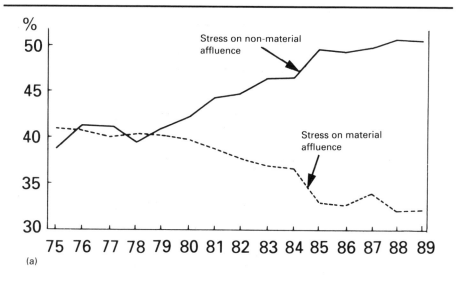

(a)

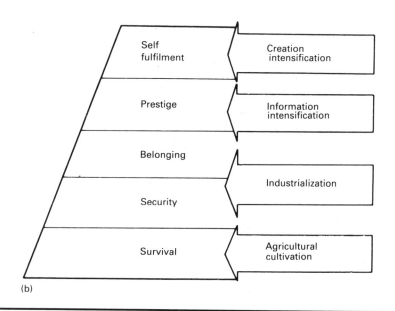

(b)

Source: Prime Minister's office 'Opinion survey on living'.

1.18(a) Consumer value systems; (b) Elevation of consumer desires and creation intensification.

industry meets the desire for security and belonging. This is because it widens the circle of ownership of goods to include the entire society, thereby enabling any consumer to feel a sense of belonging to the same community of mass-consumption.

By endowing products with various types of additional informational value, information intensification enables consumers to set themselves apart from others through consumption, and therefore meets the desire for personal prestige. Once the desires up to this level have been satisfied, the consumer will no longer

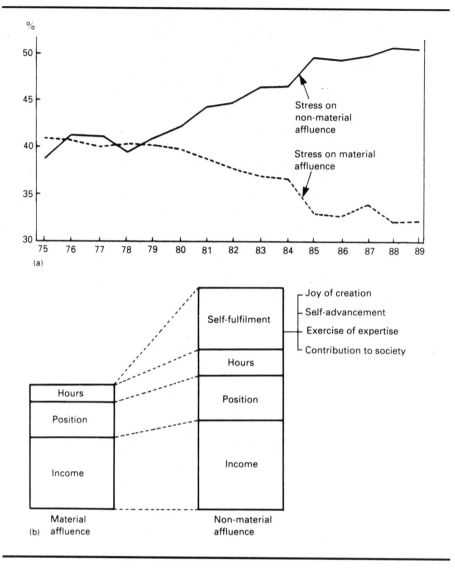

Source: Prime Minister's office 'Opinion survey on living'.

1.19(a) Employee sense of values; (b) Elevation of employee desires and creation intensification.

pursue goods or services merely for the sake of further material affluence, and will seek those whose appeal lies in non-material aspects.

If matters proceed according to Maslow's scheme, consumers will attempt to satisfy their desire for self-fulfilment next. Assistance in satisfaction of this desire by suppliers will not be possible without product and business development through creation intensification. This is because the goods and services in question will have to support the identity of the individual consumer in question, and will therefore have to be truly unique, i.e. tailored specifically for that consumer. Only creation-intense companies will be capable of supplying such goods and services.

The aforementioned shift from material to non-material aspects in consumer sense of values is of great interest to personnel engaged in marketing, who are making great efforts to respond to it.

By the same token, however, the individuals composing the pool of consumption also make up the pool of labour. As such, the aforementioned changes are also changes in the values held by employees, Fig. 1.19, and consequently must be heeded by managers as well as marketing personnel. Priorities, therefore, are changing not only outside companies, but also within them. This change takes the form of an increase in the share of the total members occupied by those seeking benefits that cannot be measured in quantified terms from their employment.

When material affluence held sway as the top priority, employee concerns were basically summarized in income, position and working hours. Once non-material affluence replaces material affluence as the top priority, however, the value attached to leisure time rises, and non-material concerns such as opportunities to feel the joy accompanying creation and for self-advancement become extremely important.

The movement toward creation intensification on the part of companies consequently is not driven solely by conditions in the market and external business environment. The changes underway in the values of the employees composing companies are themselves promoting the evolution of creation-intense companies.

In the age of creation, recruiting creative personnel is of crucial importance for corporate growth. However, a company must prepare a creative working place where creative persons will wish to work. Figure 1.19(b) presents four elements of the 'fulfilling' company that could induce such an environment.

2

Creation intensification in society - images of the creation society

Images of the creation society

In his book by the same title, Alvin Toffler expressed the then-impending arrival of the information-intense society as the coming of a 'third wave'. This book foresees a 'fourth wave' of creation intensification following in the wake of the third and rippling throughout the whole of society in the same way. Figure 2.1(a) depicts all four waves in relation to time and value. On the corporate level, creation intensification refers to a switch from efficiency to creation as the guiding principle of corporate activity. Implicit in the fundamental reordering of priorities it entails is a power sufficient to transcend the corporate level and inundate society as a whole.

If the values and roles stressed were those of manufactured goods in the industrial society and those of information in the information society, the creation society (creation-intense society) would stress those of creative activities, which would occupy a great part of the allocation of working hours and of added value.

While some are of the opinion that creation intensification is but a subphase of information intensification, NRI take the view that a clear distinction must be maintained between the two. This is because creation intensification represents a further step in the process of the progressive externalization of human functions that humankind has undertaken in its quest to acquire more freedom and to satisfy its own desires, Fig. 2.1(b). In addition to creative use of information, the concept of creation intensification also encompasses the recombination of all that has been achieved in the ages of agriculture, industry and information on a higher level in order to expand upon and produce new value from them.

Creation intensification is not a replacement of industrialization or information intensification. Instead, it can be viewed as injecting the element of creation

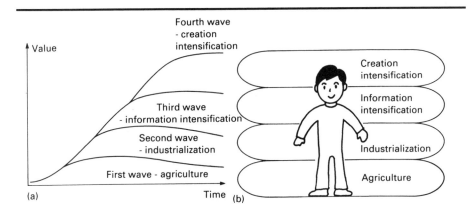

2.1 Creation intensification: (a) The 'fourth wave'; (b) Externalization of human functions.

into the continuing evolution of these two processes. In so doing, it would enhance the value afforded by both.

With the transition from hunting and gathering to co-operative cultivation, which took place around 3000 BC, it became possible for people to abandon migration in favour of a sedentary existence. By transforming land into the capital needed for production, this change represented an externalization of pedal functions. To apply the same metaphor, the industrial revolution of the 18th century represented the externalization of manual functions, which were taken over by various kinds of machines and energy sources that pushed forward the frontier of human activity.

The information intensification of the late 20th century can be seen as externalizing the functions of the human eye, ear, mouth and part of the brain in the form of computers and communications networks, and the time may come when this externalization reaches the mental function most characteristic of man; that responsible for the creation of something new. This is the significance of the arrival of the creation society.

The agricultural society arose around 3000 BC with co-operative cultivation of crops and developed through the use of iron and tools. The industrialized society may be traced to the invention of the steam engine in the 18th century and developed through innovation that successively harnessed coal, oil and nuclear power. In this century, the advances in computer and communications technology have given birth to the information society. The creation society would be a more highly developed form of society that assimilates and balances the elements of these preceding forms.

If the key word in the information society is 'data', the word in the creation society would be 'idea'. Similarly, the 'conceptor', a system supporting conception, would come to occupy the place of today's computer as a tool. 'Idea engineering', an engineering-type exploration of the relationship between cerebral functions and creative ideation, could constitute an important foundation of economic activities, Fig. 2.2.

Just as each of the preceding forms of society devised units of measure for

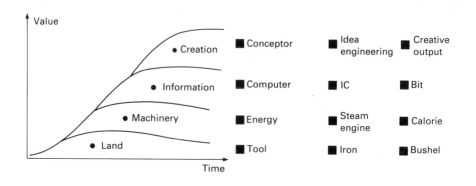

2.2 Creation.

its output, i.e. bushels in the agricultural society, calories in the industrial society and bits in the information society, the creation society could be expected to devise similar units for volume of creation.

In the agricultural society, management pursued the optimal 'co-work merit' (systems of co-operative cultivation) in production of a small range of items (crops) in small quantities. In the industrial society, management pursued the optimal 'scale merit' (economy of scale) through standardization in production of the smallest possible range of items in the largest possible quantity. In the information society, management pursues the optimal 'scope merit' through systematization and extensive use of microchips in production of a wide range of items in small quantities to accommodate the diversifying consumer preferences.

In the creation society, management would pursue the optimal 'originality merit' based on production of items not available from others. By networking heterogeneous items, it would aim for the ultimate system of production, yielding a vast range of 'one-of-a-kind' items and enabling consumption in accordance with the consumer's creative choice.

In both low-diversity, long run production and high-diversity, short run production, the supplier attempts to derive an economic merit by organizing final consumers into a group that reflects his logic and then selling the same product to this group.

By contrast, there would be no grouping of consumers in high-diversity, one-off production, Fig. 2.3. The supplier would deal with each consumer as an individual, and attempt to provide a unique item for each according to the needs of each. As a result, the quality of the production system would be measured not in terms of speed or quantity of production, but in terms of its degree of flexibility.

The key words in the agricultural, industrial and information societies could be regarded as 'fertility', 'massiveness' (heavy, thick, long, large) and 'compactness' (light, thin, short, small), respectively, each with a highly materialistic or quantitative connotation. In the creation society, however, the key word would be one with a highly non-material, qualitative connotation expressing values sought by the inner self, such as 'fulfilment' with the attributes of 'pleasure/comfort', 'beauty', 'love' and 'truth', Fig. 2.4.

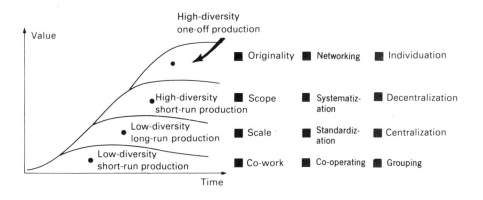

2.3 High-diversity, single-item production.

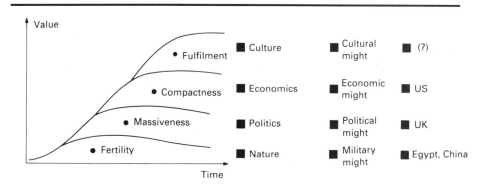

2.4 'Fulfilment'.

Of these attributes, 'pleasure/comfort' refers to a rise in the quality of use of time and space that is already surfacing in the trend toward amenity-rich environments and recreational resorts. This trend is already well underway especially in the last several years in Japan. The aspiration toward 'beauty' would transform art per se into a fully-fledged industry linked with advanced technology. The signs of this trend can be seen in the rising importance of video and the spread of computer graphics, in which work requires not only artistic sense but also advanced technology. 'Love' refers to the rising importance of communication and amicable ties between people, organizations, and between the two. The quest for 'truth' would make a separate industry of science itself.

In passage from the age of agriculture to the age of information, the laws or rules to which society marched changed in succession from those of nature to those of politics and economics, and the nature of 'power' from military might to political and economic might. In the creation society, the counterparts would be 'cultural rules' and 'cultural might'.

The most prominent pioneers of agricultural society were mainland countries such as Egypt and China. The industrialization of the 18th century was led by the UK, and the information society, by the US.

Who will open up the age of creation? Rather than a specific country, it could be that group known as the 'invisible empire', the multinational or transnational corporations. Similarly, it could be the group of countries making up the European Community upon the unification of its market in 1992. It could also be Japan, a country somewhat distanced from the western civilization that has been dominating industrial society or it could be an amalgamation of the creative edge of all. Table 2.I outlines the creation society in relation to the other three significant societies and the possible images it may bring.

Table 2.I Images of the creation society

	Agricultural society	**Industrial society**	**Information society**	**Creation society**
1 Wave	First wave	Second wave	Third wave	Fourth wave
2 Emergence	3000 BC	18th century	Late 20th century	21st century
3 Social change	Cultivation	Industrialization	Information intensification	Creation intensification
4 Revolution	Agricultural revolution	Industrial revolution	Information revolution	Creation revolution
5 External-ization	Feet	Hand	Eye, ear, mouth	Brain
6 Value	Co-operation	Standardization	Systematization	Networking
7 Merit	Co-work	Scale	Scope	Originality
8 Measure-ment	Bushels	Calorie	Bit	Volume of creation
9 Law	Nature	Politics	Economics	Culture
10 National might	Military	Political	Economic	Cultural might
11 Produc-tion	Low diversity small-lot	Low diversity large-lot	High-diversity small-lot	High-diversity, single-item
12 Technol-ogy	Iron Tools	Steam engine energy	Communication network Computer	Idea engineering Conceptor
13 Attri-butes	Land Tools Grouping Feudal authority Natural time	Machinery Energy Centralization Central authority Simultaneity	Information Data Decentralization Decentralized authority Multi-time	Creation Ideas Individuality Optimization Free time
14 Key word	Fertility	Massiveness	Compactness	Fulfilment
15 Pioneer	Egypt China	UK	US	(?)

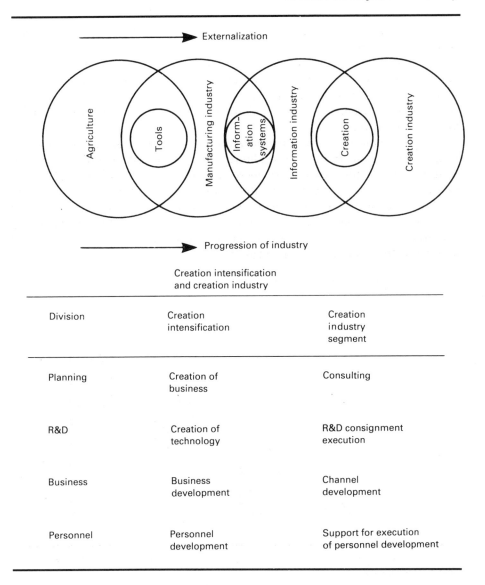

2.5 Stages of industry and externalization.

The rise of creation industry

The aforementioned progression of industry and society (agricultural, industrial, information) is at the same time a progression of externalization, Fig. 2.5. With progression to a new stage, certain functions that were of prime importance in the previous stages are externalized and it is the rooting and spread of this externalization that ushers in the new stage. In the progression from the information society to the creation society, corporate business planning functions would be externalized in the form of a separate consulting industry, and research and development functions in the form of a separate R&D industry.

In reality, such activity has already begun to surface over the last two years. Cases in point include the widespread establishment of new think tanks, Osaka Gas's KRI (which are instituted for performance of consigned research and development), Science Service Co (which executes research consignments) and Animal Care Co (which manages laboratory animals for clients). All may be viewed as forerunners of a creation industry that conducts creation-related business for other companies.

One indicator of this externalization of corporate research and development activities is the trend of expenditures for consignments of research off company premises. This expenditure increased at an annual rate averaging 17% through the 1980s. In the process, the consigned research market surged from 170 billion yen in 1980 to 600 billion yen at present. If this trend continues, it will reach about four trillion yen in the year 2000, Fig. 2.6. Inevitably, this increasing externalization of corporate research activities generates the growth of external industry as the vessel to accommodate it.

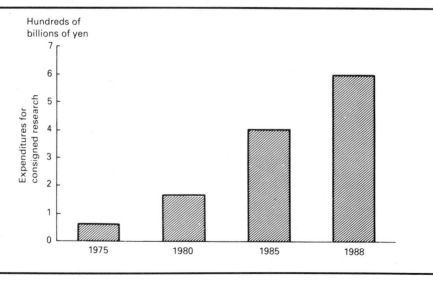

Source: Prepared by NRI from 'Survey of scientific and technological research', Management and Co-ordination Agency.

2.6 Trend of expenditures for consigned research.

At this point, the information society from the standpoint of industry should be considered. The information explosion of the late 20th century stimulated companies to embark on programmes of information intensification. For the overall industrial structure, it meant the birth of an overall information industry comprising a group of growth industries. The share of the value of all industrial production occupied by the overall information industry, which was estimated about 10% in 1985, is projected to reach about 15% in the year 2000, Fig. 2.7.

Only a certain segment of the information industry actually produces value in the form of information. As of 1985, this segment was estimated to make up about 14% of the industry. In other words, more than 80% of the so called

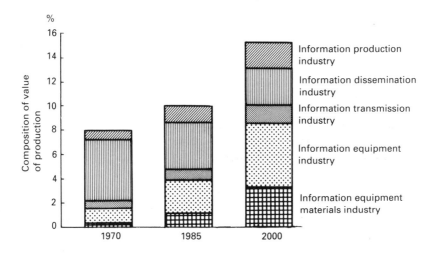

2.7 Share of total industrial production occupied by the information industry.

information industries do not produce information, but support corporate or private information intensification through information dissemination or production of required equipment, and would more properly be termed 'information support industries'. The activities of these information support industries promote information intensification in society as a whole, which in turn results in expanded production in the overall information industry, setting in motion a synergistic effect.

The emergence of such information industries has motivated companies to implement their own information intensification programmes. With the approach of the 21st century, however, society has begun to move toward creation intensification. In the creation society that will result, the industrial structure may be expected to undergo significant changes, as occurred in the case of the information society.

The wave of creation intensification coming in the wake of information intensification is anticipated to spread on both corporate and individual levels, generating a group of growth industries (comprising the overall creation industry) which will drive further creation intensification in society as they grow.

What kind of industry will the creation industry be? In the information society, the overall industry consists of a segment supporting corporate and private programmes of information intensification and another segment producing information. This suggests that the overall creation industry (as viewed from the standpoint of corporate activities, the term 'creation support industry' would perhaps be more apt) would consist of a segment executing corporate creative activities on consignment (creation execution industry), a segment supporting corporate or private creative activities (creation service industry), and a segment handling the establishment of rights to value produced by creative activities (patents and other non-tangible property as well as highly creative products) and the commercialization, distribution, and marketing of the same (creation distribution industry), Fig. 2.8. While few existing enterprises could be placed into the creation

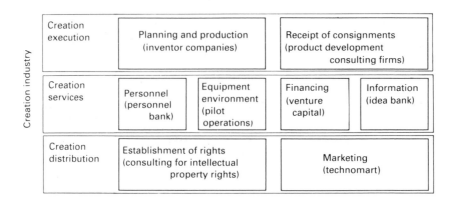

2.8 Segments of the creation industry.

distribution industry, many could be expected to emerge in the process of creation intensification in society.

The creation execution industry could be divided into the subsegments of planning and production industry which would independently produce creative value and supply it to others; and of consigned production industry which would produce such value in response to corporate or private requests.

As the segment supporting creative activities among companies and individuals, the creation service industry could be similarly divided into the subsegments of personnel, equipment/environment, financing and information in accordance with the types of business resources required for such support.

While its fully-fledged emergence still lies in the future, at present the creation distribution industry consists of enterprises engaged in the establishment of rights to creative value (in the nature of consulting firms for intellectual property rights) and of those engaged in the marketing of creative value (on the order of technomarts).

The creation industry would constitute a representative aspect of the creation society, see Table 2.II. For this reason, the scale of the creation industry would serve as a barometer of the importance of creative activities in that society.

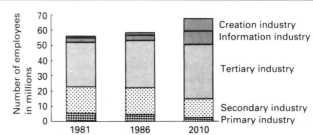

2.9 Structure of employment in the creation society.

Table 2.II The creation industry in the creation society

The creation industry

Creation execution

Planning and production	Consignment	
• R&D • Planning formulation • Inventor companies • R&D seeds suppliers	• Agency business • Industrial design companies • Think tanks • Simulation companies • Demonstration agencies • Corporate identity consulting firms	• Convention bureaux • Design offices • R&D consulting firms • Product development consulting firms • System development consulting firms • Business development consulting firms

Creation services

Personnel	Equipment/environment	Financing	Information
• Training in specialized fields • Business schools • Specialized schools • CAI firms • Dispatch of specialized technicians • Personnel banks • Management placement services • Private occupation stabilizers • Fitness clubs • Recreation centres	• Manufacturers of R&D equipment • Manufacturers of R&D instrumentation • Manufacturers of measurement devices, analysers, and testers • Manufacturers of acoustic equipment • Engineering • Manufacturers of pilot products and systems • Developers • Facility planners • Office planners	• Venture capital business • Financial consulting firms • Financial planning firms • Accounting consulting firms	• Survey organizations • M&A mediators • Consulting firms • Translation/interpretation services • Suppliers of life information (ticketing, etc.) • Idea banks

Creation distribution

Rights	Marketing
• Law offices • Patent offices * Appraisers of intellectual assets * Consulting for intellectual property rights	• Technomarts * Knowledge marts * Auction of intellectual assets * Intellectual personnel banks

Source) NRI
Note: Asterisks indicate enterprises that do not yet exist but are expected to emerge in the future.

In this connection, Fig. 2.9 presents estimates of the trend of the structure of employment in Japan as a quantified image of the growth of the creation industry. It can be seen that the number of creation industry employees, which stood at an estimated 1.7 million in 1986, is projected to increase about five-fold, to eight million, by the year 2010.

In the process, the share of the total number of employed occupied by creation industry employees, which is estimated at 3% for 1986, would rise to about 12% as of 2010. If so, one out of every eight Japanese employees would be working in the creation industry, i.e. engaged in creative activities of some sort as an occupation, by that year.

3

Corporate response to the age of creation - strategy for creation

The dawning of the age of creation and creative corporate activities

As described in the previous sections, creation intensification may be regarded as the next stage in the progression from industrialization and information intensification in industry and society. Through its contracting effect on product life cycles, information intensification is prompting companies to develop new product and business concepts on a continuous basis. Although the advanced industrialized countries of the West have been the source of the seminal product and business concepts that powered global economic growth during the postwar period, their capability to continue to perform this role appears to be declining. In this situation, the role of this type which must be discharged by Japanese companies is steadily expanding.

The changes taking place in the realm of values are making it increasingly vital for employers to provide work offering the opportunity for exercise of creativity if they want to recruit quality personnel. Pursuit of creativity is assuming rising importance as a corporate priority alongside expanded sales and profit and higher rank in economic society.

The new stress on creativity in corporate activities translates directly into an extensive provision of opportunities for satisfaction of the need to exercise creativity on the part of their constituent members; their employees. In society as a whole, increasing affluence is bringing exercise of creativity to the fore as a key concept. The status which has been termed the 'creation society' is gradually taking shape. If so, the present could be termed the 'dawn of the age of creation', in which the social currents of transformation into the creation society are steadily beginning to swell, Fig. 3.1.

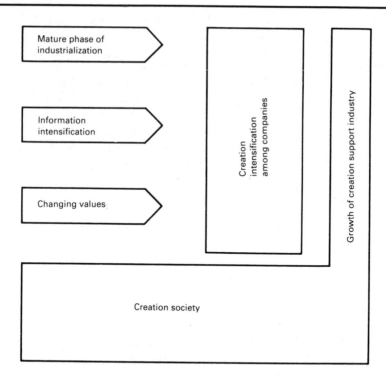

Forces behind the age of creation

	Companies	Society in general
Organization	R&D Product development System development Business development	Governmental institutions Universities Research agencies Mass media Economic organizations
Individuals	Researchers Planning developers Managers Ordinary employees	Consumers Scientists Artists Specialists Bureaucrats

3.1 The dawning of the age of creation.

At the vanguard of the procession into the age of creation will be companies. To date, creativity has been a focus of concern mainly in connection with science, art and technology. In other words, creativity has generally been treated as something in the province of individuals such as scientists and artists. However, the main forces behind the dawn of the age of creation will be companies themselves, through the creative energies cultivated by their researchers, planners, top executives, middle management and regular employees.

The movement toward the creation society will be provided with real thrust when creation ceases to be regarded as something in the realm of individuals and becomes the key concern of companies as organizations devoted to the creation of value.

The kernel subjects of this effort to intensify creation will be the four corporate activities of R&D, product development, system development and business development, Table 3.I. At the same time, however, this effort will encompass all aspects related to the generation of products and business, embodying new concepts without parallel in other companies.

The creative corporate activities that are the subject of this project are therefore those that derive new technology, products, systems and business from the theories, ideas, concepts and know-how spawned by this creation.

In a presentation at NRI offices, Dr Mete of the Rochester Institute of Technology likened the attempt to evaluate corporate creativity in real time to 'trying to drive a car with an opaque windshield at full speed, looking only at the rear view mirror'. The point is that creation cannot be evaluated while still in progress; evaluation is only possible when the results are in. Table 3.II presents a comparison of Japan and the US in terms of R&D creativity.

A framework like that shown in Fig. 3.2 could be used as a kind of conceptual yardstick for measuring the degree of creativity. In this framework, creativity is expressed as a vector in a space of two dimensions: the originality of the concept and the magnitude of the impact.

The conceivable parameters of originality are the lack of existing models, the degree of discontinuity with what has gone before and the inclusion of elements of self-negation. Those of impact are degree of improvement in growth/profit, the degree of improvement in the company's position in society and degree of contribution to the intracorporate vitality.

Table 3.I Subjects of creation

	Subjects of creation			
Corporate activities	R&D	Product development	System development	Business development
Intellectual product	Theories	Ideas	Concepts	Know-how
Results of corporate activities	New technology	New products	New systems	New business

Table 3.II Comparison of Japan and the United States in the aspect of R&D creativity

	US			Japan		
	Basic	**Applied**	**Development**	**Basic**	**Applied**	**Development**
Government	○	–	△	–	–	–
Companies	△	○	○	–	◎	◎
Universities	◎	–	△	△	△	△

Note: Meaning of symbols is as follows (relative comparison)
  ◎ excellent
  ○ good
  – mediocre
  △ inferior
Source: Presentation at NRI by Dr Mete, Asst Prof of Rochester Institute of Technology (12 Sept 1989).

In this context, general corporate activities can be grouped into three basic categories, as shown in Fig. 3.2 and as follows:

1 Imitation
This is the pole opposite to creation, and refers to the copying of promising concepts created by others and marketing them at lower prices or with more skillful campaigns in order to increase sales and profits. Although the impact may be considerable, the originality is negligible.

2 Improvement
This is the partial modification or elaboration of basic concepts already in existence in order to induce an impact of increased sales and profits, etc.

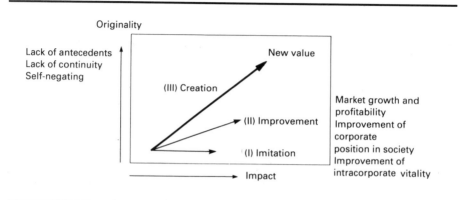

3.2 Yardstick of creation.

3 Creation

This is the production of completely new value or concepts that exert a great impact on society.

Our concern here is (3), creative activities.

The need for strategy for creation

The rooting of creation intensification and construction of creation-intense companies must be approached in a manner that differs fundamentally from that applied in building companies in the ages of industry and information, in which the main parameters were productivity, quality control and price competitiveness. The requirement is the preparation of an environment conducive to creation in the company. The scheme for executing this preparation in the most effective way is the central theme of this book; strategy for creation. The means of this strategy, which will be particularly important for Japanese companies, is termed 'management for creation', Fig. 3.3.

To date, Japanese companies are said to have achieved growth through management that is neither of the 'from-the-top-down' variety nor of the 'from-the-bottom-up' variety, but rests primarily on the self-organizing efforts of middle management. In the process of creation intensification as well, success could hinge on the ability of middle management to organize themselves in pursuit of this target. If so, there would be a need for means that will make a direct contribution to creation intensification in the middle layer of management. This brings us to a third requirement for Japanese companies (in addition to strategy and management for creation): a concrete methodology of support for the promotion of creative activities, or 'method of creation'.

The remainder of this book will explore this method of and management for creation through a case study of various moments of significant creation and their context in Japanese and US companies, and an analysis of the results of a questionnaire survey with leading companies in both countries. Figure 3.4 illustrates the literal Japanese meaning for creation.

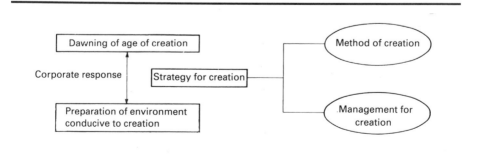

3.3 Corporate response to the age of creation.

The Japanese word for creation is a compound of two characters: '創',
meaning 'first', and '造', meaning 'make'.
'創' : 'first' (no antecedents)

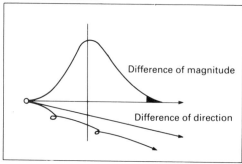

'造' : 'make'

(1) Pursuit of the ultimate

Examples

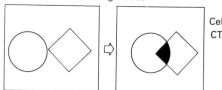

Smallest size
Lowest pressure
temperature and
speed

Super conductivity (Onnes)
IC, LSI, VLSI

Greatest size,
Highest pressure
temperature and
speed

(2) Combination of the heterogeneous

Cell fusion (Yoshio Okada)
CT scanner (Cormak, Housefield)

(3) Structuring of the peculiar

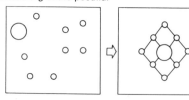

Elucidation of the double-helix
structure of DNA (Watson & Crick).
Nylon (Carothers)

3.4 創造 (creation).

Process of creation

4

Process of creation in research and development

Creativity in research and development

Profile

The constituent factors of creativity in R&D are of two basic types: personnel and environmental. In other words, the exercise of creativity is greatly influenced by individual capability of the researcher (personnel factors) and by the organization surrounding him (environmental factors).

The following can be cited as examples of momentous exercise of individual creativity in research:

- Einstein's formulation of the theory of relativity
- Shockley's invention of the transistor
- Onne's discovery of superconductivity
- Fineman's reconstruction of quantum mechanics
- Watson and Crick's discovery of the double helix structure of DNA

The acquisition of personnel with a superior capability is, of course, a vital prerequisite for vigorous promotion of research and development. To a great degree, however, this individual capability itself is beyond control as a subject of management related to R&D. By contrast, management can control the environmental factors (the organization) to a far greater degree than the personnel factors.

It can also be noted that the exercise of creativity by talented individuals (individual creation) must be distinguished from creation effected as an organization (group creation). Since our concern here is strategy for creation in corporate research and development, it would be more effectively approached by focusing on the environmental as opposed to the personnel factors.

Model for the process of research and development

IGKP model

There are basically three types of personnel involved in any given process of R&D: those who are the source of the idea that provides the basis for creation (idea generators), those who support the idea and attempt to nourish it to fruition (idea promoters), and those who are opposed to the idea and try to squash it (idea killers). This categorization forms the basis for our 'IGKP model', a conceptual model that can be used to describe the process of creation in general terms, Fig. 4.1.

Of all creative activities, the IGKP model stresses the group personnel aspect, particularly the process of creating problem-solving measures and new concepts.

In the following discussion, the term idea generators (IG) refers to the individual personnel whose conceptions generate ideas that are the seeds of creation: the term idea killers (IK), to those personnel who try to suppress the idea, are opposed to the change it represents, or otherwise have a negative reaction to the prospect of its execution, and the term idea promoters (IP), to those personnel who support the idea, try to protect the IG from the IK, and attempt to foster the growth of the idea through such means as proposal of visions incorporating it and presentation of opportunities for commercialization based on it.

Generally speaking, IGs are prevalent among members of the lower age groups who are blessed with a high degree of creative ability as individuals. Although it may not be entirely impossible to cultivate and reinforce this creative ability on the individual level, the more realistic approach would be use of IPs to prepare an organizational and personnel environment that would facilitate exercise of their ability by the IGs.

This arrangement of the organizational and personnel environment consisting of IGs, IKs and IPs may be referred to as 'idea co-ordination' (IC). Analysis of the process of creation in R&D must view the functions of IGs, IKs, and IPs not in isolation from each other, but in terms of this co-ordination.

The performance of IKs and IPs also depends on individual capability, but the functions they represent can be more easily cultivated and reinforced through

---

IG (idea generator):
  Generation of the ideas forming the seeds of creation

IK (idea killer):
  Orientation toward preservation of status quo; negative
  reaction to implementation of idea

IP (idea promoter):
  Fostering of the idea by protecting IGs from IKs, proposing visions
  incorporating the idea, and presenting opportunities for commercialization
  of the idea

IC (idea co-ordination) = (IG,IK,IP)

4.1 Co-ordination of creation in research and development.

experience and training than those of IGs. In addition, although a single IG rarely achieves great results, a single IK or IP generally can do so.

Idea killers can be characterized as oriented toward preservation of the status quo and reacting negatively to the implementation of the new idea. Researchers who have been working in a single field of research for a long time, in fields where the technology has already been established to a great degree, or have achieved great success in past research naturally tend to acquire a more pronounced orientation of this type and to function as IKs.

Generally, IPs are not naturally equipped for their function, but are 'made' through extensive experience in decision-making related to R&D and of management of research organizations spanning several fields. This sets them apart from IKs, who tend to arise as natural products of their own experience.

The range of management control in cultivation and reinforcement is greater in the case of IPs than in that of IGs, but the degree of difficulty is about the same in both. Functions IG and IP are performed by specific individuals, but IK is in many cases performed by organizations. In companies with a great dependence on a long-standing business, the management culture tends to be highly conservative and control-oriented. In such companies, the atmosphere itself functions as an IK, and it may often be unclear which individual or individuals are functioning as IKs.

The starting point for creative activities is the activity of the IG. If this individual creativity (individual creation) is to exert an influence on corporate activities, it must be elevated to the level of group creation through interaction with IKs or IPs.

In creative corporate activities in R&D, product development, system development or business development, the role played by IKs and IPs is as important as that played by IGs. The fundamental concern in management of creative activities is therefore an optimization of the relative balance of power among IGs, IKs and IPs in accordance with such factors as the subject and stage of development.

Nevertheless, this optimal balance or co-ordination of IGs, IKs, and IPs is not a static, fixed form; it changes depending on the circumstances of development.

In R&D of technology, for example, for which the research process and approach are clearly defined, adherence to the path shown by the stock of results obtained to date would generally be more effective than a departure relying on creative ideas. In terms of the disparity of the relative strength of IGs and IKs, the advisable mode of co-ordination in this case could be expressed as 'IG < IK'.

Conversely, in R&D of technology such as neurocomputers, for which the research process and approach are not clearly defined, the possible paths are various and progress could very well be determined by the degree of the creativity of the ideas generated. In such cases, the co-ordination should place IGs in a position of strength relative to IKs. Table 4.I outlines the possible relationships between IGs and IKs subject to the varying forms of companies and technologies entered into.

Naturally, the circumstances of neurocomputer R&D may be expected to change as such programmes progress. As neural-type information processing technology comes into use in more and more application fields, the process and approach of neurocomputer research will gradually become better defined. In step with this change, the role of IGs would contract, and the type of co-ordination employed in the case of established technological fields would become more feasible.

As compared with the other categories of corporate creative activities (product development, system development and business development), R&D generally requires a strong position for IGs.

In sum, the nature of 'optimal co-ordination' even for the same theme of development will change as the work proceeds from the stage of R&D to that of business development.

Four-stage model

A four-stage model of creation in companies, Table 4.II, is proposed. In research and development activities, in which the individual element looms larger than in the other categories of creative corporate activities, creation is divided into two basically 'individual' stages and two basically 'environmental' stages (a detailed explanation of this model is presented in Chapter 8).

The stage of hypothesis construction for research and devlopment, for example, is regarded as a basically individual stage. Although environmental and organizational factors also operate in it, the dominant element is the creativity of ideas generated on the individual level.

The stage of 'chain of empathy', on the other hand, is regarded as a basically environmental stage, in which the activity of IGs is elevated from the level of individual creation to that of group creation within the organization as the corporate environment.

In Table 4.III, the line intersections indicate the birth of a relationship between IGs and IKs/IPs. The nature of the relationship and the identity of the intersection differ depending on the case of research and development, Table 4.1.

When the time required for movement from the stage of hypothesis construction to that of the chain of empathy is long, a single IG working on a single theme of development may form a relationship with several IKs and IPs. In addition, a person who functioned as an IP at one stage may function as an IK at another as the work progresses.

As noted above in connection with neurocomputers, even in research on the same theme, the advisable form of co-ordination of IGs, IKs, and IPs may change as the work progresses, setting in motion a corresponding change in the relationships shown in Table 4.III. This change in the aspect of co-ordination may

Table 4.I Idea generators and idea killers

	Country	Company	Technology
IG<IK	Japan	Large companies	Established technology
IG=IK	US	Medium-scale companies	Advanced technology
IG>IK	UK	Venture companies	Futuristic technology

Table 4.II Four-stage model of creation

1 Construction of hypothesis	Group/organizational atmosphere Individual enthusiasm/ambition/competitive spirit Business needs/imperatives Accommodation of needs, expansion upon seeds Suggestions from outside, new knowledge Deliberate challenge to accepted notions Individual insight, discussion
2 Dissimilation	Draft of image Association, analogy Ideation, conception Combination Theorization, calculation Experimentation Learning from mistakes Hints from other fields Discussion, criticism Self-negation
3 Concept creation	Continuity Flash
4 Chain of empathy	Information sharing Logicality, corroboration Harnessing of specialized knowledge and technology Education, training Diffusion activities Communication

Table 4.III Relationship of four-stage model and IGKP model

Idea generators	Idea killers	Idea promoters
1 Construction of hypothesis		
2 Dissimilation		
3 Concept creation		
4 Chain of sympathy		

be viewed as a kind of 'shake-up' that is needed to maintain the vitality and dynamism of the various research activities. Figure 4.2 provides further expansion of the IGKP model.

The need for creativity

Japan's weaknesses in research and development can be seen as follows:

- Lack of experience in business development rooted in independent research and development
- Shortage of personnel specializing in research evaluation
- Low priority attached to distinctiveness of concept
- Low ability to cope with freedom and isolation
- Weak position of idea generators

The factors cited above as Japan's 'weaknesses' in R&D are not necessarily 'problems'. However, if Japan is to grow out of its traditional role as a product supplier and into a new role as concept supplier, and to promote a constructive relationship of co-existence with the newly industrializing countries that are stepping into the role of product supplier, it must have a firm grasp of the weaknesses as well as strengths of its R&D. These weaknesses are of two basic types: those which were spawned by the environment surrounding Japan, and those which derive from 'Japanese characteristics', i.e. characteristics generally associated with the Japanese personality.

The two major environmental factors are the process of the development of Japan's industry, which was one of 'catching up' with the advanced

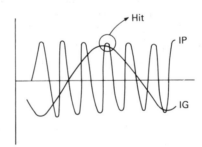

Note: Expressed as waves, IGs, by nature, ordinarily have a long period (cycle).
IPs must therefore be constantly reinforced in order to ensure that IGs will have a sufficiently ample opportunity for creation. Conversely, if the unit functioning as an IP conducts activities at a low frequency, the emergence of a single act of creation could require an extremely long period of time. To obtain the maximum frequency of creation, the company must produce a situation in which the IP function is maximized. This could be done by having numerous IPs working in relay.

Source: NRI.

4.2 Expansion of the IGKP model.

industrialized countries, and the availability of a huge, open market overseas for the products of this industry. In effect, these factors made it possible to develop business without independent efforts beginning right from the phase of R&D, and to maintain the viability of the business even without concepts that were distinctive or otherwise set apart from counterparts.

Japan's industry has been particularly inexperienced in nourishing developmental themes right from the phase of R&D through to commercialization (business development). As a result, it has also been inexperienced in the evaluation and screening of themes in this process, and has not developed effective programmes for the cultivation of personnel qualified for such evaluation and screening.

These circumstances are reflected in an insufficient appreciation of the importance of R&D as a support of sustained growth and source of intellectual assets. This point is evidenced in the practice of diverting research personnel to the business division, even if it entails the suspension of an in-progress research programme, when the expansion of the existing business produces a shortage of personnel in that division. As such cases suggest, R&D has not always been accorded a high strategic priority.

Characteristics of high-tech industry can be seen as follows:

- Small scale of production
- High rate of growth
- Deficit-ridden unless the entrant ranks among the top three
- Supply from a single country can meet the worldwide demand
- 'Spiciness'
- Need for expanded basic research as the industry expands

The 'Japanese characteristics' include an insufficient ability to cope with situations of freedom and isolation. If placed in a situation that is highly unstructured or in which the work is to be pursued by only a small team, Japanese researchers tend to be incapable of demonstrating their full ability. In addition, Japanese IGs tend to be in a position of weakness relative to IKs.

These weaknesses can be particularly critical in research activities in fields directly related to advanced technology. Since the scale of production in such fields is still small in comparison to established fields, distinctive concepts are vital for acquisition of a market share sufficient to assure the viability of the business. Furthermore, companies must possess the developmental capability that will enable them to keep constantly abreast of the steep growth rates.

Another characteristic of advanced technology is that basic research becomes increasingly important as the market expands. For this reason, companies must be endowed with the research and development capability to keep themselves in the vanguard of efforts to blaze the field's frontier.

Domains with strong R&D needs can be seen as follows:

- Information
- Electronics
- Comfort/leisure
- Biotechnology
- New materials
- Industrialization of art

More dynamic research and development activities are indispensable for Japan's transformation from a supplier of products to one of concepts and for a constructive coexistence with new product suppliers.

The need is particularly strong in the advanced domains noted above. These fall into two basic categories: those concerning the industrialization of advanced technology, and those concerning the industrialization of art. The industrialization of advanced technology is the aggregate of efforts to enhance functions, boost speeds, enlarge capacities, increase densities, attain higher levels of refinement and specialization, etc. The main domains are those of information, electronics, biotechnology and new materials.

The industrialization of art expresses the response of industry to the elevation of what constitutes appeal in the eyes of customers from the level of needs to that of wants and further to that of tastes. It is deeply intertwined with the trend toward amenity-rich environments.

This distinction could be reinforced by use of new terminology for the products of this industrialization. On the analogy of the terms 'hardware' and 'software', the products of the high-tech industry could be termed 'intelligenceware', and those of the art industry as we have described it, 'artware'.

The subjects of the case study of research and development presented in the following section are themes selected from the domains of information, electronics and biotechnology. It should be noted that, since the themes in question are still at the stage of research and development, an effort has been made to keep the respective accounts abstract without sacrificing the description of the notable features of each case.

Case study of research and development

Neural network R&D organizations

Neurocomputers rest on a principle of computation that is different from that of the Von Neumann computers now in general use. They are beginning to receive great attention as a means of elucidating human intellectual activity (the fundamental principles of the activity of the brain) and of application of the results in the field of computers.

Neural networks are one of the major technological supports of neurocomputers. Endowed with the faculties of learning and self-organization, neural networks reportedly hold the key to the construction of next-generation computers that will transcend the limits of the Von Neumann machines.

The brain, the model for neurocomputers, is an assemblage of neural networks constructed from a mass of neurons that enables a high level of performance in complicated reasoning and decision-making on the basis of vague information. In order to assure the same overall functionality for computation that characterizes Von Neumann computers, adaptation to the external world and performance are improved by the combination of learning and self-organization as the counterpart of switching programs in the case of Von Neumann computers.

Research of neurocomputers is being approached by researchers representing many different fields. The work spans the fields of not only mathematical science and computer science but also neurophysiology, cognitive science and others, Fig. 4.3.

The case accounts attempt to identify the vital factors in each stage of the four-stage model and the relative interrelationship of IGs, IKs and IPs in the process of research to date.

Organization A

This case concerns neurocomputers in the information domain and exemplifies a research situation in which the research process and approach have not been clearly defined, Fig. 4.4.

At the stage of hypothesis construction, the vital factors are suggestions from outside sources, discussion, new pieces of knowledge and new phenomena,

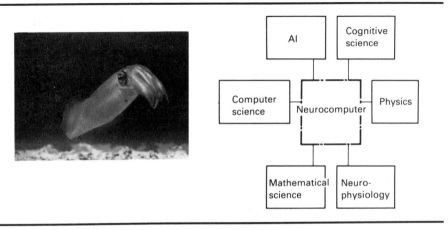

Source: Kazuyuki Aihara 'Neural computers – learning from the brain and nervous system', Tokyo Denki University Publishing Bureau.

4.3 Fields of research into neurocomputers.

$IC=\{IG>IP>>IK=O\}$

1 Construction of hypothesis
— Suggestions from outside sources
— Discussion
— New knowledge and phenomena
— Challenge to accepted notions

2 Dissimilation
— Association, analogy
— Theorization
— Calculation, simulation
— Discussion, criticism

3 Concept creation
— Discussion
— Continuity

4 Chain of empathy
— Information system

4.4 Case A.

and a deliberate challenge to certain commonly held assumptions. Due to the extremely advanced nature of this domain, the activities of the organization to which the researchers belong are not in themselves sufficient for collection of information of the required quantity and quality, and therefore suggestions from outside the organization are exceedingly important.

The advanced nature of this domain results in the unearthing of new pieces of knowledge and new phenomena at a high frequency. This has the effect of increasing the vitality of the research activities. Since the domain is subject to the appearance of much new knowledge and phenomena, exercise of originality is a vital requirement in the research work. This is why deliberate challenge to accepted notions is also cited as an important factor.

As discussed, neurocomputer research spans many different fields. In the case in question, the theme is approached from the standpoint of mathematical science, and the work at the stage of dissimilation is centred around theoretical calculations and numerical simulations conducted to corroborate these calculations.

In the second and third stages as well as the first, 'discussion' is cited as an important factor. Like the second stage, the discussion in the third stage includes specialists not employed by the company, but the emphasis remains with members of the intracorporate team.

Another factor of importance related to discussion is 'continuity'. The IGs in this case actively encourage young researchers to work on themes conducive to the composition of research theses even if there is no direct connection with the main theme, and formulate conceptions of the final research results in as much detail as possible in order to make it easier to receive backing from IPs.

The idea co-ordination for this case is expressed as: $IC = (IG > IP >> IK = 0)$. In essence, IKs do not exist in the research environment of the IGs. The environment is extremely favourable to heuristic research; it assures the research freedom of the IGs, who are encouraged to give free rein to their creativity. The only potential restraints are external factors such as cutback of funds or reduction in the amount of time alloted to research due to manpower needs associated with some other work.

The research themes can therefore be quite freely selected by the researchers themselves, but this also means that IGs must function as 'player-managers', i.e. leaders of their own team. At the stage of dissimilation, for example, the IGs themselves would have to evaluate the research themes from a perspective of critical objectivity.

For the sake of convenience, IG, IK and IP functions have been described as being discharged by different individuals or groups of individuals. However, in cases such as this, in which they act as player-managers, the IGs would also have to discharge an IK-type function in order to provide the team with a continuity of direction.

The stages of hypothesis construction and dissimilation consist mainly of exchange of views at learned societies and discussion sessions within the institute in question. In many cases, the hypotheses are constructed through analogy with the work of other researchers. These other researchers are generally those whose work also represents a challenge to accepted notions.

Organization B

Like case A, the research in this case, Fig. 4.5, also concerns neurocomputers, but is being promoted with application to the existing business as the foremost concern. Furthermore, projected contribution to this business is a major criterion in selection of research themes.

Of the aforementioned fields of neurocomputer research, the themes in this case belong to that of neurophysiology, but also are related to neural information processing (visual and aural perception) and computer graphics. Although there is no great difference from the previous case in respect of the factors of importance at each stage of the four-stage model, the idea co-ordination may be expressed as: IC = (IK > IG > IP). In short, the environment is harsh as far as IG activity is concerned.

Because the IK forces are strong, the overall research activities tend to be exclusive. There are tough restrictions imposed on participation in learned societies or seminars and on publication. There is also little opportunity for discussion with researchers from other institutions, which is vital in promoting neurocomputer research. These circumstances therefore impede the research progress.

In addition, it is difficult for researchers to win permission to travel abroad for the purposes of work or study. The low degree of researcher freedom also extends to the selection of research themes; it is difficult to gain recognition or funds for themes judged to be out of conformance with institute policy. Since there is thought to be no great difference from the last case in regard to IG ability, there is a good possibility that the research could achieve landmark results if the IC is revised.

The strength of the IKs in this case stems from the conservative, closed atmosphere and culture of the organization itself. The IGs encounter different IKs at every stage, and may be unable to tell just who their 'real opponents' are. IPs would have to play the major role in efforts to improve this situation. Prospective remedial measures include organization of an in-house movement making an appeal for the importance of the IG research themes and the formation of new

IC={IK>IG>IP}

1 Construction of hypothesis ———————— Suggestions from outside sources
  ├— Discussion
  └— New knowledge/phenomena

2 Dissimilation ———————— Association, analogy
  ├— Theorization
  ├— Calculation, simulation
  └— Discussion, criticism

3 Concept creation ———————— Discussion
  └— Continuity

4 Chain of empathy ———————— Information system

4.5 Case B.

research teams to induce a sympathy with the same. In reality, however, the organization does not contain any individuals who could step into this role.

A similar situation is apt to take shape in other organizations like the current one, which has an extensive record of achievement in the business in question and in research related to it. An added complication is the fact that, when the research themes are of a highly advanced nature and the research managers cannot find any cases to serve as precedents, the IP function is liable to be suppressed, leaving the IGs in the position of having to wage their battles alone.

A prospective countermeasure in such cases is a shift to a policy of 'incubation outside the organization'. If the IGs can cope with the idea of going it alone, it would be advisable to remove their activities from the direct supervision of headquarters and site them at related national/public laboratories, universities, or even research institutes in foreign countries.

Organization C

This case also concerns research related to neurocomputers, but in the fields of artificial intelligence and cognitive science.

Reflecting these fields, discussion counts more highly than calculation as a factor in the stages of hypothesis construction and dissimilation. The line-up of factors in the four-stage model resembles those of the preceding cases, but the idea co-ordination differs from both, and could be expressed as IC = (IG > IP > IK), Fig. 4.6.

In approaches to neurocomputers from the field of cognitive science, stress is laid on matters such as analysis of the human thought process and relations with grammar. Discussion remains a vital factor at virtually all stages, i.e. the entire process of creation.

In the stage of dissimilation, models may be formulated on analogy with the results of other research, but a great part of the work is taken up with case-study-like investigations of the actual human thought process.

As in case A, discussion plays a vital role in the research process, but more importance is attached to discussion with outside parties rather than the research group or company members.

The IG in this case has already scored great success in related fields, and

IC = {IG>IP>IK}

1 Construction of hypothesis
— Suggestions from outside sources
— Discussion
— New knowledge, phenomena

2 Dissimilation
— Association, analogy
— Theorization
— Experimentation (case study)
— Discussion, criticism

3 Concept creation
— Discussion
— Continuity

4 Chain of empathy
— Information system

4.6 Case C.

his activities have received considerable recognition both inside and outside the company. He is consequently accorded ample opportunity for participation in discussions off company premises. In addition, the researcher temperament is one of eagerness to challenge themes in frontier areas. The in-house atmosphere consequently leaves little room for the emergence of IKs.

For the above reasons, selection of research themes is generally left to the discretion of the researchers themselves. As a result, there is a high degree of freedom in the research activities and IG activities.

As the IG himself has already acquired a significant stature, the need for IP functions is reduced. In cases such as this, the established reputation of the IG can function as an IP. In Japan in particular, once an individual is acknowledged as an authority in a given field, his stature as such tends to remain intact over the long term and to extend to other fields as well. Just as a corporate atmosphere or culture of a closed nature can function as an IK, this abstract stature can function as an IP.

There is, however, a difference between the two: as IK forces, corporate atmosphere and culture are truly 'faceless' entities, but stature as an IP force is always tied to an individual or group of individuals. While the IG doubles as IP in this case, this suggests that it could be effective for institutes to invite persons who have scored great success at other institutes to serve as IPs at their own. Figure 4.7 outlines IG, IP and IK rhythms in relation to creative potential.

Method of and management for creation in research and development

There are basically three means of cultivating and reinforcing creativity in research and development: cultivating and reinforcing IGs, cultivating and reinforcing IPs and weakening the power of IKs relative to that of the IGs and IPs. The result is the formation of a situation in which the power of IGs is greater than that of IKs (IG > IK). In other words, the cultivation and reinforcement of creativity can be viewed as a shift from the status of 'IG < IK' to that of 'IG > IK', Fig. 4.8.

The role which must be played by IPs changes as the research proceeds, in accordance with the relative strength of the IGs and IKs. As a result, there is a need for a 'shake-up' of the actual operation of the research and development organization in this process, in order to keep the IC, i.e. balance of power among IGs, IKs and IPs, in the optimal status. The following is an account of methods of producing the status 'IG > IK' premised on this need for shake-up.

As seen in the previous cases, discussion among researchers is an extremely important means of expediting the progress of research and development in fields of advanced research.

Theoretically, it would be possible to reinforce IGs by bolstering the strength of the individual IGs themselves, i.e. qualitative reinforcement. In reality, however, a quantitative approach to reinforcement would be more effective, e.g. an increase in the corps of researchers attached to the IG group and provision of ample opportunity for free discussion on the research themes, in view of its aforementioned importance.

Generally speaking, it is difficult to formulate a sequence of research

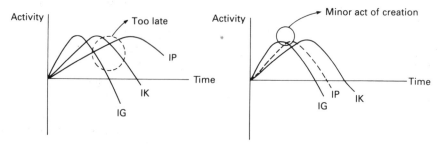

Note: In this model, the size of the result of IG + IP − IK expresses the
creative potential of the organization in question.

In the event of a radical reorganization, IGs, IPs, and IKs would each
start from a zero status. In this event, it is clear that IGs must be provided
with a margin relative to IKs. IPs must be in a position to protect IGs
before the power of IKs crests.

4.7 IG/IP/IK rhythms.

themes and to induce a self-proliferating effect in research and development
unless the research group is composed of at least three members.

The corps of researchers on the level of the entire organization (research
institute) must also be of a sufficient size. This also applies to the number of
researchers who do not directly involve themselves in discussions but conduct
research that is just as advanced or heuristic.

More specifically, at least 10 - 20% of the researchers in organizations
such as the central laboratories of major companies should be committed to
programmes in the most advanced areas.

It would be possible to induce the same effect by reinforcing the IPs and
leaving the IG power as is, Fig. 4.8. Nevertheless, it is extremely rare for a single
research theme to involve more than one IP.

Reinforcement of IPs should consequently be approached by such means
as qualitative improvement, explicit IP assignments for a given theme, or
placement under the jurisdiction of other individuals functioning as IPs.

As already described, IPs function to protect the IGs from IKs, to formulate
visions incorporating the new idea, and to furnish the opportunity for
commercialization of the same. In the first respect (protecting IGs from IKs), this
function can be regarded as amounting to an in-house campaign.

This is because the IP must work to deepen understanding of the IG
research and to make a case for its merits and necessity in order to foment an
atmosphere of respect for the IG activities.

Quite often, research and development in advanced fields may go on for
years without achieving any tangible results with a business value. To maintain a
high level of researcher and IG vitality in such cases, the IP must formulate visions
and targets that will act to spur them on. Even if the research results ultimately fall
short of the original targets, the IP must provide opportunities for their presentation
or publication and promote their reflection in the company products.

The IP must also work to increase IG participation in learned societies and other venues when IG reinforcement cannot be affected through quantitative means, i.e. an expansion of the corps of researchers.

In most cases, no more than one IK is involved with a single theme or IG; the IK function is usually performed by a single person or the corporate culture itself. In such cases, the weakening of the IK power could not be approached by quantitative means. Instead, the power of the IK could be effectively weakened by reinforcing that of the IP or broadening the distance between the IK and IG.

Action of the latter type may be exemplified by the establishment of new research institutes located at a sufficient distance from the headquarters, dispatch of researchers to universities, and siting of the research activities at companies that are tie-up partners of the company in question. In any case, the object is incubation of the research and development off the company premises.

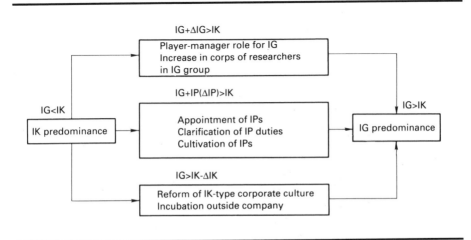

4.8 Reinforcement of creativity in research and development.

CREATION ENGINEERING AND SYNECTICS
creation in stages

| **Researcher** | W J J Gordon |

| **Subjects** | Researchers, developers |

| **Basic perspective** | Systemology, cybernetics |

Substance: 'Synectics' is a coinage from the Greek referring to the linkage of heterogeneous elements that appear to be unrelated at first glance. As a process, it consists of the generation of something new by deliberately viewing the 'familiar' as something 'unfamiliar'. The reverse act of viewing the 'unfamiliar' as something 'familiar' is also important in this process, but in the course of creation, the key factor is not the analytical capability required for such 'accustomization', but the capability to integrate previously disintegrated concepts required for the former.

The synectic process can be described in terms of the following five psychological states.

Practical mechanism of creation and basic psychological states

Psychological state	Anthropomorphic analogy	Direct analogy	Symbolic analogy	Description of psychological state
Detachment		O	O	Detachment from object for view from 360 degrees.
Involvement	O			Active involvement with the object through integration with and personification of it.
Deferment	O	O	O	Deliberately circuitous approach to problem in order to avoid rushing the solution.
Speculation	O		O	Detachment from the object allowing the mind to play freely.
Autonomy of object	O	O	O	Once problem-solving reaches a certain point the idea takes on a life of its own and begins an autonomous movement.

Synectics is a methodology for the discovery of 'something new' of value amid the familiar, and could exert a great influence on future creative research.

Source) W J J Gordon, 'Synectics – the Road to Creation Engineering'

5

Process of creation in product development

Creativity in product development

FINDS - a new way of apprehending creativity in product development

Creativity in product development has conventionally been demonstrated in connection with: (a) exploitation of seeds, (b) accommodation of needs and (c) development of channels to fill the gap between demand and supply. Today, however, the modes of product use are far more diverse than any conceptions formed by suppliers, and in many cases, the products do not meet all user requirements. It is gradually becoming impossible for companies to supply products that satisfy customers merely by probing their seeds and the market needs.

The progress of information intensification is driving a constant increase in the variety of products that suppliers must develop and accelerating the contraction of product cycles. Under the current systems, suppliers are becoming unable to maintain the proper level of progress, and their new products are not keeping pace with their targeted applications. This situation also stems from the underdimensioned information disseminated by the suppliers, attributable to the lack of a well-defined philosophy to underpin their activities, and from the confusion induced among consumers by the flood of similar products that results from this defect.

NRI propose FINDS as a new approach to developing what is truly needed today, Fig. 5.1, when genuine contentment seems curiously absent amid the abundance of goods and services. FINDS may begin with the identification of only those trends in needs that are in agreement with the company philosophy. Products would then be developed for these needs through the application of a technologically advanced developmental capability (seeds exploitation) in order to equip them with a level of function or performance far higher than that attained by

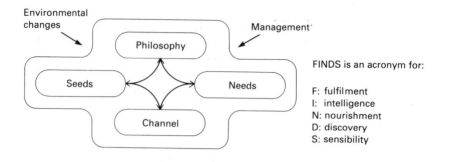

Environmental changes

Management

FINDS is an acronym for:

F: fulfilment
I: intelligence
N: nourishment
D: discovery
S: sensibility

5.1 FINDS (development of what is truly needed).

their antecedents. FINDS may also take the form of providing products with a distinctive significance in a context that is deeply intertwined with intellectual or cultural settings, in order to satisfy needs on a wholly different order from those to which conventional counterparts are directed. In short, FINDS may be defined as the discovery and creative development of what consumers are seeking from products.

Product life cycle and creativity

Creation in product development can be categorized in terms of the phases of the product life cycle, Fig. 5.2. While there are basically four such categories, the fourth (FINDS creation) must be regarded as the most important for the future.

Seeds-type creation

Creation of entirely new functions based on technological seeds in the form of patents, etc. It includes the injection of entirely new concepts through such activities as exchange with companies in other industries.

Examples: Xerox, colour laser copier

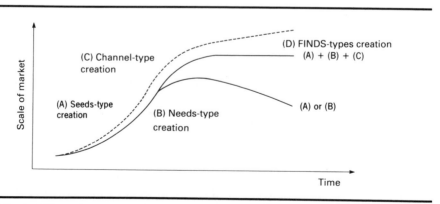

5.2 Product life cycle and categories of exercise of creativity.

Needs-type creation

Accurate determination of the trends in needs in the market and development of products attuned to them with a distinctive edge over competing counterparts based on improved productivity or enhancement of function/performance, etc.

> Examples: Attack, Walkman, Asahi Super Dry (see later in this chapter), refrigerators with 'magic doors' that can be opened from the left or right side

Channel-type creation

Linkage with new distribution channels for development of goods or services that cannot be supplied by competitors.

> Examples: Courier Service, Cool Home Delivery (refrigerated parcel service)

FINDS-type creation

Reflection of the corporate vision or philosophy in addition to exploitation of seeds and accommodation of needs.

Flow of creativity in product development

In postwar Japan, the mode of exercising creativity in product development has passed through four stages that correspond to four periods of economic growth and four stages of change in the level of value, Fig. 5.3. A key background factor shaping each stage was the balance of the demand and supply.

Filling shortage

The immediate postwar period was one of serious shortage of goods, and the balance was one of demand surplus in virtually every product field. During this stage, the most pressing agenda item was acquiring the ability to supply the demand for

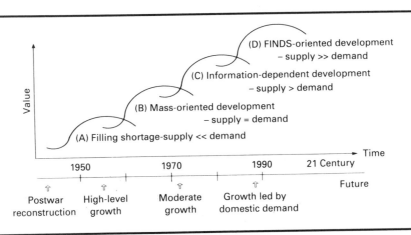

5.3 Flow of creativity in product development.

essentials. The product development typifying this stage was improvement of varieties of crops and other activity aimed at increased production. The representative cases include the development of fertilizers, agricultural chemicals, durable synthetic textiles with a long service life (e.g. nylon, vinyl), sausage made of fish meat, and margarine. In each, the aim was keeping the supply of necessities on a sufficient level. Around the mid-1950s, the home appliance boom erupted as refrigerators, washing machines and vacuum cleaners were added to the list of necessities for every home.

Mass-oriented development

In the ensuing phase of high-level economic growth, the demand and supply were balanced and the overall market expanded as suppliers made the most of the mass-production merits of mass-market products such as colour televisions, air conditioners and economy-class cars. The expanded export of compact cars to the US that began in this stage can be viewed as the result of exercise of creativity in coping with various needs associated with improved quality control and productivity. A representative case is the development of the rotary engine before the onset of the first oil crisis.

Information-dependent development

Levels of supply and penetration of durables in the consumer market have risen further, spawning a situation of surplus that has forced suppliers to use an information value as a means of setting their products apart from those of competitors. In the clothing field, for example, 'one-point shirts' (with a solid colour and only one small insignia on the chest, along the lines of LaCoste shirts) found an expanding circle of buyers along with the spread of golf as a form of recreation. Their popularity may be interpreted as having rested on affinity for the significance and information value attached to brand-name merchandise. Subsequently, the value of one-point shirts in consumers' eyes declined as DC (designer and character brands) apparel experienced a booming popularity. And the upward revision of the yen against the dollar triggered the influx of prestigious brand-name items of clothing that are international status symbols. In the field of automobiles, there is also a growing preference for models with options that set them apart from mass-market versions. It has become increasingly important for suppliers to deploy a systematic information strategy that includes transmission of information about ratings of their models in circumscribed segments targeted for sales in limited quantities.

In the distribution field, convenience stores have sprouted up all over Japan, and the spread of POS systems has made it possible for managers to identify fast and slow-moving merchandise in real time. Department stores as well have begun to expand the range of mail-order sales and to draft plans based on the collection and analysis of customer information. These activities depend on the existence of extensive information networks and high levels of productivity among the distributors. Although the scale of the business is still small, the rise of special services such as performance of personal import upon request is worthy of note as a development symbolizing this stage. In short, the development of goods and services is now highly dependent on information; the use of information resources provides the main venue for the exercise of creativity.

FINDS-type development

In FINDS-type development, the supplier would identify the essence of what custom-ers are looking for in products (needs) and determine those areas in which this essence fits in with the company vision (philosophy). Concepts would be formulated with attention to various environmental changes and social or cultural contexts. Finally, the concepts would be transformed into products through co-ordinated action in seeds exploitation and channel development. Needless to say, the target products would embody a value far greater than conventional versions as far as physical functions and performance are concerned.

With the approach of the 21st century, Japan's economy has turned to the home market as its main source of growth and export activities have been moder-ated. Customers who are capable of accurately evaluating products and purchas-ing products only if they suit them perfectly are coming to constitute the core of the market. Once this stage appears in a fully-fledged form, very few big-selling products are likely to arise. Suppliers would instead concentrate on providing products to those consumers with lifestyles attuned to the company philosophy. Products would be evaluated in terms of their creativity and the degree to which they assist the consumer's pursuit of self-fulfilment. In such a setting, the relent-less push for a greater share of the market that characterized the mass-market stage would be devoid of meaning. The thrust of competition would switch to demonstration of originality and creativity. 'FINDS orientation' may be viewed as a collective term for all of these trends.

Case study of product development

Handycam 55 (Sony 8 mm video camera)

Process of creation

The Sony Handcam 55's basic product concept was its compactness, lightness and size, being the same size as a Japanese passport. Sony emphasized the fact that it could film for two hours without a cassette change and that, despite its compact size, offered high-performance features such as a × 6 power zoom lens and a 1/4000 shutter speed, Fig. 5.4.

Basic product concept
1   Compact, lightweight, easily
    taken by women on vacations,
    passport size, no protruding parts

2   2 hours of filming without reloading,
    perfect for wedding receptions

3   High performance despite compactness
    X6 zoom
    1/4000 shutter speed

5.4 Development of Sony Handycam 55.

At present, most video camera manufacturers are working to boost the performance of their models while making them smaller and lighter. At the same time, they are trying to offer lower prices that will accelerate their penetration of the market. This was the background of the development of the Handycam 55, which has grown into a remarkably successful product. The process of development was as follows.

The 8 mm video format was determined in 1984, and the international standards in 1985, thus paving the way for fully-fledged commercial products. At this point, Sony personnel became interested in developing a supercompact video products that would take full advantage of the merits of 8 mm video. The thinking was that, since they are designed mainly for use outdoors, portable video cameras should ideally be as compact as possible. This dream of attaining the ultimate in compactness touched off a desire to try to realize it using 8 mm technology, which afforded the best prospects for doing so.

In late 1986, a proposal of the head of the Personal Video Division led to the institution of the 88 Project for the development of the required basic technology. The Project's stated aim was the development of an incredibly compact 8 mm VCR to be unveiled sometime during 1988. The Project team was composed of more than ten specialists in the range of fields instrumental for new VCR development, including IC technology, video tape drive mechanisms, packaging, set design and product design. The average age of the Project members was 31.

The first model made its debut in May 1988. Technical innovation in the early stages of the development was exemplified by the extensive use of multilayer PCBs to save space and make possible the landmark compactness. A crucial element in this process was the know-how about 'conception and style' gained from the audio development staff.

The group was renamed the '55 Project' in January 1988 as matters moved into the stage of product development. At this time a 29-year-old planner who had participated in the Walkman planning and also had field experience, was appointed as Project co-ordinator.

One of the major aims in design was realization of the aforementioned passport size (plus the size of the drive unit) without sacrificing the targeted performance levels ($\times$ 6 zoom, playback capability). Reflection of the results of exchange of creative ideas with the respective specialists enabled a reduction in volume to one-third and in weight to one-half the levels of conventional counterparts.

Handycam 55's passport size evoked a great reaction among consumers soon after the first models were placed on the market in June 1989. In response, Sony began running carefully constructed commercials showing typical scenes of use for the product that centred around travel as their key concept and set the product apart from others in the minds of consumers.

Management for creation

The following can be cited as the notable characteristics of Sony's management for creation in the development of the Handycam 55.

1   Creation of markets through new product development

Sony regards the creation of new markets through the development of new products as a genuine concern. During the aforementioned period of steep economic growth, it accorded greater priority to new product development than channel control in its efforts to cultivate the market. Its president sees Sony's role as one of constantly striving for excellence by testing the limits of its creativity and posting ever more successful results through creative management.

2   Appointment of young employees to lead product development

The corps of personnel in their twenties has consistently provided the power behind Sony's new product development. In the case of the Handycam 55, the developmental setup was co-ordinated by the head of the Product Business Division, who had formerly worked at one of the company's Kyushu stores. This enabled the reflection of business know-how in the development.

3   Personnel exchange and transfer

Sony provides for the diversion of personnel resources in accordance with the needs of major projects of product development and similar undertakings. Project leaders may actively recruit members from among the in-house staff. If a certain employee wishes to participate and is regarded as a good candidate for participation by the leader, the head of the unit to which the employee is attached generally will free the employee for this participation.

4   Sympathy of consumers gained through adverts portraying typical scenes of use

The Handycam 55 is not only directed to the family segment (i.e. used mainly for the video equivalent of baby pictures, etc). The concept was a portable, compact, high-performance camera that youth and women could take on vacations. This also formed the basis for the distinctive commercials, which feature a personality who is popular among young women going through customs on her way to boarding an international flight.

5   Effective use of know-how concerning high performance in compact packages acquired in other divisions

In attempting to realize a model that was far more compact than the 8 mm models already on the market, the development came up against technical barriers on several occasions. However, breakthroughs were eventually achieved thanks to the know-how accumulated in connection with the development of compact products in other fields (transistor radios, Walkman).

Asahi Super Dry (Asahi Breweries)

Asahi Super Dry is brewed using a new type of yeast, with appropriate changes in the brewing process. At about 5%, its alcohol content is higher than that of the average Japanese beer (about 4.5%). The adjective 'dry' was chosen to express its unique bite (sharp flavour). It was first marketed in March 1987 as a new 'sharp-tasting' beer that represented a challenge to the staid lagers which dominated the Japanese market, Fig. 5.5.

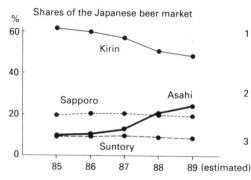

Shares of the Japanese beer market

Key concept of Asahi Super Dry

1 Alcohol content of 5% dryness with emphasis on pleasant sensation when swallowed ('bite')

2 A new, sharp-tasting beer to counter staid lagers dominating the market

3 New yeast, new brewing process

5.5 Development of Asahi Super Dry.

Process of creation

The development of Asahi Super Dry was made possible by a decision at the top rungs of management which fused the previously independent processes of market surveys concerning 'body' and 'bite' and technical studies. A new synergistic organization was formed to exercise creativity in developing a new product and constructing the system needed to keep it in stable supply. The following process led up to the development.

1   Institution of 'Flavour Reassessment', a study group composed of 15 members from technical, production and business units
The diverse membership of this group analyzed dietary patterns among the generation that would constitute the major demand segment in the coming years, and found an inverse correlation between consumption of 'light' foods and drinks on the one hand and that of meat on the other.

2   Survey of flavour preferences among 5,000 consumers implemented by the marketing division and production project division
In the conventional view, bitterness and robustness were the standards by which beer was judged in the Japanese market. However, the survey discovered that the majority of younger beer drinkers judged beer not only by its bitterness but also by its flavour when held in the mouth (body) and by the pleasantness of the sensation when swallowed (bite). It also found that beer drinkers in their twenties and thirties stressed bite over body.

3   Brainstorming sessions between the head of the marketing division and the production side (in the person of the assistant plant director)
These sessions culminated in the concept of dry beer with both body and bite.
    It should also be noted that Asahi Breweries was equipped with the technical capability needed for the concept's materialization.
    The following points may be cited as background factors in the research and development:

- A difference in flavour depending on type of yeast was confirmed through activities made possible by a technology tie-up with Lowenbrau Beer.
- A probe was made of the yeast bank of the company's central laboratory. Thirty different strains of yeast were identified as offering the desired body, bite, flavour, aroma and fermentative action.

Management for creation

Characteristics of Asahi's management of creation can be seen as the following:

1 Chain of empathy through commitment on the part of top management

Since 1986, Asahi Breweries has been expanding its share of the market at a pace no one in the industry would have believed possible. The key element in this performance has been the commitment by the top levels of management to the change represented by Super Dry, which has rippled through each division in a kind of chain reaction. This change has taken such forms as a revamping of flavour and labels, product development integrating R&D and business staffs, extensive use of various media, intensive investment in advertising, an 'all-Japan taste test campaign' involving a million consumers, new investment on large scales, priority on Super Dry in production, reinforced quality control and even removal of 'old beer' from the market through prompt rotation of stock on the retail level, Fig. 5.6.

Asahi Breweries was established in 1949 upon the dismemberment of DaiNippon Beer, and had initially enjoyed a 36% share of the market. For the following thirty years, however, the company's share continued to inch downward, fueling fears that, if nothing were done, it would fall below 10%, positioning the company behind Suntory in the industry for the first time.

In the face of this crisis, the then-president, Murai, decided to buck the conventional industry wisdom and completely revamp the contents and label of the company's products as part of a new CI program to renew morale. He was succeeded by president Higuchi, possessed of a buoyant, charismatic personality, who personally made the rounds of wholesalers and special contract liquor stores across Japan to ensure rotation of stock and end sales of 'old beer'. Higuchi also believed in direct dialogue with employees, and began the practice of general

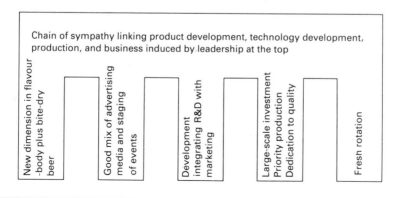

5.6 Management of creation in development of Asahi Super Dry.

morning meetings which he addressed through the medium of video. He also forbade the practice of 'cram' selling, abolished the system of profit-based control in plant operation and reassigned 600 of the 3,000 employees. The unity of purpose instilled by this rapid series of measures forged a chain of sympathy linking the planning, development, production and business divisions.

2 Management in the aspect of product development

Upon the transition from Murai, who laid the groundwork for the company's revitalization with the new CI campaign, to Higuchi, the current president, the in-house setup underwent a programme of reform aimed at establishing a dynamic communication between the marketing and development staffs. The new concept germinated in this new environment.

Although the new concept was actually proposed by the marketing staff, its formulation involved co-ordination with other divisions. More specifically, the following can be cited as background factors: (a) in-depth surveys related to flavour and consumer preferences and a developmental setup integrating R&D with the business end, and (b) assurance of the quality by brewing technicians, building confidence in the ability to market a substantially different product. The company's marketing division can be regarded as having hit upon 'FINDS' in the concept of 'body plus bite – dry beer', and as having then driven full-tilt towards the realization of this concept.

3 Management in the aspect of marketing

In advertising, a distinction was drawn between ads placed in newspapers and magazines, which were to present descriptions, and TV commercials, which were to convey an image. The campaigns portrayed Super Dry as the beer for contemporary preferences, and worked a fundamental change in consumer perceptions of beer. Realizing that the future of the company could hinge on Super Dry's success, Higuchi kept the advertising, which taken together formed a series with a narrative content, continuously before the public from January into autumn, despite the enormous expense entailed. In addition, the company staged a nationwide taste test campaign that was billed as the world's first of its kind and attracted a million participants.

4 Management in the aspect of production

With the backing of the resolute decisions taken at the top, the system of production was reinforced by assignment of priority to Super Dry and by new large-scale investment. An additional key factor was the successful effort to convey the personality of the new product to the neighbourhood liquor store owners and consumers in general.

Higuchi's policy on plant management was one of dedication to quality. In effect, he told his plant managers to turn out the finest product possible using the finest materials available, regardless of the cost. Quality replaced profit as the bottom line in plant management.

5 Management in the aspect of logistics

Higuchi also prepared the logistical framework needed for maintenance of quality and for 'fresh rotation', by which 'old beer' (beer left unsold for more than three months) was taken off the market. He demonstrated his seriousness by personally making the rounds of certain liquor stores and loading old beer into his car for return to the company.

Attack (Kao Co, compact detergent marketed in 1987)

Attack is a detergent with a great power to remove perspiration stains and other dirt. This power derives from application of biotechnology; Attack contains an alkaline cellulase enzyme that is able to break down even firmly set dirt. The detergent is offered in a small package that easily fits into a bicycle basket. In addition, technology was developed to coat the surface of the detergent granules with a non-viscous builder, so that a single spoonful of Attack delivered the same cleansing effect as four spoonfuls of regular detergents, Fig. 5.7.

Basic concept of Attack

1   Small package
    Box easily fits in a bicycle basket

2   Cleaning power of four spoonfuls of
    regular detergent in a single spoonful
    Unique coating of the granule surface

3   Ability to remove even firmly set dirt
    Application of biotechnology

5.7 Development of Attack.

Process of creation

The process of creation at Attack can be seen as follows:

1   Scientific elucidation of the structure of dirt

Kao Co made exhaustive studies of why certain kinds of dirt are hard to remove and scientifically elucidated the structure of dirt. Focusing on the fact that patches of dirt soldified by cellulose could be broken down by the action of enzymes that dissolve this cellulose, Kao directed its energies to the discovery of the optimal cellulose yeast for this purpose. This effort spanned many years and drew upon the participation of regular staff employees. Soil samples were collected from various parts of Japan for analysis. Microbes discovered in the process were cultured and stored. The store of microbes was then searched in an attempt to identify those that were suited to the purpose and application in question. The development of Attack also drew upon Kao's extensive experience in research and trial commercialization of detergents employing enzymes.

2   Positioning of detergent product and functions within the context of the consumers' total daily life

Kao realized that conventional detergent boxes, which are bulky and hard to carry, were out of step with the performance-oriented trends in other product segments of the market. In view of this need for more compact packages, it embarked upon the development of technology to deliver the same cleaning power in granules of a smaller size. It also realized that consumers were more concerned about 'cleanliness' than ever before, and that a detergent more capable of removing dirt would be highly valued.

3   Appeal to consumers through effective advertizing depicting scenes of use

In its advertizing, Kao presented Attack in a manner designed to change conventional perceptions of detergent among consumers.

4   Empathy among distributors

Detergents, soaps and similar products have been unpopular with distributors since the prices are generally not commensurate with their space requirements. The small boxes were consequently welcomed by wholesalers and retailers who must make the most efficient use of a limited store space.

Management for creation

Characteristics of Attack's management for creation can be seen as the following:

1   Five guidelines in product development and leadership at the top

Kao has formulated five guidelines for product development. Its top-level management exercises a formidable leadership to ensure that these guidelines are strictly observed.

- Is the product of value to consumers?
- Does it apply some distinctive technology?
- Does it deliver a good cost/performance?
- Did it gain a favourable reaction from consumers in preliminary surveys?
- Can the product be effectively promoted at every stage of distribution?

    If the answer to any of these questions is 'no', there is no point in product development in Kao's eyes.

2   Commitment to fundamental, key elements

Kao attaches great weight to technical originality in the belief that it will not be able to set its products apart from others on the retail level unless they are marked by some independently developed, unique feature. (The importance of unique technology to back up products was driven home to Kao during the oil crises, when even supply of resources from other countries appeared to be in jeopardy.)

    This commitment is exemplified by Kao's stress on basic research that begins not on the level of needs perceptible by consumers, but on the deeper level of skin metabolism and physiological mechanisms. In marketing as well, it supplements the usual approaches with cultural scientific studies of human emotion, belief and aesthetics. Its product development capability is therefore rooted in the most basic layers. In addition, the company attempts to induce an overall synergy in product development by linking efforts to create key chemicals and technologies with its TCR (total cost reduction) campaign. (Kao's production technology division and R&D division were consolidated in June 1988).

3 Consistency with the company philosophy takes precedence over share

The company's philosophy amounts to a dedication to the creation of unique products with a real value, and therefore de-emphasizes the activities of competitors or the size of the company's share of the market as determinants of policy (stress on the 'philosophy' portion of the FINDS model).

Utsurundesu (Fuji Photo Film, photographic film with lens, first marketed in July 1986)

Basic concept of Utsurundesu

1   A new dimension in cameras – film with a lens

2   Disposable camera

3   Pocket-size

4   The camera you don't have to remember to bring from home

5.8 Development of Utsurundesu.

The concept of Utsurundesu, translated as 'it really works!', was four fold. As a camera, it could be seen as disposable. Being the size of two boxes of film, it was compact, lightweight and when the film had been used, the entire product could be given to the developer. Utsurundesu developed as the camera which you didn't have to remember to bring from home, Fig. 5.8.

Process of creation

The following cites the process of creation in the development of Utsurundesu.

1 Sense of crisis, easy-going creation

The background of Utsurundesu's development was an awareness that the film market had passed its peak and that consumers were shifting to electronic cameras, giving rise to a sense of crisis about the prospect of a contraction of the film demand. Nevertheless, the development itself was promoted not in a heavy-handed fashion, but with an easy-going attitude designed to encourage creation.

2 Development in small ad hoc team

A project team composed of about ten members was formed to develop a new-idea product that would breathe new life into the film market. None of the members participated in the project full-time; all worked on the project during spare moments of their respective jobs. The team objective was an expansion of the segment of film purchasers, i.e. widening of film's niche in the market, through the marketing of a new-idea product.

3 Flexibility in concept formation

In the process of concept development, the focus in studies first fell on the means of equipping high-sensitivity film with a picture-taking function. In other words, the concept of a disposable camera was originally not under consideration. Actually, the company had researched disposable cameras some years before, and decided to abandon plans to go ahead with commercialization for reasons associated with cost and marketing. By this time, however, the company had developed the low-cost high-sensitivity film that paved the way for commercialization. Utsurundesu's time had come, and the target concept was reoriented accordingly.

4 Stress on ease of use

In order to identify the direction in which the segment of film purchasers was to be expanded, a series of studies was conducted concerning the characteristics and behaviour patterns of prospective new customer segments. The team decided to adopt high-sensitivity film for the product, in the belief that, whatever the segment, the photos taken would have to be of a high quality. It also decided to equip the camera proper with only the minimum requisite functions. Ease of use took the place of functional sophistication as an object of concentration. The team strove for a camera that virtually anyone could use and to make it easy to carry around and to purchase when the occasion of use arose, the camera was to be no bigger than two boxes of film.

Management for creation

The following can be seen as the three main characteristics of the management for creation at Fuji.

1 Small, flexible organization open to serendipity

Utsurundesu was developed by a small team working in their spare time who were not made to feel a heavy burden of responsibility. The concept has a light, playful feeling that probably would not have taken shape in a grim, high-pressure atmosphere like that of the manufacturing industry.

At one point in the development, a sceptic commented, 'Does this thing really take pictures?' A team member replied, 'Believe me, it really works! (utsurundesu)'. This casual reply was seized upon as the name, which has acted to stir curiosity about the product.

2 Dedication to quality and exclusion of superfluous functions

While Utsurundesu is a 'playful' product, the team realized that it could not be of a low quality. No compromise was made on the quality of the developed pictures, which is about the same as that afforded by ordinary cameras. Functions, on the other hand, were pared to the minimum required. A year after the original Utsurundesu debut, Fuji Photo Film came out with a 35 mm full-size version and a version with a flash in November of that year. Around the same period, cameramakers were unveiling sophisticated models along the lines of Minota's alpha-7000, and the thrust of competition in the market lay in enhancement of photographic functions through the use of microelectronics.

3 Mood of experimentation in development

The process of development included test marketing conducted merely as a kind of experiment. Once it was discovered that it had a strong appeal for women and high-schoolers, Utsurundesu moved into full-scale production. In addition, it was decided to expand the target segment gradually outward from these demand niches through publicity stressing the product's convenience.

Cima (Nissan Motor, luxury car in the +2,000cc class, first marketed in January 1988)

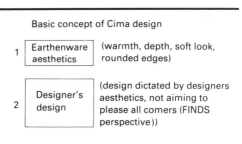

Basic concept of Cima design

1	Earthenware aesthetics	(warmth, depth, soft look, rounded edges)
2	Designer's design	(design dictated by designers aesthetics, not aiming to please all comers (FINDS perspective))

5.9 Development of Nissan Cima.

Before Cima, most Japanese luxury cars with an engine displacement in excess of 2,000cc were developed on the assumption that they would be chauffeur-driven, and great emphasis was consequently laid on the comfort of the rear seat area. By contrast, Cima was developed as a luxury car affording a sense of complete satisfaction for the owner as driver. In the design aspect, it is claimed to exhibit a novel styling and form that have no parallels, Fig. 5.9.

Process of creation

In the case of passenger cars, a great deal of the creativity in development involves the design. The following is an account of the process of creation in the development of Cima's design.

1 Development in a high-pressure situation

The development of Cima's design took place in an atmosphere of extreme pressure. In the first place, there was great apprehension about the future course of the company as a whole. Nissan's midterm statement released in September 1986 showed an operating deficit of 19.7 billion yen. To compound matters, its share of the domestic passenger car market dipped below 20% in October of the same year. The sense of crisis that welled up in these unprecedented straits spread to the design centre and created an awareness that some decisive, bold action had to be taken.

Second, there were great temporal constraints placed on the work due to the fear that competing automakers might come out with a formidable model of a similar type before Nissan. As a result, the development of the Cima design had to be achieved in an extremely short time. Designers were asked to perform work that ordinarily requires a year in 3.5 months, in order to move as rapidly as possible from the modelling stage to production.

These two factors imposed an enormous pressure on the designers, but also appeared to have inspired the novel Cima design. The designers literally had no time to stray in a mass of details; they had to decide promptly upon a basic concept and then concentrate on refining it.

2 Concept refinement

The person in charge of the Cima design work was Noboru Wakabayashi, then a senior designer in the design centre (now manager of the centre). Wakabayashi focused on the following two features as the target concept: a) a model with 'earthenware aesthetics', i.e. that looked as if it had been crafted by hand and was not the result of some 'cold' mechanical process, and b) a model that reflected the designer's view of what a luxury car should be as opposed to the manufacturer's desire to 'sell'.

The attempt for earthenware aesthetics was an attempt for a design avoiding the hard, cold look of steel and imbued with the warmth, depth and rounded edges of pottery. In this connection, the team addressed a question bearing on a difference between European and Japanese culture: 'Just how much of the massiveness embodied by West German luxury models, which conveyed their sturdiness, should be incorporated in a Japanese-style luxury car?'

This question emerged in Wakabayashi's mind on a trip to Europe during the hiatus between the development of the Cedric and that of the Cima. While travelling through West Germany and Spain, Wakabayashi felt a ponderous heaviness in the air which he had not felt in the US and which he saw as manifested in automobile design as well. Reflection on the nature of this heaviness and the difference from Japan led him to the key concept of a 'Japanese-style massiveness'.

The second feature meant that the development was to proceed not with a view to satisfying a wide range of consumer preferences, but with an unswerving commitment to a coherent aesthetic concept shaped by the designers themselves.

This stance stemmed partly from the limited time frame. There was no margin for digestion of a host of 'needs' factors; the designers had to take the shortest path to what they perceived as the most important features and priorities.

Time was also a factor in the decision to design only one model as opposed to the usual practice of designing several models and then choosing one. This approach apparently contributed to the translation of the concept's aesthetics in a pure, intact form. This is because aesthetics rarely survive the rational dissection occurring in competition among designs with their vitality completely intact. In addition, the design of several models is often accompanied by a kind of mutual complementation of ideas that leaves the one eventually chosen with some kind of incoherency. Since this cannot occur with only one model, the designers' sensibility has a better chance of being carried over into the design without losing any of its vitality.

Management for creation

The following can be seen as the notable characteristics of Nissan's management for creation in the development of Cima.

1 IPs supporting a setup that left the design to the designers

Prior to the development of the Be-1 and Cima, Nissan's design staff tended to turn out designs that were basically expansions upon previously successful designs and could easily have cases built for them. This tendency was a product of the system requiring all designs to undergo a procedure of approval by parties including non-designers. This system acted to exclude designs that were truly innovative and to encourage the proliferation of those that could hardly be termed creative but were liable to win approval.

The picture changed when Wakabayashi began working on the Cima. Non-designers were no longer given a say on matters of the design per se, which was to embody a high degree of creativity and superb aesthetic sense. The design work was left to the designers themselves.

The entire process from design to development was the responsibility of the director of the development group (now director of the product division), Yasuhiko Misaka. Up to that time, Misaka had worked exclusively in marketing and came to this assignment with virtually no experience of design. This unprecedented shuffling of personnel across divisions was implemented in accordance with the policy of Yutaka Kume, who assumed the post of president in 1985.

Misaka noticed that Nissan's designers had been doing their work without any contact with the people who would be driving the models they were designing. He therefore encouraged the design staff to get out of the office and meet with potential customers for direct dialogue. However, except for laying down a basic orientation, he said absolutely nothing about the nature of the design, leaving the substance of the work completely to the designers, and concentrated on providing them with the funds and supplies they needed.

Misaka's policy heightened the sense of responsibility and authority felt by Wakabayashi and his staff, and contributed to the birth of a creative design. When told that the Cima design had been completed, Misaka's first comment was reportedly, 'Well, have you done everything you wanted to?'

Referring to the Cima development, vice-president Sonoda (now advisor), who had jurisdiction over the design research division, reportedly told some of his peers to 'let the youngsters do as they please'. This remark was apparently motivated by a fear that the design would only suffer from interference by senior executives out of touch with the trend of the times.

This atmosphere is also illustrated by the turn of events when Kume decided to visit the design centre. Standing before the row of clay models in the studio, Kume was on the verge of making a pronouncement when Wakabayashi stepped up and said, 'If you have anything to say, please don't say it here; it's bound to affect the design'. The daunted Kume emitted a long 'hmmm' and walked back out of the studio.

The stance of top-level management is now one of getting the designers to make the most of their creative potential. This stance is undoubtedly a major factor in the great turnaround in Nissan's business in recent years.

In short, there were plenty of people playing an IP role in middle and top layers of management in the case of the Cima development.

2   Management reform supporting 'design by designers'

The adoption of the policy of non-interference in design by management was accompanied by a multifaceted reform in management.

This management reform, in turn, resulted in an organizational reform that accorded a greater degree of freedom to employees and provided for recognition commensurate with individual achievement.

Various measures were taken to create a freer atmosphere more conducive to creation. Uniforms were made optional and working hours were made more flexible. Employees were encouraged to drive models of competing automakers to get first-hand experience of their ride and suspension, etc for research purposes. The circle of those eligible for a loan of test models from the company, which was formerly confined to executives, was broadened to include ordinary employees.

In the field of development, the reform included replacement of rigid adherence to the seniority system with a system whereby a given task was placed into one of seven ranks in terms of degree of difficulty, with ability rated accordingly, in order to create an environment stimulating exercise of talent, individuality and creativity by the individual. Promotions and rises were now made on the basis of merit. The designers responsible for the successful Be-1 and Cima were rewarded with ample recognition that further whet their incentive.

With the success that began with the Be-1, the approach in Nissan's sales strategy shifted from one of 'product-out' to one of 'market-in', i.e. the sales staff abandoned the 'hard sell' and became accustomed to letting the models sell themselves. This shift was in agreement with the stance in Cima design, which was one not of pandering to the widest possible needs, but of an uncompromising commitment to the aesthetics of the 'Japanese-style massiveness' conceived by the designers themselves. In this respect, Cima can be viewed as an expression of a coherent philosophy on the company side, which we have termed one of the elements in a FINDS perspective.

3   Re-creation

Since Cima, Nissan has been working to develop a stream of equally novel models. The question is the extent to which this creation can be sustained. Wakabayashi has stated that he has no particular intention to 'groom' his successor. In work aimed at achieving advanced design, there would be no point in inculcating one's own ideas in the successor's mind.

This is because advanced design is 'advanced' with reference to 'the present'. It will cease to be advanced if it stays tied to 'the present' as it moves into 'the future'.

For this reason, what Wakabayashi intends to impart to his successor is an uncompromising attitude, commitment to one's aesthetic stance, and other matters regarding the designer's approach, not his own aesthetic sense.

In Wakabayashi's view, the task of a manager of creation-related work would presumably lie in an accurate perception of the trend of the times, identification of individuals with the sensibility required to lead the way in the coming years, and the provision of formidable support for the activities of those individuals.

US manufacturer of control equipment

Management for creation

The subject of this case is the development of a product (machine vision) by a leading US manufacturer of factory automation (FA) and computer-integrated manufacturing (CIM) equipment (referred to here as 'A Co'), Fig. 5.10.

A Co's range formerly consisted mainly of factory floor sensors and other mechatronics components. As this equipment began to enter the mature stages of its life cycle in terms of both the related technology and market, A Co realized that it had to develop new products promptly in order to expand its range. It consequently conducted a survey of the entire sensor-related market, which revealed bar code, machine vision and data carrier systems as the most promising fields. By acquiring certain small-scale entrants, these new fields became a new division for A Co.

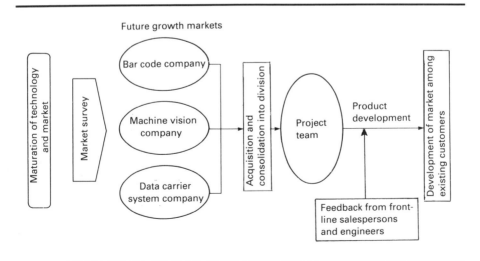

5.10 Management for creation in machine vision development.

In its approach to machine vision, A Co instituted an in-house team for product development composed of six members, including product design engineers, marketing personnel and sales staff. The team implemented an indepth field survey that centred around analysis of the trends in technology (e.g. price, performance). Meanwhile, the plant engineers and marketing staff did their utmost to ascertain the reactions and needs of the customers they encountered during performance of their routine duties.

In cultivating the market, A Co's biggest customers were made the subject of intensive campaigns deployed by means of developing the applications they desired and accumulating the know-how they needed.

The notable features of the management for creation in this process can be summarized in the following three points.

1 Identification of keys for success

A Co's construction of strategy for the development was grounded in a firm grasp of the keys for success in that development. It is characteristic of the FA field that: a) the selling points are a good match with the technology already in use and development of relevant applications, and b) the domain of FA technology is far-flung and evolving independently. As a result, one of the major keys for success is a thorough familiarity with a wide range of customers and of the 'seeds' of new FA technology, and the accumulation of a vast store of know-how related to application. A Co has consequently placed in-depth knowledge of its customers as its top priority in several respects.

In the first place, its promotion of product development is keyed by dialogue with customers. A Co conducts no basic research. By the same token, however, it harnesses the energies of its front-line staff to assist product design engineers in ascertaining the nature of customer needs, as noted above. This has enabled A Co to turn out products that offer customers a greater freedom of use and expansibility through integration with other systems than those of competitors. This factor has supported its ability to stay on top of the FA market.

In the second place, A Co's product development is conducted with sales to its existing customers in mind. In the case in question, the cultivation of a market for the new product took the form of a buildup of application know-how and of a record of 'little successes' in application through interaction with customers willing to work with it. This effort gradually expanded the circle of customers inclined toward purchase of A Co's products.

2 Communication of mission to each employee

A Co makes sure that each of its employees understands its mission.

The role of managers is regarded as consisting of: a) instilling in employees a shared, lucid understanding of the basic mission of their division, b) explicit statement of goals and the time by which they are to be attained, and c) allocation of resources accordingly.

3 Divisional managers picked from pool of employees with experience of several divisions

Only those who have acquired experience of several divisions are appointed as division managers. Most of A Co's divisional managers worked in product development, market development and production before they became managers; very few came straight from the financial division. A Co has also prepared a programme complete with manuals to assist the career development of individual employees. The success of this programme may be gauged by the incidence of leaving at A Co, which is extremely low as compared with that at the average American company.

US manufacturer of chemicals and pharmaceuticals

This case concerns the development of new herbicides (products A and B) by a US manufacturer of chemicals and pharmaceuticals (here referred to as 'B Co').

B Co's development of herbicides dates from the 1950s. Since the prospects for its subject were unclear, the early product development was not allocated a sufficient amount of resources by management. The work was tackled by a team of four developmental personnel (biologists and chemists) and 30 marketing personnel and culminated in the announcement of product X. This product met with failure due to the combination of difficulty of use and the lack of instructions concerning the product for wholesalers and farmers.

B Co unveiled an improved version of product X in 1965, but this too failed to achieve success, due to the lack of sufficient backing in the form of instruction for users. Meanwhile, the herbicide market was rapidly expanding and numerous competing products had appeared.

At this point, B Co took a lesson from its failures and adopted a 'mixture strategy', aimed at achieving a mixture of product A with the products of other companies in the market that would act to expand the range of herbicide application. This shift in strategy was accompanied by one from sales to actual degree of use on farms as a criterion for judging salesperson performance. It also adopted a firm policy of taking insufficiently effective products off the market, and initiated programmes of detailed instruction in use for farms. This strategy rocketed B Co from the fifteenth to the first spot in the industry, see Fig. 5.11.

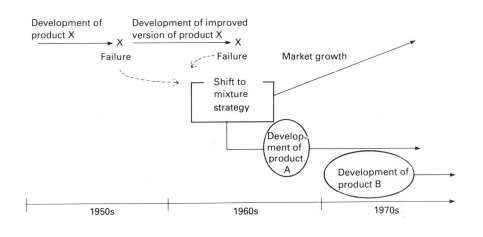

5.11 Flow of development of herbicides.

Nevertheless, B Co did not stop here; it went on to develop product B, which applied biotechnology and had an even greater range of application, in the 1970s. Although it began with a team composed of only four technicians and one marketing employee, right from its start, the development of product B was premised on sales around the world. Ultimately, the team succeeded in developing more than 100 applications for product B in a total of 110 countries.

Management for creation

The following four points can be cited as the notable features of the management for creation in this development.

1 Shift to user needs as the bottom line in development

The adoption of the mixture strategy was preceded by about fifteen years of consecutive failure. The major causes of this failure were an insufficient grasp of the users' actual needs and insufficient programmes of instruction in product use for users. The mixture strategy consequently attached prime importance to effectiveness and ease in actual use on farms. The system of evaluation of salesperson performance was reoriented in line with this strategy. In addition, instructional programmes were reinforced and various activities carefully monitored.

2 Conquest of NIH, 'not invented here', syndrome

Researchers and technicians plagued with the NIH syndrome are content to continue in the orientation of the products which they have already developed and are reluctant to challenge a new orientation. In the case in question, this syndrome was detected in two locations of development, and B Co took action to rid them of it. In terms of the IGKP model, this may be regarded as IK containment.

The NIH syndrome surfaced in the form of in-house opposition to the idea of a mixture strategy. Technicians in particular were staunchly opposed to the coexistence and co-prosperity with competing products that are implicit in this idea. In response, B Co deepened its contact with the University of Illinois and fed back the results of research of the compounding of competing products conducted there into its own programme of product development. In so doing, B Co formed an 'idea bypass' off its premises.

There was also the opposition of marketing personnel and technicians to the commercialization of product B. The marketing personnel could see no need for commercialization at a time when product A was selling well thanks to the success of the mixture strategy. However, they were eventually persuaded to co-operate in the effort by a programme of education about the reasons for commercialization. As a group, the technicians tended to resist any idea that did not fit in with the notions and knowledge they had acquired in their work. The company dissolved this resistance by bringing out the advantages that could be expected from the development and the unique features of the product. In the end, the technicians as well became convinced of product B's merits, and diligently applied themselves in its development.

3 Transformation of IG into IP

Specifically, the manager of the product B development project was the inventor of product A, which originally led the mixture strategy to success. He had therefore experienced first-hand just how strong opposition to new ideas within the company could be, and was able to protect IGs from IKs during the development of product B.

4 Preparation of environment conducive to creation
In this connection, it cited the following as conditions which project leaders must assure in promoting the creativity of the project team: a) provision of ample opportunity for desired activity, b) avoidance of outright rejection of ideas, c) flexibility in operation, d) sufficient degree of freedom of activity for individual members, and e) sharing of ideas among members.

RESEARCH OF JAPANESE-STYLE CREATIVITY

creation psychology

Researcher   Akira Onda

Subjects   Educators, developers

Basic perspective   Psychology, philosophy

Substance: His quest to discover the essence of creativity has led Akira Onda into a wide range of areas, including creativity development, the relationship between dreams and creation, creativity among the Japanese, and education for creativity. In the process, he has built a record of significant and diverse achievement. Of particular interest is his research of approaches to cultivating creativity in education through the use of origami, the traditional Japanese art of folding paper into various figures.

The common thread running through all of his work is an exploration of the connection of Zen, Buddhism in general, and other branches of Oriental thought with creativity. This perspective also colours his views of origami. He sees in origami a means of fostering in children the power of concentration and intuition needed for creation, and suggests Zen meditation as a means of doing the same for adults.

Oriental creativity has often been described as differing from the Occidental variety in that its substance is creation growing out of imitation. Onda's work is an attempt to go beyond this view and establish a methodology of Oriental creation.

Source: Akira Onda, 'Research of Creativity Development'

Method of and management for creation in product development

Based on the previous cases, the following five points can be cited as requirements for creative promotion and management of product development from a
FINDS perspective.

Uncompromising commitment to essence

Products that the consumer will feel inclined to purchase have been developed
with an unswerving attention to their essence.

Such products have some kind of intrinsic appeal. Seeing the Handycam
55 for the first time, consumers cannot help but be impressed that the video camera
has become so compact. Super Dry offers a new flavour that is changing ideas of
what a good-tasting beer is.

Attack demonstrates a greater cleaning action in smaller quantities than
conventional detergents. Detergents applying biotechnology and packaged in
small boxes are now acquiring an increasing share of the market, and the big box
of detergent is beginning to disappear from shelves. In this way, Attack has made
the detergent business over in its own image.

Cima avoids the clutter of options which might have been incorporated if
the design had been approached with 'sell' uppermost in the mind. Instead, it
remains steadfastly faithful to the earthenware aesthetics concept that proceeded
from the designer's own sensibility, and thereby makes a statement about what a
luxury car should be.

Similarly, the herbicides developed by B Co had something that the farmers
wanted; a greater herbicidal effect.

FINDS is the exercise of an overall perspective and discernment in product
development. FINDS-oriented development begins not with a grasp of superficial
needs, but with a probe of the essential needs. The object is determined with reference to the company philosophy. A coherent, kernel concept is formed, and
then approached through innovation using technological seeds. FINDS perspective and discernment are reinforced through this uncompromising commitment
to reaching the essence of the product.

Positing of scenes of use

Once the major target segment is decided upon, the company should posit scenes
of the product's use that take into account the nature of the aspirations, the
emotional colouring and the sense of values in that segment.

This requires the ability to paint a detailed portrait of the user's character
and behaviour that includes not only his lifestyle and environment but also
sociocultural elements not under his individual control.

If the company can equip it with a level of function or performance far
above the level of counterparts used in the scene in question, the product will
doubtlessly be perceived as a creative one with a formidable attraction. And by
skillfully presenting it in the scene, the company can cloak the new product in a

persuasive image; the product will 'make sense' in the eyes of the target consumers.

The advertising for the Handycam 55 is built around the theme of travel. The number of Japanese going abroad each year is now in the order of ten million, and young women account for a great share of this number. The TV commercials consequently depict a young woman who is asked to present her passport at customs and instead presents her Handycam 55. The scene of use is adroitly tied to the product's most distinctive feature; its passport-size compactness.

The development of Attack was approached by positioning detergent in the context of all relevant daily life activities. A wide-ranging survey implemented by Kao to this end found that consumers disliked big boxes of detergent because they didn't fit into the baskets of the bicycles many of them used to go shopping and because they made the already cramped area around washing machines, which are generally installed next to bathtubs or sinks, even more cramped. This information about the scenes of use and handling formed the starting point of the product development. And the technology developed to resolve these difficulties applied innovative seeds gained from basic research in the fields of physics and chemistry.

In the case of Utsurundesu, the team posited scenes of high-schoolers and young women playfully posing before the camera on an outing. The test sales were launched to learn if the product would really be accepted by this segment, i.e. would really fit into these scenes.

Cima's originality lies in the earthenware aesthetics and 'Japanese-style massiveness' pictured by the designer that did not characterize models of European or American manufacture. The scene of use was not that of the chauffeur-driven owner dominating previous luxury car development but that of the owner-driver.

A Co, the US manufacturer of control equipment, approached machine vision by developing system applications and acquiring know-how especially for the scenes of use among its major customers.

Use of highly distinctive technology

Each of the companies described in the case study has a store of distinctive technology that constitutes its strength. In the case of the Handycam 55, making an 8 mm video camera of passport-size compactness required an extensive reduction of the size of the cylinder head drum, a flat loading format and positioning of operation switches on the side of the main unit. In addressing these items, Sony drew upon what might be called its tradition of making equipment smaller than competitors can. Its ability to surmount the many obstacles and realize a camera that is far more compact than competing counterparts can be equated with an ability to reinforce further its greatest strength. Attack and Utsurundesu were both preceded by attempts to commercialize products along similar lines that either were discontinued or ended in failure. Both came to fruition through reinforcement of technological seeds (discovery of highly effective enzymes and an enhancement of film sensitivity, respectively), which made it possible to attain the required level of quality.

Reinforcement of key technology paved the way for the development of

Kao's Attack and Sofina as well. Key technology also formed the basis for the product development of A Co (FA & CIM technology) and B Co (biotechnology).

Recognition of personnel achieving creative product development

A company cannot expect to develop creative products on a continuous basis (as opposed to big sellers that suddenly vanish) unless it can keep personnel who are up to the task and can maintain their incentive for creation. Sony has given the leaders of its product development, who are generally in their twenties, a considerable amount of authority and responsibility. Its internal setup is geared for receptiveness to the sensibilities of its younger employees; its corporate culture is youth-oriented. The members of the teams responsible for Super Dry and Cima were rewarded with handsome bonuses that have fired the incentive of their successors. In short, such specialists must be given recognition commensurate with their achievement.

This is also true in the case of the management performing an IP function and seeing that the creative work reaches fruition.

Harnessing of organizational and individual assets

Sony's projects of product development are bolstered by the system of in-house recruitment of the most suitable members, regardless of their division. This is a key pillar of developmental capability in a company that prides itself on development of original technology.

In the case of Asahi Super Dry, the wave of support that rippled across divisional boundaries and led to the birth of a successful product would not have been set in motion without the company's solidly established brewing technology.

Companies developing expertise and distinctive technology within the conventional vertical arrangement of organizational units can induce a demonstration of genuine creativity if management can induce an interaction between market information gained from analysis of needs and unique elemental technologies. This point is illustrated by the case of Super Dry development. In the case of Utsurundesu, the development was achieved by a small group of employees, some of them amateurs as far as product development was concerned, who worked on the project in their spare time and were not made to feel intense pressure. Here, success rested on the existence of a high-sensitivity film that made commercialization of the unique concept possible and on effective use of the company's marketing channels. The very idea was creative; in all other respects, the success depended on the marshalling of the company's existing resources.

A Co provides for the muster of interdivisional resources by appointing personnel with experience of several divisions as divisional managers.

Effective use of product-development-related informational resources in the broad sense, including the induction of an interdivisional sympathy toward the work, the participation of younger and female employees, attention to the opinions of employee family members and constructive response to complaints, is vital for the elimination of the fixed notions, commonly-held ideas and preconceptions that block the exercise of creativity.

6

Process of creation in system development

Creativity in system development

Characteristics of systems in companies

With the progress of information intensification, economic and social activities are coming to depend more and more on the related (information processing and communications) systems. A case in point is the spread of ATMs and other on-line systems in the banking business. In the distribution field, great penetration is being made by POS-based inventory management systems and on-line dispatching systems for home delivery services.

Positioning

Systems process information promptly, accurately and in great quantities, and in effect compress time and distance. Their capabilities far outstrip those of the individual employees operating them. Nevertheless, the systems themselves do not produce value for management; they are only a means of attaining business objectives set by management.

As a result, system development must be conducted as an integral part of larger programmes of innovation of the corporate system of distribution, marketing techniques and new tie-ups with other companies.

Ultimate aim

The ultimate aim in system development is the establishment of a competitive position of clear superiority relative to other companies through supply of unique goods and services that would not exist without the system and that offer the customer a greater added value in both quantitative and qualitative terms.

Problems

As systems become more sophisticated, extensive and complex, the system division necessarily becomes more specialized as a group, and there is an increasing possibility of estrangement from or a gap in perception with other divisions.

Table 6.I Characteristics of systems in companies

1 Positioning	The means of attaining an object
	Inseparable from the system of business
2 Ultimate aim	Establishment of an overwhelmingly superior competitive position
3 Problems	Need for information literacy
	Time lag between construction and surfacing of effect
	Funding for required investment

There will also be a greater time lag between the system's construction and the surfacing of its desired effects. A lack of mutual understanding or co-ordination at any of the stages of system planning, development and use may rule out attainment of the initial objectives. Similarly, a tardy decision to use or construct systems can make it extremely difficult to regain ground lost to other companies as a result.

In addition, system development requires sizeable investments, and by extension, a firm commitment by the top level of management to the development. However, such a commitment may be difficult to obtain, since executives at the top are likely to lack a deep understanding of the system.

Stages of creativity in system development

Stage 1 Improved efficiency through information processing

Figure 6.1 shows the change in the use of systems to improve corporate efficiency.

Systems originally attracted the attention of companies mainly in connection with use for individual work. The systematization of routine work enabled a labour reduction and improved efficiency in individual work. Systematization gradually spread to more diverse work, thus contributing to upgrade the overall level of office services.

Next, the focal point of systematization moved to integrated control. Systems came into use as means of consolidating various types of control information and managing it in a unitary form. Use on this level greatly improved the efficiency of organization operation.

Individual work	○ Large loads of routine work -> 　　　　reduction of labour, improved efficiency ○ Small loads of diverse work -> 　　　　improvement of service
Integrated control	○ Consolidation of control information -> 　　　　improved efficiency in operation of organization
Linear information use	○ End users-> supply of information to end user
Respect for individuality	○ Personalization-> system as everyday tool

6.1 Stage 1 – Improved efficiency through information processing.

This was followed by the rise of linear-type use of information. Unlike the consolidation of all information in a central entity characterizing the previous one, this phase was marked by supply of information in the opposite direction; to the end users. Systems were employed to facilitate use of information by the company's end users themselves.

Today, system use has entered what might be called a phase of greater respect for individuality. Both information and systems are undergoing a kind of personalization; adaption to the individual operator or user. In the process, systems are becoming a larger, more familiar part of the daily corporate routine.

Stage 2 Strategic use of systems for business innovation

System development is currently graduating to a new, second stage of strategic use for business innovation, see Fig. 6.2.

In virtually all recognized cases of exercise of creativity in such system development, the developing company was able to generate a new market or build a position of clear superiority in the existing market through effective use of information processing and communications equipment or technology in business development or corporate management activities. The systems in question are the so-called 'strategic information systems' (SIS).

The coming years are likely to see continuing efforts to develop systems aimed at setting the company apart from competitors and giving it an edge in competition. The main forces behind such efforts are the top level of management and enterprising managers.

Stage 3 Business development through system creation

Certain companies pioneering a strategic use of systems are developing unique goods and services based on fuzzy logic and other advanced system application technology.

As a third stage, NRI envisage the rise of systems embodying highly creative concepts that transcend the level of individual products and create an entire

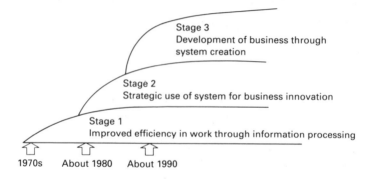

6.2 Stages of creativity in system development.

ANALYSIS OF HUMAN INTELLECTUAL ACTIVITY
balance between concentration and diffusion as a key

Researcher J P Guilford

Subject Researchers, developers

Basic perspective Cognitive psychology

Substance: A trained psychologist, Guilford produced a model that views the thought process as a sequence of five operations.
• Recognition of some problem (or topic)
• Committing of the problem to memory along with related problems
• Circumscription of the problem and concentrated contemplation of it
• Freer, diffuse consideration of it
• Final evaluation

He has also proposed a structural model of intellect (SI model) incorporating productions and contents along with these operations.

Placing memory at the core of thought, Guilford distinguishes two mnemonic segments, one being the reservoir of concentrated (logical) knowledge, and the other, of diffuse (empirical) knowledge. In addition, he links these respective segments to the concentrated and diffuse operations noted above.

Concentrated thought is exemplified by the typical thought used in calculation, e.g. addition and subtraction. Diffuse thought includes the kind of thought that generates ideas for new product development.

Guilford's subject is the thought of individuals such as researchers and developers. The notion of striking the proper balance between concentrated and diffuse thought, which is obviously important for individual creativity, also contains valuable suggestions for creativity on the organizational level. For example, the layers of corporate organization could be viewed as corresponding to the sequence of five operations. In this scheme, the creativity of the organization as a group would depend upon a balanced capability for each operation, as in the case of individual creativity.

Source) J P Guilford, 'Three Faces of Intellect', Am Psych, 14, 469–479 (1950) business or enterprise. Today's private parcel post business and convenience stores laying in stock three times a day would be inconceivable without the support of their systems. Nevertheless, in such cases, it would be more accurate to say that the business concept came first, and was followed by the use of systems in an extremely sophisticated way in order to realize that concept.

Our third stage is therefore characterized by the proposal by system developers of new business concepts per se in a form that makes the fullest use of the power systems possess, i.e. the proposal of business like today's parcel post service and convenience stores from the system side.

The premise in this stage would be an extremely keen awareness by companies of the importance of exercise of creativity in system development.

In addition, as the role of system development expands and deepens, the role played by the systems in corporate management would also undergo a fundamental change. The originality and creativity of systems (e.g. neurocomputer systems, fifth-generation computers) could constitute the main force behind business development.

If this stage in fact materializes, creativity in system planning could no longer be separated from creativity in business planning; the two would only be significant if they could be induced in co-ordination with each other.

GROUP THOUGHT
system thought and SINIC theory

Researcher Isao Kon

Subject Researchers, developers

Basic perspective System theory, cybernetics

Substance: How can a group systematically achieve creation? Kon attempts to answer this question by viewing the group of individuals as a single system operating through a distribution of roles among its components. To minimize the conflict between the needs of the individual and those of the group, he proposes the formation of subgroups, each composed of a few individuals, and repeated discussion within each subgroup that eventually leads to an overall group consensus.

Known as the 'KPS Method', this approach aims at a dynamic intragroup communication effected by a division of group members into three classes: panel leaders (PL), panel members (PM) and other members (M), each with their own distinctive roles. It differs from brainstorming in this explicit demarcation of roles and its total systematization. The group generates a concept by rhythmically performing Guilford's cycle of diffuse and concentrated thought three times in succession. He also proposes the institution of a 'think module' (TM), a standing in-house organization constantly engaged in KPS activities (in contrast to the sporadic convening of brainstorming sessions) in order to enhance the creativity of the organization as a whole.

Source) 'Developing Creativity', edited by R&D Study Group

Case study of system development

Toyo Sash

A revolution sparked by the use of innovative systems is quietly underway in the household-use aluminium sash business. The revolution's standard-bearer is the leading entrant in this business, Toyo Sash. In the process, Toyo Sash's share of this market continues to rise.

In 1981, Toyo Sash began operating an in-house on-line system for distribution known as TRAIN. This was followed in 1985 by the initiation of service around its TOPICS system, which is also used by stores and other businesses outside the company. These two systems have worked a dramatic change in the nature of Toyo Sash's distribution.

TRAIN has greatly rationalized the company's internal distribution. Covering 50,000–60,000 different types of items, distribution of the related construction materials by conventional means was, not only extremely complex and time-consuming, but also made it difficult to optimize production and inventory. The installation of TRAIN cut the time required from order placement to delivery from over two weeks to one night at a single stroke.

As shown in Fig. 6.3, TRAIN has streamlined the flow of materials from the company's 37 plants to its seven distribution centres, and finally, via its sales arm, to the 20,000 stores handling its products across Japan.

This system was extended to the stores which are Toyo Sash's customers by TOPICS, the name given to its VAN services. On-line TOPICS terminals have now been installed in more than 1,000 of these stores. TOPICS has won high marks from these users for its effectiveness in rationalizing their own business and enabling them to monitor inventory in real time.

These systems have come to the fore as tools of innovation in distribution that are making conventional approaches to distribution obsolete. This innovation is spreading among its customers, plants and at its headquarters.

While these systems, which are expanding by the year, harbour various elements of creativity, of particular note is the creativity exercised in the initial period of TRAIN development.

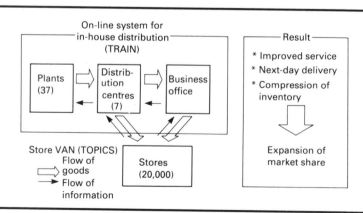

6.3 Distribution innovation at Toyo Sash.

Management for creation

Toyo Sash would never have been able to compress its delivery term from two weeks to the next day, something no one would have imagined possible at the time, if it had not prepared a unique in-house environment conducive to creation in the system field.

The following four points, shown in Fig. 6.4, can be cited as the major features of the process of creation of this system.

1 Formation of a definite vision for development by top-level management

In 1974, Toyo Sash instituted a special committee that drew the participation of all divisions to deliberate upon innovation. After a period of in-depth investigation, the committee cited distribution intensification and the construction of a system to support distribution as the most critical needs. In response, top-level management hammered out a vision of innovation with a clear-cut target, next-day delivery anywhere in the country. This declaration of the target, which appeared virtually unattainable at the time, at each stage of the development and on each level of the organization may be regarded as the first key to success.

2 Cultivation of personnel needed for system planning

A coupling of business strategy and system strategy is indispensable for creation in system development.

Toyo Sash reinforced its information system division with an additional 30–40 employees. The sole focus of their initial education was increasing their awareness of the need to offer the customer a greater benefit.

Today as well, Toyo Sash attempts to produce system engineers that do not immerse themselves in their field of expertise, but constantly remain attuned to the needs of the front-line business. This has effected an organic linkage among

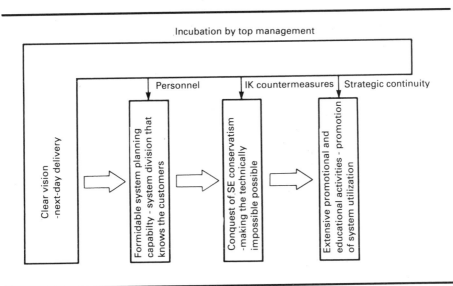

6.4 Management for creation in system development at Toyo Sash.

the functions of business planning, system planning and system design, which are prone to disjunction, within a single organization; its information system division.

3 Containment of technical idea killers (IKs)

Whether they are on the company staff or attached to manufacturers, system engineers with many years of experience as such tend to have a conservative outlook on the subject of innovation in the aspect of technology.

This is particularly true of those who have worked on large scale systems. Such system engineers are keenly aware of the difficulty of developing a defect-free system even of the conventional type, and are reluctant to venture into fields of new technology in view of the risks. In the development of TRAIN as well, certain technicians stated flatly that the proposed system was 'technically impossible'. The opposition of such technicians was pushed aside and the system planning began.

This containment of technical IKs would not have been possible without the existence of a clear vision and a system planning staff versed in both the business and technical ends.

TRAIN represents the realization of a complex system of on-line, real-time processing in a decentralized environment that had been labelled as impossible by some technicians.

4 Launching campaign to promote utilization and understanding of TRAIN

Innovative systems are often not well-received by their prospective users, both inside and outside the company. Toyo Sash realized that promotion of system utilization is both vitally important and requires efforts on a par with or greater than those expended in development. For this reason, it is conducting a vigorous campaign designed to increase utilization and understanding of both TRAIN and TOPICS.

Seven-Eleven Japan

Seven-Eleven Japan Co took its start from a tie-up with the US company Southland, and has since blossomed into a rapidly growing Japanese-style convenience store business thanks to its innovative techniques.

As of the end of November 1989, there were 3,815 Seven-Eleven stores in Japan. Some 98% of this total were franchise operations run by retailers who had formerly operated liquor stores and other small neighbourhood businesses. The spread of Seven-Eleven stores has therefore meant a revitalization and modernization of small retail businesses. Figure 6.5 shows the systems of Seven-Eleven Japan.

In addition, the company has prompted the implementation of various new kinds of distribution techniques among its vendors (the wholesalers and manufacturers that are its sources of stock). While it does not see itself as such, Seven-Eleven could be regarded as the instigator of nothing short of a revolution in the distribution business.

All of its actions are built around a policy of 'viewing things from the consumer's perspective and keeping abreast of the consumer's needs'. To live up to this policy, however, it has had to adopt a host of new schemes, i.e. systems.

A prime example is its system of physical distribution, especially for fast

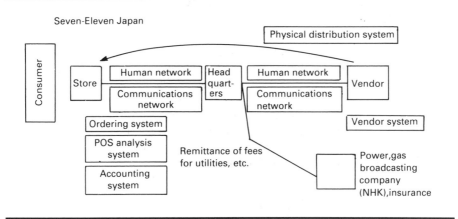

6.5 Japanese-style convenience store business created by systems.

foods and perishables, where freshness is a must. The company has taken various steps to ensure the freshness demanded by consumers, including delivery of box meals and similar items three times a day, delivery of hot and cold items separately, and alteration of delivery routes depending on the day or hour in order to avoid traffic congestion.

The company's systems do not consist merely of various computer systems and communication networks linking the stores, vendors and headquarters. They also encompass a 'human network', i.e. a corps of counsellors who explain POS data and systems to member stores and help them to make the best use of the same.

Seven-Eleven Japan pioneered Japan's convenience store business, which now contains many competing entrants. Nevertheless, the company's development of this business should not be viewed as a thing of the past, but as an on-going process.

Management for creation

The following four points which are also shown in Fig. 6.6 can be cited as the major characteristics of creation at Seven Eleven Japan.

1   Rigorous, customer-oriented operation

Seven-Eleven Japan has expanded by transforming Japan's petty retail business, but not as part of a strategy developed with large-scale supermarkets in mind. President Suzuki asserts that the biggest force the company has to contend with is 'changes in consumer preferences/needs'. In effect, its stated aim of keeping up with the ever shifting needs and preferences of consumers has committed the company to a never-ending creation.

2   The company is not afraid of disrupting the status quo

The line followed by the company represents a challenge to the existence of conventional distribution routes, and in this sense may be viewed as 'creation

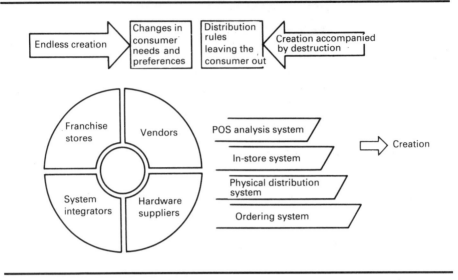

6.6 Management for creation at Seven-Eleven Japan.

accompanied by destruction'. Suzuki has told his employees, '70% of our work is destruction'.

3 Mission is seen as innovation/creation

As noted above, the vast majority of the company's stores are franchises, and therefore out of its hands. In addition, the entire daily routine is systematized, so that the company's role lies in refinement of the systems. But it is not only the operation of the stores that is left to others. The company also leaves shipping to the vendors, the information systems to system integrators, and the array of in-store equipment to hardware suppliers. While positioned at the hub of the business, the company is free to concentrate on such matters as providing guidance in effective use of the systems, detecting problems and innovation. In short, its mission is limited to innovation and creation.

4 Creation is driven by systems

The course of Seven-Eleven Japan's development of business is one of expanding its distribution and in-store systems. At the same time, this course has entailed the dismantling of the former distribution routes. Underpinning its creative activities are systems that replaced outmoded business practices and enabled rapid response to changing consumer needs.

Do house

A marketing firm, Do House Co has constructed an entirely new type of network in which the nucleus is composed of housewives. At the request of its clients (mainly food product manufacturers), Do House introduces new products to consumers, analyzes their reaction, and supplies the results to the client, Fig. 6.7. One of its chief means of doing so is the holding of 'culinary classes'.

These 'classes' are held in the homes of 660 housewives, mainly in Tokyo and Osaka, who were recruited by the company for this purpose and are known as the 'Do-san' ('Mrs Do') group. The class participants merely prepare dishes using the new products, sample the results and express their views about it; no attempt is made to sell the product to them. In other words, the classes are held only for the purpose of gathering information.

Do House now conducts market surveys for not only food product manufacturers but also manufacturers of electrical/electronic appliances.

Today, when changes in the market are becoming increasingly diverse and unfolding at an increasing speed, 'it is no longer possible to acquire valuable information about products from retailers', in President Ono's view. He sees a shift from the retailer to the home as the reservoir of knowledge and information about products. The question is how to tap this reservoir.

Do House formulated an answer in the person of the Do-San. The Do-San takes note of the casual conversation about the product in the class and organizes these on about 200 cards. The cards are then analyzed according to the KJ method in order to produce qualitative information. Needless to say, the key element in this setup is the Do-san herself. In this sense, the company has created a business operated mainly by the housewife.

Information network of Do House

Figure 6.8 shows the notable characteristics of the information network constructed by Do House which can be further expressed as follows.

1 The information funnelled through the network is based on opinions
To determine how a product is selling, one need only assemble information on

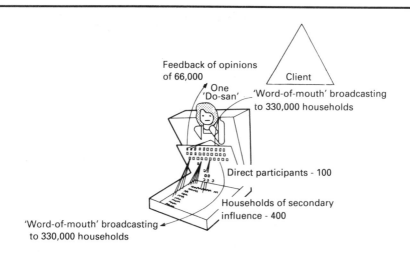

Feedback of opinions of 66,000

Client

One 'Do-san'

'Word-of-mouth' broadcasting to 330,000 households

Direct participants - 100

Households of secondary influence - 400

'Word-of-mouth' broadcasting to 330,000 households

6.7 Do House's information network.

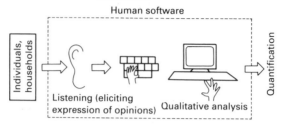

Information processing: Fact-data-quantitative analysis-information
Information creation: Opinion-qualitative analysis-quantification-information

6.8 Creation of an 'aural network'.

the actual fact; the sales. The point in such activities is assembling the information as quickly as possible, and POS systems are consequently used for this purpose today. To determine whether or not a product will sell, however, requires not information on facts, but on opinions.

2 The network is based on 'listening' as opposed to 'asking' as a means of acquiring the subject opinions

The approach is not one of questionnaires bluntly asking respondents if they would be inclined to purchase the product. The class participants can experience the product first-hand and express their opinions of it in any form they wish. The company acquires valuable suggestions precisely because of the unstructured form of the conversation that takes place in the classes.

3 The network stresses qualitative analysis

Information about facts can be gained by defining a subject segment, assembling the corresponding data and analyzing these data in quantitative terms. To gain information about opinions, however, the surveyor must first induce their expression. And the expressed opinions cannot be quantified; they are only amenable to qualitative analysis.

However, the value of this information can be increased by quantification of the results of the qualitative analysis. Ono calls the Do-sans who elicit opinions and perform the qualitative analysis 'human software'. In the context of this network, they do not simply function as nodes or switching equipment; accommodating various situations, the function they perform is on a par with, if not beyond, that of software.

Originally introduced to link internal divisions together, information networks have spread outward to link companies with their clients. In the coming years, they are anticipated to spread further, to the level of households and even individuals. As shown by the difficulties encountered in information network system (INS) testing, however, penetration to this level will by no means proceed smoothly. Networks of dialogue in yes/no formats may do for business, but not for the home.

As noted, Do House has created a new marketing technique that has, in turn, created a kind of housewife-based business. In so doing, however, it may also be regarded as having created a futuristic network system that will serve as the cornerstone of its business in the information society.

A US airline company

C Co operates a forerunning computer reservation system (CRS) that is not confined to its own flights, but extends to its suppliers, customers and even its competitors, and so also functions as a strategic information system.

At present, the system's network consists of more than 100,000 terminals installed in some 15,000 travel agencies around the world. It handles reservations and ticket sales for the flights of some 300 airlines as well as reservations for 20,000 hotels owned by 150 companies, for about 50 rent-a-car businesses, and for concerts and other events, all in real time.

The system began with a conversation in 1953 between the president of C Co at that time and one of IBM's senior salesmen who met while occupying adjacent seats on one of the company's flights.

Before CRS, the company reservation system was one of pen and paper. Reservations were entered on cards in the order received and checked against the seating chart. The process required three hours' worth of work by 12 employees per flight.

The actual development of the company's system began in 1959. When it was first put into operation in 1963, it was positioned as a means of internal rationalization that would streamline reservation work and enable the employees to ascertain the status of reservation promptly and accurately. The development reportedly required an investment of about 40 million dollars, an amount which at the time would have bought four Boeing 707s. The cumulative investment on the system to date is said to be in the order of 500 million dollars.

In the early 1970s, C Co's lead was followed by U Co and T Co, each of which developed their own separate systems. The existence of three CRSs gave rise to the notion of constructing a joint network to travel agencies, but this idea was abandoned in the face of opposition from other airlines companies. As a result, each of the three built independent networks to travel agencies.

In 1978 and 1982, two additional companies joined, bringing the total number of entrants in the airline CRS business to five. Nevertheless, the business is dominated by the systems of C Co and U Co, which command respective shares of 40 and 30% of this market.

The prime factor behind C Co's dominance is the extension of its system to include reservations for other airlines. The customer can use C Co's system to reserve seats on flights making up the optimal route for his trip, regardless of the identity of the airline. Initially, the system was designed to put C Co's flights at the top of the list of candidate flights, but even this practice has since been discontinued. C Co is paid one dollar for each reservation made through the system, which has moved from the loss to the profit column as a result.

Management for creation

There are three features to be noted in the management for creation in the development of C Co's CRS system.

1 Steadfast commitment at the top

The top-level management never wavered in its commitment to the system. The system only began to function as the strategic information system it is today around the late 1970s. From the inception of development in 1959, the president was actively involved in the project and supported it with the necessary investment. The initial outlay of 50 million dollars (about 18 billion yen at prevailing prices) and the cumulative investment of 500 million dollars (about 100 billion yen) could have been used to purchase several new aircraft.

The support came not only in the form of funds; talented system engineers were recruited to promote the development and reduce dependence on IBM.

In addition, the current president was formerly assigned to the computer division, and has supported the system development unit since his years as vice-director of the marketing division.

2 Top priority on service at the counter

C Co made every effort to see that the system reflected the needs expressed by its users, meaning travel agencies and its own reservation service counters. This stance in effect quickened the tempo of the network's expansion among travel agencies and also led to the participation of competing airlines, hotel operators and rent-a-car firms.

It was a stance that grew out of C Co's corporate culture, which is coloured by the same priority. C Co realized that, in the service industry, the main determinant of the degree of customer satisfaction is the treatment received from the employee on the other side of the counter. For this reason, it accords the greatest possible range of responsibility and authority to the personnel dealing directly with customers, and performance is judged in terms of the quality of service. In addition, the employees are encouraged to bring questions directly to the president.

3 Hybrid team of system and service personnel

The system development was conducted by a team composed of both system engineers and front-line personnel. Initially under 50, the number of personnel involved in the development now exceeds 5,000.

The decision to involve marketing personnel, accountants, and other employees who know the situation at the counter along with system engineers made possible the development of a system that is highly convenient for its operator and the customer.

CREATIVE PERSONALITY

desire to think as a yardstick of creativity

Researcher Shinichi Nakayama

Subject Developers

Basic perspective Cognitive psychology

Substance: Shinichi Nakayama (a professor of the University of Library Information) delves into the relationship of personality and creativity, and suggests that a desire to think (thought motivation) is the link between the two.

'Individual personality' is of course an extremely hazy concept, and its interpretation will vary widely depending on the affinity with and viewpoint of the interpreter. Results of recent research, particularly CAB studies, posit the following three groups of factors as manifestations of human personality.

- Basic factors (e.g. emotional capacity, sense of responsibility, sincerity, cheerfulness, self-discipline)
- Interpersonal factors (e.g. co-operativeness, openness, leadership, sense of propriety, empathy)
- Goal-oriented factors (e.g. planning capacity, creativity, power of execution, power of concentration, adaptability)

Here as well, creativity is treated as a function of the desire to attain a certain goal.

An evaluation of several subjects in terms of these factors and investigation of their respective interfactor correlations with a view to identifying those factors heavily bound up with creativity produced the following portrait of the personality adapted to creation:

Cheerful, independent disposition, ability to lead others, no grim sense of responsibility, no strict observance of proprieties.

Obviously, since it rests on mere hypothesis, this conclusion should by no means be applied as a standard in actual personnel evaluation, but nevertheless may warrant some consideration.

Source) 'Research and Measurement of Creativity', in 'Research of Creativity vol 6', edited by Japan Creation Study Group

Method of and management for creation in system development

Method of creation

Figure 6.9 at upper left plots the positions of the companies covered in the case study with reference to co-ordinate axes. The vertical axis indicates the intensity of the impact exerted by the system in question on the business, and the horizontal axis, the degree of advancement of the company's objective in using the system.

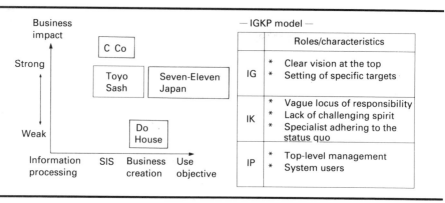

6.9 Positioning of cases.

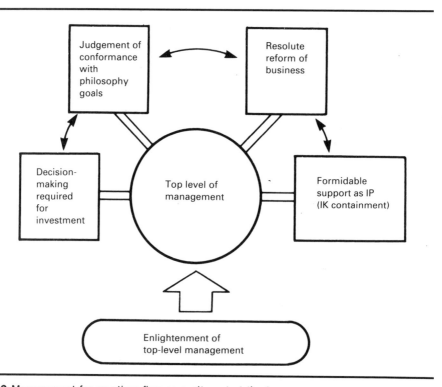

6.10 Management for creation; firm commitment at the top.

Toyo Sash's system was designed for strategic use and has had a strong impact on the aluminium sash industry. C Co's system forms a network linking the company to travel agencies. In the case of Seven-Eleven Japan, it is the system that is creating the business.

By contrast, Do House's system represents a special case. It has had a relatively small impact on the business, but may be regarded as a futuristic network of 'meaning-rich' information.

Figure 6.9 at upper right shows the roles and characteristics of IGs (idea generators), IKs (idea killers) and IPs (idea promotors) in system development.

In system development in particular, it is important for IGs to have a clear vision/philosophy and set a specific objective for the development. Toyo Sash's president Asada has built a vision around 'co-action', and set a target comprehensible to any employee; 'next-day delivery anywhere in Japan'.

IK factors appear in the forms of a lack of understanding of or co-operation with the system on the part of other divisions and a vague locus of responsibility for the development. In addition, personnel who cannot see beyond their own field of expertise and tend to be averse to significant change or departure from the status quo generally function as IKs in system development. A case in point is the vendors who refused to co-operate with Seven-Eleven Japan in its programme of distribution innovation. The company responded by resolutely terminating its contracts with them.

To achieve creative system development, the top level of management generally must play an IP role. This is because the development exerts a companywide impact, entails massive leading investment and running costs, and requires close interdivisional co-ordination (IK containment).

The system's prospective users may also function as IPs. In each of the four cases studied, the work advanced in response to the needs of the system's prospective users and customers.

Management for creation

Firm commitment at the top

The first prerequisite of management for creation in system development is a firm commitment at the top to the development, see Fig. 6.10. Regardless of whether the IG function is played by the top-level management, system division personnel, or personnel in some other organizational unit, investment required for system development must ultimately be approved at the top. In addition, it is liable to be unclear if the system will deliver a commercial benefit commensurate with the investment. For this reason, the decision to invest must be made largely with reference to the corporate philosophy/goals harboured at the top. In some cases, system development may also require a radical reform of the prevailing mode of doing business.

Furthermore, once the development is decided upon, it must be backed by potent IP forces that can contain IK forces until the benefits of the system clearly surface. This observation is corroborated by the cases of Seven-Eleven Japan, Toyo Sash and C Co.

In sum, creative system development would be impossible without a firm commitment by top-level management throughout the work.

Nevertheless, system development is an inherently high-risk undertaking, and top-level management is therefore apt to be reluctant to make such a commitment. Even if the system division succeeds in formulating a creative system plan, it may be promptly dismissed when submitted to the top. And as a result, the company may find itself outdistanced by rivals and placed at a serious disadvantage in competition.

This prospect suggests the need for enlightenment at the top, as indicated by the arrow pointing upward at the bottom of Fig. 6.10. The presentation of plans must be accompanied by an exposition, in as much detail as possible, of the benefits that may be expected from the system and its aims, illustrated with references to the benefits other companies have derived from similar systems.

The presentation should also include a comparison of the company's existing information system with those of other companies in the aspect of performance, a description of the related activities among competitors and the danger that could result from procrastination.

Management for dissimilation

A second prerequisite of management for creation is effective management for dissimilation. As used here, the term dissimilation refers to the merger of the diversity of priorities and perceptions among the various divisions and organizational layers throughout the entire sequence from system planning, design and development to promotion among the prospective users and the creation of new business and markets. Management for dissimilation is the deliberate incorporation of this dissimilation in management. The following can be cited as means to this end.

The first is 'fusion of the heterogeneous', to which there are two approaches. The first approach is the cultivation of transdisciplinary personnel. It may be exemplified by Toyo Sash's policy of hammering away at the need to offer the customer a greater benefit in its programme of education for its new system division recruits.

The second approach is familiarization with the scene of use. In the development of its business support system, Toyo Sash had its developmental personnel accompany its sales corps as they made their rounds in order to familiarize them with the business-end needs.

The second is the appointment of an official IP. The aim here is keeping the IK forces in check by, for example, placing a member of the board who wields great influence within the company in charge of the entire process of system development. In fact, in one of the aforementioned cases, the system development was placed in the hands of a director possessed of a great capacity for leadership who had come up from the business planning division, knew the problems of the system users, and had always been speaking about system development. His presence was instrumental in the attainment of an apparently unattainable goal. This IP therefore functions as a kind of general project manager.

The third is qualitative refinement (purging of elements working against the development). Preparation of an environment in which the various elements composing the information system will show a respect for each other's opinions (as opposed to an obdurate attitude precluding dialogue) is surprisingly important for the induction of a full dissimilative effect. While it may appear to run counter to dissimilation, this qualitative refinement of the entire body involved in the development is a precondition for the occurrence of an effective dissimilation. Examples include the exclusion of unco-operative vendors and the holding of companywide meetings every Tuesday to ensure a shared perception of the basic orientation in system development at Seven-Eleven Japan, and the termination of assignments to non-productive Do-sans at Do House.

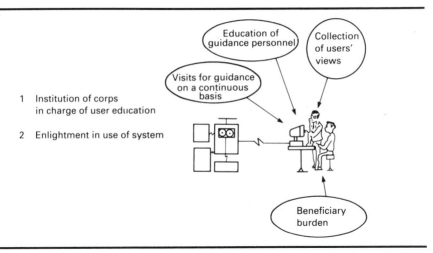

1. Institution of corps in charge of user education
2. Enlightment in use of system

6.11 Management for creation; boost in user capability and motivation to use the system.

Boost in user capability and motivation

A third prerequisite of management for creation is a boost in the capability and motivation of the prospective users to use the system. The fruits of creation in system development only appear when the system is used to its fullest potential. Assurance of full use must be placed at the top of the list of agenda items in management aimed at inducing a 'chain of empathy.'

Various programmes of education and enlightenment for users are conceivable to this end. An obvious step is the institution within the organization of a corps in charge of user education, Fig. 6.11. The crucial factor would be the mode of corps operation, as follows.

First, members of the corps should visit users to provide them with guidance on a continuous basis. In the case of Seven-Eleven Japan, this function is discharged by its operation field counsellors (OFC). Each OFC is assigned to seven or eight stores which he must visit at least once every two weeks. Toyo Sash also has a team of consultants who advise customers on the use of its system.

Second, the corps itself must be thoroughly trained. Seven-Eleven Japan has become famous for the district manager and OFC conferences it holds every Monday and Tuesday, respectively.

Third, programmes of user education must be paralleled by others aimed at ascertaining the actual needs at the site of system use and reflecting them in the system development. The institution of a career development programme should also be considered in order to groom and keep personnel with the ability needed for this task.

Another measure that could be taken to motivate active use of the system is having the system's beneficiaries (users) assume part of the burden of the system's cost. In such a scheme, a failure to make the most effective use of the system would have an adverse effect on the user's profits. By charging a dollar for each reservation made through its system, C Co has heightened user awareness of cost/performance considerations. This step also transformed its information system division from an expense burden to a profit earner.

7

Process of creation in business development

Creativity in business development

Outline

Creativity in business development is the ability to develop entirely new goods and/or services that rest upon systematic use of the creativity demonstrated in technology, product and system development and that, taken together, constitute an entirely new business. This definition excludes the creation of goods and/or services that suddenly generate a vast demand among a certain type of customer and then just as suddenly vanish; the substance is continuous supply of goods and/or services that offer a high value-added to a wide range of customers. Similarly, development of business through the imitation or improvement of existing technology, products, or systems is not creative. There are five basic patterns of such creative business development:

- Establishment of venture company by an enterpriser – Apple, Federal Express, Secom
- Reinauguration in form transcending the original business – Yamato Transport, Meitec
- Development of business through in-house venture or subdivision – great synergy with the company's main line
- Development of business through outside venture or other detachment from the company – low synergy with the company's main line
- M&A – Misawa Homes

The development of business through in-house ventures, subdivisions, detachment and outside ventures that make use of the company's business resources as well as through M&A (merger and acquisition) strategies that make use of the resources of other companies is assuming increasing importance for continued growth and advancement, Fig. 7.1.

Flow of creativity in business development

The evolution of business development in Japan may be divided into the three major phases of imitation, improvement and creation as shown in Fig. 7.2.

The phase of imitation extended from the immediate postwar years to the period of high-level economic growth in the 1960s. During this phase, business development was based upon the transplantation of business seeds to germinate Japanese versions of forms of business that had been developed in the advanced industrialized countries of the West.

This development of business through the wholesale import of technology and know-how required little investment on R&D, and the business was able to get on track in a short period of time. Whole segments of Japanese industry in the manufacturing sector, such as chemicals, food products, automobiles, machinery and home appliances, as well as in the service sector, such as supermarkets, mail-order sales, leasing and rent-a-cars, began from such imitation.

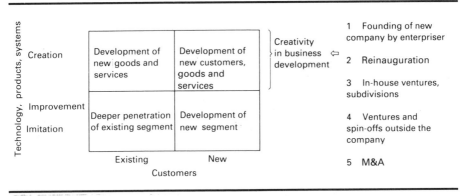

7.1 Creativity in business development.

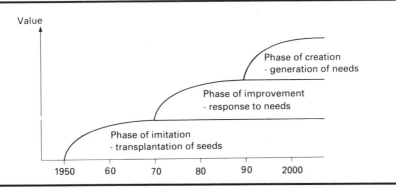

7.2 Flow of creativity in business development.

The phase of improvement lasted from the first oil crisis in 1973 into the 1980s. It was marked by a shift away from wholesale transplantation of Western business concepts and toward improvement of the same for adaptation to the needs of the Japanese market in development of new business.

The factors forming the background of this phase included diversification and elevation of the level of consumer needs as Japan's economic power grew. In addition, Japan's industry had acquired a greater capability for independent development of technology and business skills.

As business development grew more needs-oriented, various companies launched programmes of diversification into growth fields, intensifying competition in them. In foreign markets, the battle among Japanese companies for a bigger share of the pie led to the outbreak of trade friction.

In the 1990s, however, business development can no longer be approached by matching the existing resources with the existing needs in accordance with existing concepts. NRI take the view that it will have to begin with the active creation of needs from a long-term, imaginative perspective and in a manner that removes the limitations associated with business resources and other conditions. In short, the 1990s is viewed as the start of a new phase of creation in business development; business development through the generation of needs.

Table 7.I presents the characteristics of the three phases of business development. The key to success in the phase of imitation was speedy import of superior technology and know-how from the West. One of the major roles of corporate presidents and division directors was scouting Western countries for such technology and know-how.

Success in the phase of improvement hinged upon ability to meet customer needs. Technology and know-how were repeatedly improved and refined for a closer accommodation of needs.

The key to success in the phase of creation would be generation of needs by repeatedly returning to the basics: why the company exists in the first place, what it is that the customers are truly seeking from it, along the lines of the FINDS perspective described in connection with creativity in product development.

In the phase of imitation, price was the main determinant of competitiveness, and profits derived from a formidable cost competitiveness

Table 7.I Characteristics of business development

Phase	Keys for success	Determinants of competitiveness	Source of profit	Risks	Return	Intensity of competition
1 Imitation	Transplantation of seeds	Price	Share	Low	Low	Medium
2 Improvement	Response to needs	Functions adapted to needs	Speed	Medium	Medium	High
3 Creation	Generation of needs	Sensibility, sympathy, image	Creativity	High	High	Medium

supported by a high share of the market. Since the technology involved was already solidly established, investment in development and facilities was low-risk, and the return was also low. While present, competition did not escalate to an excessive degree, since the overall pie was expanding due to the high-level economic growth.

In the phase of improvement, stress was placed on the ability to accommodate needs, i.e. the level of functions/performance in goods and/or services. Profits depended on developing a higher level of functions/performance and supplying them to customers faster than competitors. This called for investment for independent development that entailed higher risks but also brought a higher return. In addition, competition was more intense than in the previous phase.

In the phase of creation, envisioned as beginning in the 1990s and continuing into the 21st century, competitiveness would be determined by factors that go beyond improved functions/performance, sensibility, the ability to elicit empathy toward the subject business among the consumers, the ability to create and convey business images. The creativity of companies would be called into account as customers look for distinctive concepts and new added value. Development of business would require vigorous investment accompanied by high risks, but success would yield high returns. And as companies vie with each other mainly in demonstration of originality, competition in the marketplace would cool off relative to the previous phase of improvement.

Case study of business development

Meitec

Process of creation

Meitec started out as a technical personnel dispatch business consisting of only president Sekiguchi and seven other employees founded in 1974 under the name 'Nagoya Technology Center'. By March 1987, when its stock was listed on the Tokyo Stock Exchange and it was renamed 'Meitec', it had grown into a software engineering firm employing about 4,500. Figure 7.3 outlines the process of creation at Meitec and is further explained in the following:

1 Starting from scratch
Meitec's predecessor was Kansai Seiki, a machine designer and manufacturer established by Sekiguchi in 1963. Kansai Seiki went bankrupt after the failure of a window frame business undertaken in a bid to expand its sales. The founding of the new company (Nagoya Technology Center) therefore represented a fresh start from scratch.

2 'All we have is . . .' -> 'at least we have . . .'
The Nagoya Technology Center was born out of the challenging spirit of Sekiguchi and seven of his colleagues. Lacking both financial and material

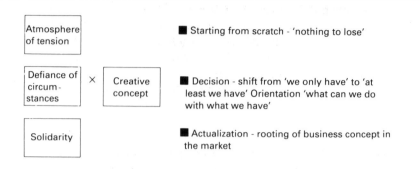

7.3 Process of creation at Meitec.

resources, the group realized that they nevertheless had valuable knowledge and technical expertise, and proceeded to found a business built around sales of the same.

Sekiguchi's generation of a unique business concept turned on a defiance of the circumstances; a shift in attitude from negative ('all we have is knowledge and technical expertise') to positive ('at least we have knowledge and technical expertise').

3   Rooting of business concept in the market

While the concept was business built around sales of knowledge and technology, a market of buyers did not exist at the time. The company consequently promoted a campaign of regular direct mailings aimed at getting this business concept to take root in the market.

Partly due to the timing of its founding, which coincided with the aftermath of the first oil crisis, the company's first two years were extremely sluggish. In the dearth of business, income was negligible, and the company struggled to meet personnel expenses. However, it was able to recruit talented personnel and also began to meet more of its personnel requirements by using the services of other personnel dispatch businesses. These and other factors eventually turned the tide and laid the foundation for its current business.

As its staff grew, the scope of the company's business, which was initially confined to the field of general machine design, broadened to include computer software development, aerospace engineering, automobiles, and electronic technology. This was accompanied by a regional expansion; in the 1980s, the company's business began to spread outward from Nagoya to include Osaka, Shizuoka, Tokyo, Yokohama and Sendai. In 1989, it established a second headquarters in Tokyo. It is also developing business overseas; it has established a US affiliate known as Yugain International, Inc and is doing business in South Korea and Taiwan.

Management for creation

The following can be cited as the notable characteristics of management for creation at Meitec.

1 Accurate reading of the trend of the times at the top

One of the most notable features of Meitec's creation of business is that it success-fully germinated business from a concept which it singlehandedly created and implanted in the market. What had been a novel idea thus became part of the norm. At the time of its founding, even technicians were being laid off as business slumped in the wake of the oil crisis. Sekiguchi had the foresight to see that many companies would be saddled with a shortage of technicians once prosperity returned.

2 Sharing of information and aspirations within a small organization

The successful translation of the business concept into reality was made possible by Sekiguchi's people-centred philosophy. Information was shared freely among the staff of seven, and funds for cultivation and recruitment of personnel were not cut back even when sales were down. This approach nourished the trust and solidar-ity that drove the generation of the new business.

In addition, its small size facilitated a close-knit communication among the initial staff, who had also gone through the previous failure together and shared an aspiration to lead the new venture to success.

3 People-centred philosophy

Sekiguchi's people-centred philosophy, which attaches top priority to knowledge and technical expertise, still permeates Meitec. The company has established a research facility for personnel education and technical training. It has also pro-vided its employees with dormitories, health care facilities and an impressive array of other facilities that would be inconceivable in the conventional company. Regarding a staff of talented personnel as its lifeblood, Meitec has actively recruited personnel even during business slumps, and this has reinforced the bonds of trust between employees and management.

Yamato Transport

Yamato Transport's business was formerly centred around parcel shipment to businesses. In 1976, however, it began a new business in shipment to homes; Black Cat Yamato Home Parcel Service. Figure 7.4 outlines the process of creation at Yamato Transport.

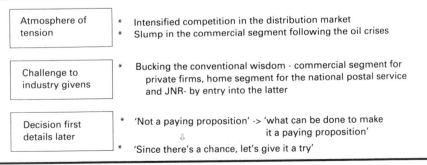

7.4 Process of creation at Yamato Transport.

The parcel post business consists of two segments: commercial (delivery service for businesses) and home (delivery service for consumers). The former had been dominated by private firms, and the latter, by the national postal service and national railways. This arrangement stemmed from the nature of business in the home segment. The incidence of orders for shipments is highly irregular, and involves delivery from a large pool of diverse sources to a large pool of diverse destinations in small and diverse sizes. For this reason, private firms had steered clear of the home segment in the belief that it was not a paying proposition.

As a result, private parcel post firms had developed their business around delivery of commercial parcels for a limited group of customers who placed orders regularly and in lots of a prescribed size. However, the competition in this segment intensified, particularly after the outbreak of the first oil crisis in 1973, when a deceleration of industrial growth contracted the commercial parcel market.

By contrast, the only entrants in the home segment at the time were the national postal service and the former Japanese National Railways. Sensing the widespread dissatisfaction with the service provided by these entrants, the company judged that quality services in this segment could command a sufficient demand, and embarked on studies of entry.

This move met with opposition within the company, on the grounds that the home parcel post business was bound to be a losing proposition. Management, however, had the studies focus not on the question of the business's viability, but on what could be done to make it viable. While there was some discussion of the pros and cons of entry, there emerged an agreement that the business had a chance of turning a profit with the right execution. It was consequently decided to make a commitment to enter and then figure out the requirements for this right execution.

Management for creation

Management for creation at Yamato Transport can be seen as comprising three key characteristics.

1 Posting of a clear watchword in management – 'density'

The studies hit upon 'density' as the key to getting the business on viable footing; the viability of the business could be expected to rise as the density of shipping consignments per unit of service area rose, and conversely, to fall as this density fell. In addition, a high density would in effect shrink the area that had to be covered per truck. The smaller this area, the more familiar the driver would become with the routes, and the speedier the service would be. The minimum requisite density could be expressed in terms of the number of consignments that had to be carried by each truck (driver) per run in order to turn a profit on that run.

Theoretically, viability came down to a simple matter of doing everything possible to increase this density. The company judged that the best means of increasing density was providing excellent service, and began making plans to that end.

The focus then shifted to increasing the volume of shipment per consignment. The solution raised by the studies was the construction of channels to liquor stores and rice dealers by offering an unparalleled convenience for such customers.

This led to the campaigns for a new service with slogans that could not be matched by the postal service or JNR – 'next-day delivery anywhere in Japan' and 'just phone for pick-up'.

2 Emphasis on service over income at the top

Another key in the building of the business was that management consistently placed quality of service over income as a priority in the operation. This was done on the conviction that excellent service was sure to lead to increased consignments, and by extension, to the rise in density that would naturally improve income. The company consequently set up offices even in outlying areas, and saw them begin to turn a profit in the second year.

President Okura explicitly stated that he attached more importance to service than the financial statement in the development of the business, and told district managers that they would not be reprimanded even if they failed to show a profit as long as they were taking measures to upgrade service. This is because he saw no chance for increased consignments in such cases if the quality of services remained unchanged.

3 Self-motivated employees – 'employee as manager'

What must not be overlooked as a cornerstone in the foundation of this business is the organizational setup. This setup was designed to involve all employees in management. While each employee had his own particular role to play, no role was put above others as being more crucial for the operation of the business. The distinction between 'manager' and 'managed' was dissolved; all roles were placed on equal footing, the aggregate comprising the management of the business. This setup, in which drivers were positioned as salespersons, acted to enhance each employee's involvement with his task, whatever its nature, and his motivation to perform to the best of his ability even without pressure or supervision from above. It also effected a smoother in-house communication and prevented the opening of the gulf that is liable to exist between drivers and superiors.

Yamato Transport successfully transformed the basic disadvantages of the home parcel segment for private firms into its basic strengths. Its exercise of creativity can be glimpsed in the process of this turnabout.

Misawa Homes

Process of creation

Figure 7.5 presents the process of creation at Misawa Homes, and is discussed in more detail below.

1 Systematic M&A

A manufacturer of prefabricated housing, Misawa Homes is employing a unique approach to diversifying its business through an expansion and reinforcement of its main line. The approach is a merger and acquisition (M&A) tactic, but one that differs from M&A as conventionally practiced.

Over the last several years, Misawa Homes acquired capital participation in various companies, each of which had been facing serious difficulties. Within a few years upon entry into the Misawa Group, however, each had improved its result, some even moving out of the red and into the black. In addition, each was earning profit in business completely unrelated to the main line before Misawa Homes' capital participation.

Part of the secret behind Misawa Homes' M&A strategy lies in the segmentation and flexible recombination of the business resources in the subject companies. The company evaluates each subject in terms of its business resources, i.e. technology/expertise, personnel, reputation/credit, funds, and reserve (land, stocks). These resources are recombined with those of other subjects and its own in a manner that will yield the highest return.

2   Long-term vision

At the same time, however, Misawa Homes' actions are not aimed merely at increased profit from the housing business. It is developing business in accordance with a long-term vision of growth from a housing-related manufacturer into a 'total residential industry' that is the goal of the Group-level strategy. The existence of this long-term vision for the Group-level activities has made each M&A subject a vital part of the overall plan. As a result, resources or businesses that were not given much attention by the subject before entry into the Group are now operated to their fullest effect.

3   Pursuit of optimal mix of resources

Other key factors can be found at the actual site of business; greater resort to mid-career hiring and non-interference in the conduct of business.

The M&A subjects were not necessarily equipped with all of the personnel needed for the new business. In order to get the new business on track in a relatively short time, Misawa Homes realized that it would be more effective to hire personnel that already had the qualifications than to train a whole new corps itself. In addition, this policy amounted to an injection of new blood that gave the corporate atmosphere a bracing edge and revitalized the organization.

As noted above, the subjects had all been struggling for many years prior to their entry into the Misawa Group. The company set targets for these subjects, but did not dictate to them on other matters. This policy encouraged an attitude of pride and independence, as opposed to dependence on Misawa Homes, among the subjects. Figure 7.6 illustrates Misawa Homes' diversification.

Management for creation

Figure 7.7 presents the management for creation at Misawa Homes which is discussed in detail below.

1   Direct linkage between top and bottom

The Misawa Group's approach to business development was conceived by president (and founder) Misawa.

Misawa's trailblazing spirit and ingenuity are well-known in Japan, and have given rise to many anecdotes that date from the founding of Misawa Home. Nevertheless, the string of successful ventures rested not on the strength of his

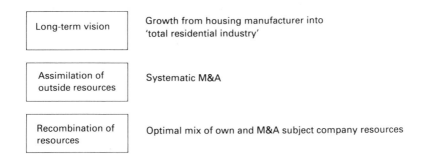

Long-term vision	Growth from housing manufacturer into 'total residential industry'
Assimilation of outside resources	Systematic M&A
Recombination of resources	Optimal mix of own and M&A subject company resources

7.5 Process of creation at Misawa Homes.

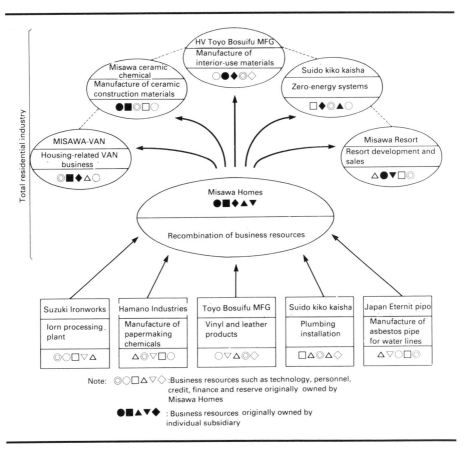

Note: ◎○□△▽◇ :Business resources such as technology, personnel, credit, finance and reserve originally owned by Misawa Homes

●■▲▼◆ : Business resources originally owned by individual subsidiary

7.6 Diversification at Misawa Homes.

creative energies alone, but on deliberate efforts made and organizational measures taken to generate and collect ideas.

For this reason, Misawa has not only gone out of his way to engage in dialogue with people outside the company, but has maintained a constant dialogue with those in charge of the actual operation within the company. If diagrammed,

* New edge to charge the corporate atmosphere with proper degree of
   tension
   Injection of new blood through greater resort to mid-career hiring

* Direct linkage between top and bottom
   Maintenance of creativity through collection of ideas directly from
   employees (idea proposal system)

* Execution by proposer to take charge of the idea execution

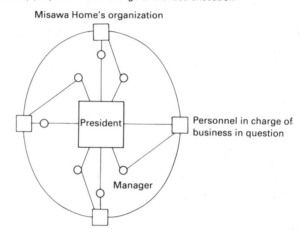

Misawa Home's organization

President

Personnel in charge of business in question

Manager

7.7 Management for creation at Misawa Homes.

Misawa Homes' organization would take the form of a pyramid. But in the minds of its employees, the organization is a wheel with Misawa at the hub, Fig. 7.8. This is because the president makes it a point to broaden his own perspective by hearing the ideas of the people under him first-hand.

2   Idea execution by the proposer

Misawa's employees are told that all promising ideas have a chance to be taken up, and moreover, that the proposer himself may be placed in charge of the project. The company is already promoting projects of new business based on ideas proposed by employees, and expects the number to increase in the coming years.

Tokuma Shoten Publishing

Tokuma Shoten Publishing is widely known as the producer of 'Nausicaa of the Windy Valley', 'Raputa, the Castle in the Sky', and other feature-length animated films that were great box-office hits, see Fig. 7.8. It stands at the centre of the Tokuma Business Group, which is developing a unique, multifaceted information business organically linking the printed word, audio and film/video and sees itself as a 'total purveyor of culture'. The current status enjoyed by Tokuma Books was engineered by its founder, Yasuyoshi Tokuma.

Tokuma Shoten Publishing's entry into the animation business was prompted by the booming popularity of animated cartoons and their characters in magazine, television, and other media. At the same time, Tokuma himself had always been interested in science fiction and animation, and was eager to enter that segment of the comic book market built around animated cartoon characters. He also realized that the company was a latecomer to the comic book market, and would have little chance of success if its entry took the form of publication of its own comic books of this type. Consequently he decided to attempt initial entry not by publishing the comic books themselves, but by providing information concerning those published by others and animation in general.

The vehicle of this entry was Animage, a magazine of animation information that was strikingly different from the ordinary comic books. Particularly notable is the fact that the strips carried by Animage were executed not by cartoonists but by animators. This gave the magazine a cinematic image that set it apart from other comic books and paved the way for the company's entry into the animated cartoon film business.

In developing the Animage business, Tokuma Shoten Publishing searched out talented young animators and other personnel and closely co-ordinated their activities. One product of these efforts was Shun Miyazaki, an animator who has brought the company much success.

Management for creation

The characteristics of management for creation at Tokuma Shoten Publishing can be seen as the following:

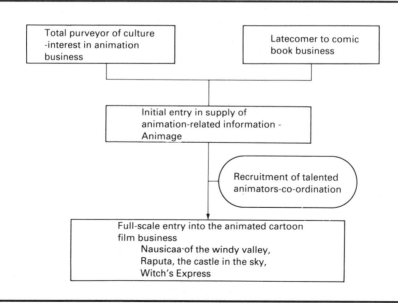

7.8 Process of creation at Tokuma Shoten Publishing.

- Challenge to accepted notions, fighting the conventional with the unconventional.
- Stress on energies of young employees, encouragement of active participation in idea generation and business planning.
- Incentive for creation, awards (President's Award, Tokuma Award).
- Speedy decision-making, swift, resolute action.
- Smooth transition from individual to group creation, excellent co-ordinating ability.
- Removal of fear of failure – learning from mistakes, failure as a stimulus.
- Face-to-face conversation between the president and new employees, personnel-oriented management.

Tokuma Shoten Publishing's resolutely positive stance in business contains a wealth of hints about how creation harbouring the possibility of failure should be managed.

Tokuma Shoten Publishing's growth into a 'total purveyor of culture' began from the publication of a host of weekly magazines, the first being 'Asahi Show Business'. In fact, many of these publications were too far ahead of the times, and ended in failure. The number of tight spots which Tokuma managed to navigate may be imagined from the fact that he is affectionately referred to as 'the man who lives on the brink'. Tokuma drew upon these experiences in constructing his current approach to management.

This approach is characterized by the generation of concepts that fly in the face of the conventional industry wisdom, the active solicitation of ideas from young employees, connection of 'creation' to 'merit' in the minds of employees, quick-witted decision-making, and a corporate culture in which employees are not afraid of failure.

Perhaps the prime benefit accruing from this approach was an ability to co-ordinate smoothly the transition from individual to group creation. This ability was instrumental in the company's success in the animated cartoon business.

A case in point was the publication of Animage, where the crucial element was this ability to co-ordinate the transition from the stage of idea generation to that of idea promotion based on the experiences of the past. And Animage's success put the company in the position to hire animators.

Tokuma has announced that he will take responsibility for any failures, which has the desired effect on employees because Tokuma has previously been true to this statement.

The success gained in the film business also owes much to skillful co-ordination within the Tokuma Business Group. 'Nausicaa of the Windy Valley', the first release, proved immensely popular, and this at a time when audiences for Japanese-made films were dwindling. It was followed by 'Raputa, the Castle in the Sky', 'Witch's Express', and other works released at roughly one-year intervals, each scoring significant success. Today, Tokuma is hailed in various quarters as the creator of a new genre of animated cartoon films that represent a progression from Disney's.

A US manufacturer of electronic measurement equipment

Process of creation

A US manufacturer of electronic measurement equipment, D Co, first entered computer integrated manufacturing (CIM) business in the mid-1980s, and has since gone on to establish itself as one of the leading manufacturers in it.

In the early 1980s, there arose a movement to expand upon factory automation (FA; consisting mainly of automation of work processes on the work site) and realize more comprehensive systems of automation in manufacturing through integration of the functions of the business, design and R&D divisions with those of factories. D Co began to hear an increasing number of its customers express needs for such CIM systems.

D Co's first response was the development of CIM systems for a prescribed circle of customers in a prescribed field. These systems lacked a general-purpose applicability, and did not find an extensive market.

In order to find a way to improve the situation, D Co implemented an in-depth interview survey with 20 different types of customers around 1985.

This survey revealed the following three requirements, for which the appropriate action was immediately taken.

1 Standardization of the system architecture
To this end, D Co devised a versatile modular structure enabling both system composition suited to the needs in question and networking between different types of plants.

2 Sales tie-up with software development firms
D Co launched a value-added business (VAB) programme by developing and marketing systems in partnership with software houses. In so doing, it chose the top-ranked software houses in the fields in question as its partners.

3 Provision of a highly operable software environment for the production system design of customers
D Co developed software for data input and output in the form of text, graphs, or images, as the user desired. The operating system was designed for a high compatibility with other systems, and the data base software was equipped with a high processing speed.

Management for creation

There are four notable points in D Co's management for creation in developing CIM business.

1 Mixed team of R&D and marketing personnel
The team originally consisted of about 10 members, including researchers versed in the related computer technology and marketing personnel with detailed knowledge of the customers' manufacturing setups.

This mixed format kept the researchers in touch with the realities of the customer needs and also spawned ideas that probably would not have taken shape without the resulting interplay of differing perspectives. Personnel with a purely manufacturing background were deliberately excluded from the team, in the belief that they were liable to act as idea killers. If the researchers functioned as idea generators, the marketing personnel were 'idea realists', in the sense that they kept the team's work tied to the realities of the business.

2　Interviews with customers

The work was rooted in a careful survey of the customer needs. The interviews with 20 different types of companies were conducted jointly by researchers and marketing personnel and lasted about six hours per company on the average. Comments from the lengthy, face-to-face discussions regarded as containing hints for new ideas were organized by field and posted on a bulletin board. Customer needs were therefore literally kept constantly before the eyes of the team members.

3　Weakening of IK forces through cross-checking

IK forces were contained by a system of cross-checking. The team members were divided into subgroups of five, and the work of each subgroup member was reviewed by at least two of his peers. This discouraged members from attempting to suppress the ideas of others unless they themselves could come up with something better, thus weakening IK inclinations.

4　Exclusions of tunnel-vision

Personnel that could see no farther than their own field of expertise were consciously excluded from the development. The team members shared the responsibility of grasping the customer needs and tackling the task of meeting them. No one was allowed to evade this responsibility with remarks to the effect, 'that's not my area'.

A US machinery manufacturer

Characteristics of business development

A US manufacturer of machinery (mainly engines), E Co's business also encompasses supply of the related systems and maintenance service any hour of the day, 365 days a year. Its sales reached 500 million dollars in 1988, and grew at an annual rate averaging more than 10% for the preceding five years, making it one of the leading companies in its industry.

Founded around the turn of the century, E Co originally produced horse-drawn carriages and horseshoes. With the appearance of the automobile, it entered the field of automobile repair. Subsequently, it began selling diesel engines and introduced a warranty system, which was a novel idea at the time.

During the Second World War, E Co supplied the government with diesel engines designed for military use. In the 1950s, it developed transport systems for airports as the US civil aviation industry began to expand. In the 1960s, it created systems for tapping oil deposits. In the 1970s, it began supplying engines and the related systems in a variety of special fields, including on-site power generation, amusement parks and refrigeration units for trucks. In short, E Co's development of business has been characterized by a flexible adaptation to changes in the market and prompt movement into fields of growth.

Unlike many US conglomerates, it did not attempt to move into fields unconnected with its existing business by taking over entrants in them. Its development of business remained firmly grounded in its core technology of engines.

In recent years, it has become increasingly difficult for entrants in the machinery industry to provide their products with features not available from competitors, since the market and technology are already in a mature stage of development. In such a situation, the focus in competition is shifting to reinforcement of sales routes, finer market segmentation, extra maintenance services and other improvements not directly concerning the product per se. With an appreciation of this point, E Co stands ready to provide its customers with parts and maintenance service at any hour of the day, 365 days a year. This arrangement has further boosted its trustworthiness in the eyes of customers.

Management for creation

The management for creation in business development at E Co can be summarized in the following two points.

1 Marketing personnel as 'market sensors'

E Co's organization consists of different divisions for different fields of the market. The arrangement is one of decentralization; the division itself is the major seat of responsibility and authority in business in the field in question. In virtually all cases, the development of new business in a given division has started with the ideas of its marketing personnel. In this sense, E Co has expanded by using its marketing corps as 'market sensors'.

The company prizes well-defined, relatively risk-free ideas arising from the contact between its people in the field and their customers. It tests such ideas by putting together a product embodying them and trying it out in the market. If it evokes a good reaction from customers, the product is then made a priority in resource allocation.

2 Trial before criticism in the manufacturing division

It is the manufacturing division's duty to give ideas a try before criticizing them. In terms of the IGKP model, the manufacturing division is compelled to act as an IP instead of IK.

E Co's plants mainly conduct assembly. In addition, this assembly generally is carried out in a shop form as there are few assembly lines. The plants are equipped with the multifunction equipment and qualified personnel required for swift response to changes in product needs/specifications. The company also has a diverse mix of sources for assembly components, enabling it to acquire the optimal combination of components for the job in question.

E Co's development of new business could therefore be viewed as a process of absorbing ideas arising out of the contact between its marketing personnel and their customers, elaborating the ideas in the manufacturing division, and feeding the results back to the customers. Elaboration of the ideas on the floor of the plant tends to produce far more workable results than could be expected from more discussion sessions.

Partly due to the nature of its business, the pillars of E Co's creation are not abstract probes in R&D, but an ability to pick up the customer's needs and to propose actual products to meet them.

CREATION OF MANAGERS

Researcher   Takeshi Oe, Shuji Honjo

Subject   Managers

Basic perspective   Method of measurement

Substance: Is there a set of characteristics that may be necessary for a creative enterpriser? If so, is it possible to identify personnel with good prospects for success as developers of new business ventures by referring to such characteristics? Can the prospects of success for a new venture by a major firm be similarly assessed? As a response to such questions, the authors have devised a method of gauging suitability for creative business development.

The method revolves around two indicators, each concerning 'difference' (DI): one for personal difference (PDI), which expresses the degree to which the subject differs from other persons, and the other for the corporate difference (CDI), which expresses the degree to which the proposed business differs from the average major company. A proper degree of difference is posited for both, on the premise that an excessive or deficient degree of difference would disqualify the subject as an enterpriser. In this scheme, success could be viewed as resulting from the maintenance of a proper balance between the distinctness (or degree of originality) of the individual enterpriser himself and that of his business.

Evaluation of personnel in terms of the two indices would presumably make it possible to distinguish those suited for management positions in major companies and those suited to start up new businesses.

As compared with the US, venture businesses are more difficult to start and slower to grow in Japan. In terms of this method, this situation results from the reluctance of personnel with high DIs to leave large companies, and the fact that personnel with high DIs would find it difficult to raise the needed funds, and even if they managed to do so, would probably end up exceeding the aforementioned 'proper degree of difference'. The method also suggests that the reason why successful ventures are still scarce in Japan is that the personnel chosen to lead ventures generally rank low in terms of both indicators.

Source) 'Creative Research and its Measurement', in 'Creativity Research 6', edited by Japan Creation Study Group

Method of and management for creation in business development

Method of creation

The case study illustrates four basic stages in the method of creation in business development.

1 Reading the trend of the times, accurately interpreting information

Meitec foresaw the arrival of an age in which it could build a business around sales of its knowledge and technology. Yamato Transport sensed a latent demand in the home segment of the parcel post market, which had been left to the national postal service and national railways in the belief that it was not a paying proposition for a private firm. Tokuma Shoten Publishing saw the opportunity presented by the booming popularity of animated cartoons and their characters on television and in comic books. D Co anticipated the elevation of its customers' automation needs from the level of FA to that of CIM, and launched in-depth interviews with them in response. E Co has always had its marketing personnel function as 'sensors' of trends in the market. In essence, the point is 'seeing which way the wind is blowing' by getting the views of customers and then erecting hypotheses for the appropriate action.

2 Trial and discussion, test of the hypothesis by idea generators

Yamato Transport implemented market surveys to corroborate its intuitions about dissatisfaction in the home parcel segment and the latent demand. D Co formed a mixed team of R&D and marketing personnel to generate and refine ideas. E Co has its manufacturing division test ideas in the market before rendering an appraisal of them.

3 Concept creation with a positive, keyed-up attitude that defies restrictions imposed by the circumstances

Meitec president Sekiguchi noted a fundamental change in attitude from negative ('all we have is knowledge and expertise') to positive ('at least we have knowledge and expertise'). Yamato Transport's president Okura countered the view that a home parcel business couldn't turn a profit by replying, 'let's think of a way to make it turn a profit'. In both efforts, this turnabout of perspective triggered the concepts.

4 Accepting the risks and going ahead with the project once convinced of its propriety

The key element in this stage is forceful promotion of the idea by top-level management or the project leader, who also assumes the burden of risk. In the cases of Meitec, Yamato Transport, Misawa Homes, and Tokuma Shoten Publishing, the president himself functioned as the IP, meaning that the single most powerful force in the company was behind the business development. In the case of the two US companies, a key factor in the successful creation was the assumption of full responsibility for the business by the project leader.

Management for creation

Four characteristics can be discerned in the management for creation in business development.

1 Creation of a managerial atmosphere charged with the proper degree of tension

In the case of the four Japanese companies, the president himself functioned as both idea generator and promotor. The new business was born in a do-or-die situation for him as owner and head of the company. In the case of the two US companies, the business was developed through an in-house venture and divisional organization, respectively. In both, however, the project was undertaken by a relatively small group working in a fairly tense atmosphere. In any case, a feeling that 'something must be done' appears to be necessary for the creation of new business.

2 The formation of teams composed of a small number of members who do not all have the same background

Meitec's business development was promoted by Sekiguchi and seven of his colleagues. Misawa Homes and Tokuma Shoten Publishing stress discussion between the president and idea generators. D Co formed a mixed team of about ten R&D and marketing personnel to tackle CIM business development. The sharing of information in small groups composed of members coming from different fields enriches the idea generation process and enables the creation of concepts with a better chance of success.

3 Input from customers

Yamato Parcel recognized the widespread dissatisfaction with the service provided by the national postal service and JNR in the home parcel market, and concluded that the provision of better service could stimulate the demand and produce the 'density' required for viable business in that market. Misawa Home's president takes every opportunity to meet and discuss business with people outside his organization. D Co began its foray into the CIM business with an exhaustive interview survey of 20 different types of customers. Selected comments elicited by these interviews were written on cards and posted on a bulletin board to keep them before the team members.

4 The exclusion of tunnel-vision

In teams that depend upon a sharing of customer information and responsibility among a small number of members, there is no place for people who cannot see beyond their field of expertise and attempt to shift responsibility to others. This is why remarks to the effect 'that's not my area' were banned within the D Co team.

III

Strategy for creation

8
Method of creation

Method progression

Part II presented a case study of creation in R&D and in development of products, systems, and business. Observations about the method of creation in corporate activities applying in some degree to all of these cases must be approached with consideration of the following two questions.

- Should the creative act be apprehended at the individual or organizational level? Should the output of the creative act be viewed in terms of the idea/concept or product/business? This is also a question of how the method of creation evolves within the framework of corporate activities and corporate organization.
- Does there exist a methodological counterpart to the four-stage structure of creative corporate activities?

These two questions constitute the perspectives for the following account of the method of creation.

Creative activity has conventionally been regarded as a function of individual personality and ability. In this view, creation depends upon a personal 'greatness' and originality; individuals brimming with ideas and a challenging spirit who see and think about things differently from the average person, Fig. 8.1. Since creativity in companies has been regarded as virtually synonymous with this individual creativity, creative activity in companies as well has been considered 'unmanageable', i.e. inherently outside the knowledge base of management.

However, the cases presented in Part II show that, while individual creation is an important element, it is not the whole story in creation in companies. Methods of creation were applied at levels transcending the individual level. The IGKP

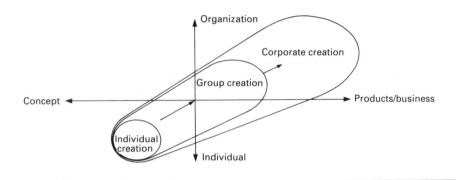

8.1 From individual creation to group creation and corporate creation.

model used to analyse the cases of creation in research and development also applies to each of the cases concerning development of products, systems and business. The thrust of the IGKP model is interaction among two or more persons, each playing a different role, with a view to inducing some larger creative activity.

NRI term this kind of creative activity and the method used to induce it 'group creation'. Once creation reaches this level, it is not only amenable to management, but also must be managed.

To carry this concept further, one can envisage a situation in which a creative orientation permeates all the company's activities and its entire organization. The method of creation in companies attaining this status is what is meant by the term 'corporate creation'.

It must be emphasized that the concepts of group and corporate creation do not imply a disparagement or negation of individual creation. They merely express a conviction that creative corporate activities, while including individual creation as a key element, also contain other aspects that cannot be reduced to individual creation and are proper subjects of management.

While the words and images used to describe the method of creation varied from case to case, the following sequence of four stages may be regarded as applying to all of the cases studied.

- Construction of hypothesis
- Dissimilation
- Creation of concept
- Chain of empathy

Table 8.I contrasts this method of creation with the corresponding methods of industry and information.

Construction of hypothesis

In all the cases, the activity was preceded by construction of a hypothesis clearly expressing the orientation of the activity. This is one of the most important requirements in creative activities in companies.

In addition, the construction of the hypothesis was prompted by weighty factors such as a sense of crisis at the top, a keen awareness of a certain problem, and a sense of mission or obligation to society.

The hypothesis construction itself was not a matter of mental gymnastics, but a serious attempt at problem-solving mounted with thorough knowledge of the specific needs and difficulties at the site of business or among the customers in question. This observation is clearly evidenced in the cases of Toyo Sash, Meitec, and many other companies.

Hypothesis construction marked by these three characteristics can be cited as the first stage of the method of creation.

Dissimilation

The second stage of the method of creation is dissimilation. However well-constructed the hypothesis on which they rest, creative activities are bound to encounter environmental changes and situations which were not foreseen by the hypothesis as they progress.

This development appeared in many of the cases. In such a situation, it is important for the personnel in question to have an attitude that will enable them to learn from their mistakes, seek a model in a different field, accept criticism and remain objective. As the project proceeds, it must actively incorporate (or be exposed to the action of) diverse views, perspectives, and values.

Dissimilation is the mechanism of such incorporation/exposure. It may be exemplified by the efforts made by Toyo Sash to familiarize its system engineers with the needs and concerns of its customers.

Concept creation

All creative activities reach a moment of creation, when it seems that all of the clouds have been dispelled and everything has come into clear view. To attain this moment, however, requires a tenacious, sustained pursuit of the problem. Moreover, this moment is born of thought not on the conscious level, but on the unconscious level.

In short, the flash of inspiration arrives precisely because contemplation

Table 8.1

	Method progression			
	Creation of goods, information, and value			
	Source	Process	Nucleus	Propagation/expansion
Method of industry	Division of labour	Control	Expansion of scale	Standardization
Method of information	Collection	Organization	Editing	Dissemination
Method of creation	Hypothesis construction	Dissimilation	Concept creation	Chain of sympathy

has been brought down to the unconscious level. The most important, fundamental product of this moment of creation is the concept. Such concept creation is the third stage of the method of creation. This stage may be exemplified by the 180-degree turn from 'all we have is . . .' to 'at least we have . . .' in the case of Meitec.

KJ METHOD

Researcher   Jiro Kawakita

Subject   Managers, developers, researchers

Basic perspective   Conception methodology

Substance: Named after its inventor, the KJ method is a systematic approach to the generation of ideas. It is based on the use of cards containing views and information aired in brainstorming sessions. The basic procedure is as follows.
- Preparation of cards – views and information are entered on cards, one for each topic.
- Card spread – all cards are laid out on the table.
- Formation of subgroups – similar cards are bundled together.
- Preparation of subgroup names – selection of names indicative of the viewpoints of each subgroup (bundle).
- Formation of nuclear groups – all card bundles are laid on the table, and nuclear groups formed by bundling similar bundles together. This is done until about ten nuclear groups have been formed.
- Diagramming (KJ method A) – a 'diagram' is drawn by arranging the nuclear group bundles on a large sheet of paper.
- Transcription (KJ method B) – the diagram is described in writing with attention to its overall layout and the interrelations between the bundles.
   There are four basic possibilities for the status of the interplay between hints in the diagram brought to light in the transcription process.
- Mutual contradiction – mutual rejection
- Lack of interplay
- Coincidence – stability
- Comprehensiveness (high-order concept) through the aggregate of the hints. In this connection, it might be noted that the following two faculties appear to reside and develop separately in the brain.

Source) Jiro Kawakita, 'Conception Methodology – Toward Development of Creativity'

Chain of empathy

Creative activities in companies are not complete merely with the completion of the sequence of planning/developing, testing and producing. They are only complete when the actual goods/services have been provided to customers who make effective use of them and place the anticipated value upon them.

Creative activities in companies may therefore be envisaged as spreading outward in succession from the individual level to the group level, corporate level and finally the user level. To achieve this expansion, an interpersonal empathy with the activities and their results must be induced at each stage of transition.

The greater this empathy is, the wider the circle of the creative activities, and the higher the value created for the company and the society.

The induction of this 'chain of empathy' is the fourth stage of the method of creation. It is particularly in evidence in the cases of Seven-Eleven Japan and Sony.

Method of creation and application levels

Method of creation

To take a closer look at the nature of the four stages of the method of creation requires a discrimination of their prospective application levels. A method of creation is, in the final analysis, a method of a type of human activity. For this reason, we may posit the existence of three major levels of prospective application distinguished on the basis of differences in the locus of the activity or in the major factors explaining the activity's substance and attendant phenomena, Fig. 8.2.

1   Overall individual personality
There can be no doubt that personality provides the foundation, energy, and stage of creative activities. The key factors supporting creative activity on this level are various, and include intellectual curiosity, a venturesome, inquiring spirit, aspiration, ambition and aggressiveness.

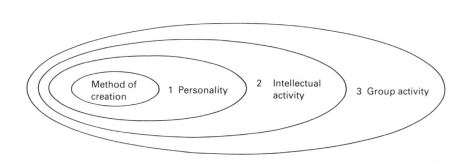

8.2 Method of creation and application levels.

2 Intellectual activity

This is ordinarily perceived as virtually equivalent to creative activity. Artificial intelligence and cognitive science are disciplines in which work is proceeding under this paradigm. However, the progress made in these fields is still far from satisfactory, and more extensive research is required.

3 Group activity

Creative activity and methods of creation can be viewed from the aspect of the activities and role assignments within a group. This level is deeply intertwined with corporate management and organization. Although its connection with creative activities per se is rather indirect, this level would consequently make a more realistic, definite subject as far as management is concerned. It may be regarded as the application level at which the method of creation is controllable.

Of these three levels, the first is a concern of the psychology of creativity. The only action which management could take on this level is the recruitment of personnel who are perceived as endowed with the creativity it is seeking. By contrast, the level of group activity falls in the province of effective managerial control, and is therefore the central concern of this book. This level is treated fully in Part III, chapter 9; 'Management for Creation'.

Intellectual activity

For the remaining part of this section, the focus will consequently be placed on the second level of intellectual activity. The following is a summary of the application of the method of creation on this level among the cases studied.

Construction of hypothesis

A typical means of constructing hypotheses is the KJ (Kawakito Jiro) method. This method is effective for fields in which a hypothesis, i.e. 'meaning-rich' information about the subject of study as a whole, can be derived by sorting out the various phenomena observed in field surveys.

In most cases, however, subjects entailing the solution of technical problems are not conducive to an approach based on the organization of observed phenomena. For example, the KJ method would not be applicable for such tasks as 'finding a simple means of measuring the adsorptive power of food product materials.'

In such cases, the person in question must conjure up from his memory images that appear to be related to the task at hand and may lead to a hypothesis idea. Such an idea may also be derived by taking leave of fixed conceptions and probing images that appear to be unrelated to the task on the surface in order to arrive at a new insight. This kind of ideation is the most effective means of hypothesis construction.

Dissimilation

The typical means of conducting dissimilation in an organized fashion is brain-storming. Since it involves the intellectual activity of more than one person, brain-storming can break through the limits of the KJ method, which is a mode of individual intellectual activity, and of individual capability of ideation. Its aim is the generation of concepts, ideas and lines of thought that are greater than the sum of those expressed by the individuals taking part in the session.

The session members must express specific ideas addressing the problem or task in question. These ideas may be distinguished from vague suggestions or hints as follows:

- They are capable of implementation (at least in principle)
- They can be explained to others
- They are logically sound

In this context, coming up with ideas consists of the recall from the memory of numerous images related to the subject, the proper recombination of the same and presentation of the recombination in a logical form comprehensible to others.

Concept creation

Concepts come in a flash of inspiration induced by bringing the mind to the unconscious level. This is the most essential portion of the method of creation. The case studies suggest that some kind of pressing circumstances or sense of urgency is vital for the derivation and refinement of such concepts. In one case that stands at the opposite pole, however, the vital factor was a sensibility that instantly seized upon a concept which surfaced casually in the course of an exchange of ideas in a more light-hearted atmosphere. Concept creation of the former type would presumably be suitable for breaking through logical impasses, and that of the latter, for aesthetic creation.

Chain of empathy

Viewed from the level of intellectual activity, the concrete means of inducing an empathy with the creation would be the sharing and exchange of the means of knowledge and of information. For the time being, this sharing of the means of knowledge as creative know-how would require direct interpersonal contact, i.e. interaction in the same place and time.

However, the horizons of creative activity could be greatly broadened if it were possible to effect the same sharing and exchange through external systems.

Scheme of conception support system

The need for a conception support system

The analysis of the four stages of the method of creation and their connection with intellectual activity underscored the crucial importance of capability for ideation and conception in creative activities.

To date, the task of generating ideas in the form of new plans and proposals in companies has depended entirely on the powers of conception of individuals such as technicians, researchers and planners.

In the coming years, the knowledge to be wielded in society as a whole may undergo a rapid increase in quantity while becoming increasingly sophisticated and complex. In the process, it will become increasingly difficult to effect an exchange of knowledge between different fields and so to discover vital interdisciplinary seeds of new technology. It would be no easy task to accommodate all of the needs arising in society as this trend proceeds, and there would be a limit to what could be achieved through the conception capabilities of individual specialists alone.

Addressing this situation would call for a systematic, engineering-type means of enhancing the efficiency of human conception and producing concepts themselves. While there already exists certain means of enhancing the efficiency of conception, such as the KJ and NM methods, these are basically empirical as opposed to systematic, engineering-type techniques.

What is being advocated here is the need for the opening of a new field of engineering, dealing with systems of knowledge encompassing seeds and needs. The achievements in this field would boost the efficiency of conception in society as a whole and enable companies to discern and meet the more sophisticated, complex needs. The implication is that companies must begin investing in the construction of an engineering-type conception support system that could have such effects.

Corporate managers have begun to acquire a keen appreciation of the importance of R&D and the development of products, and to stress these activities in their allocation of funds along with improved production facilities. Nevertheless, the same managers are apt to be under the impression that they must rely on the talents of individuals for the generation of the seeds of new technology and ideas for new products. With the approach of the age of creation, it will become crucially important for companies to boost the quality and efficiency of the ideas and concepts that form the starting point for the actual programmes of R&D and product development. Managers must therefore invest more resources in this area.

The main tool of human activities in companies was the machine in the age of industry and is the computer in the age of information, see Fig. 8.3. The counterpart in the age of creation would be this conception support system, which shall be termed a 'conceptor'. Companies should be working to develop this kind of tool as early as possible.

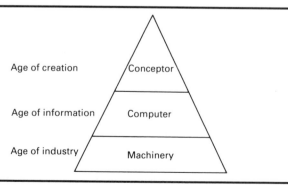

8.3 Evolution of the tools of human activity.

If man is an animal that uses fire, he may also be described as a conceiving animal. In this sense, man is a born conceiver. At the same time, it is also true that many, if not most, people believe they lack a good power of conception.

The following can be cited as factors impeding conception.

- Fixed ideas – 'That kind of thing is impossible'
- Self-repression – 'That idea would only make a laughingstock of me'
- Self-limitation – 'That's out of my field'

The most fundamental of these is perhaps self-limitation, which amounts to a neglect to exercise the power of conception in areas where the individual is not, or believes he is not, competent to do so.

Obviously, no individual is so versed in all fields that he knows all there is to know in each and understands the interfield correlations. A logical exercise of the power of conception, therefore, is bound to centre in the fields in which the individual is most at home. By the same token, the individual is apt to steer clear of conception involving areas perceived as being out of his line, where he lacks background knowledge. The conception, therefore, ends up being confined to his forte.

However, this orientation is not in keeping with the spirit of creation, and will not lead to the birth of good concepts.

There are basically three processes leading up to the birth of concepts.

- Motivation – recognition of a problem and an incentive to solve it
- Ideation – inflation of the sphere of images associated with the problem and for-mation of some combination of heterogeneous elements as a possible solution (human experience comes into play in the selection of these heterogeneous elements)
- Conception – use of store of knowledge to assemble a logical construct out of these elements

Of these, it is clear that the processes of ideation and conception will become more difficult as the knowledge required to perform them expands and becomes more complex.

If computers could be used to automate these processes to a certain extent, it would alleviate the burden of conception work to be performed by the individual and enhance the efficiency of conception. The conceptor is a system that would actually be capable of producing this effect.

Harbingers of the conception support system

In recent years, several companies have begun to develop systems that appear to be harbingers of this conception support system. The following is an account of two such systems.

Gennai – a system supporting word/image association

The advertising firm Dentsu has developed an experimental AI system known as Gennai to help copywriters come up with catch phrases. The point in advertising copywriting is hitting upon short phrases or sentences that will conjure up various positive images in the mind of the consumer and associate them with the subject of the advertising. In short, copywriting is a kind of word/image association game.

Gennai was designed to support the copywriters in this work, not to supplant them. It supplies the copywriters with hints, which they use as raw material in composing their own copy. For example, Gennai might suggest the phrase, 'a newspaper is a love letter', which its inspired operator might rewrite as 'a newspaper is a love letter of truth'. Gennai is designed to propose several tentative answers that suggest various possibilities, as there is no single correct answer in the world of ideation/conception.

Although Gennai is not yet commercially available, it could come into use in the future not only for copywriting about an existing product, but also to provide hints for ideas for new products. Table 8.II illustrates the basic pattern of Gennai output.

Packaging the problem-solving know-how of technicians

Fujitsu intends to incorporate a knowledge data base in its Kawasaki plant, which is its centre of technology department. The proposed data base would contain the knowledge, know-how and ideas of its individual technicians, the process leading up to the development of new products, the particulars of past failures and the latest technical information, all in textual form.

Fujitsu's aim in this activity is the concentration of personnel in its development division for intensive creative activities in parallel with its programme of further automation to reduce (or even eliminate) plant personnel requirements.

It is hoped that the use of this data base will enable young researchers with only a year or two of research experience to do the work of ten-year veterans.

Concept of the conception support system

Concept

In high-level knowledge information processing, a concord among the personnel involved is not necessarily important, or even advisable, partly because discussion among personnel with different perspectives is usually more productive than that among like-minded personnel. The difference of opinion can often be resolved on a higher plane through repeated discussion.

The process of conception assisted by computer should also make use of such dissimilarity through a division of roles between the operator and the computer. The system should enable each to take advantage of the other's forte, seeing that the weak areas of each are covered by the other, and that the work of each is monitored by the other. A system incorporating such techniques could prove highly effective and capable of producing practical results within a feasible time frame.

Generally speaking, a realistic support of knowledge information processing would require a knowledge of such processing by humans and an incorporation of an analogous version in the machine.

However, the focus in the development of this system must not be imitation of the human faculty of knowledge information processing, but support of this

Table 8.II

	Basic pattern of 'Gennai' output (modified in terms of English grammar)	
Pattern	Structure	Copy (key word: 'sports')
1 Metaphor	N - V - N	'Sports is a weather map'
2 Noun-oriented	N + N	Pyjamas and practice
	N of N	
3 Adjective-oriented	A - N	Exhilarating door-to-door sales
4 Verb-oriented	N - V	A nude is streaking
5 Compound	N - V - N	A Marine swims Marina del Rey

Note: N: Noun, V: Verb, A: Adjective

faculty. In short, the development must proceed from what may be regarded as the basic principle in utilization of machines:

• Machines are made to support humans. Utilization by humans elevates the capability of the machines, and humans grow as they become more skilled in using this capability.

In addition, the system would not be designed to produce total solutions or correct answers. Instead, the aim would be an output of several meaningful hypotheses of tentative answers to stir the exercise of creative conception by the operator. The system would therefore pursue not comprehensiveness but meaningfulness.

This concept would be embodied in our 'conception support system'. In the process of conception, its operator could leave the assemblage of logical constructs from a vast pool of complex knowledge to the machine and concentrate on the assemblage of elements where human intuition must come into play.

Basic functions

The core of the system would consist of the following three types of basic functions:

• Assemblage of logical constructs of knowledge (within a feasible time)
• Conception enlightenment
• Highly operable user interface

The first function would be indispensable. The second would be required if the system is to fulfill its mission of supporting conception. The system must not merely execute a task and produce an output; it must also provide an environment that will actively enlighten the operator as to the input needed for conception.

A system that would perform in the same manner regardless of the identity of the operator would be out of keeping with the objective of supporting conception. The system must be designed to make the best use of the particular talents or individuality of the operator in question, otherwise, the result will be a run-of-the-mill conception regardless of the operator that is inconsistent with the originality implicit in creative activities, which are the system's raison d'être.

The third function stems from the need for the system to provide an environment that makes it easy for the operator to furnish the system with hints needed for conception. This input process must be as natural as possible for the operator, and could not be effectively performed with an unwieldy interface.

Actual mode of use

The system could actually be put to use in a number of applications such as: proposal of plans or ideas for new products based on newly developed technology; discovery of constituent technologies of value for technology development; proposal of R&D subjects and support of R&D work; concentration and sharing of in-house know-how; education and training.

The impact of the system would not be confined to such operational innovation. It could, most importantly, be expected to upgrade the human role within companies and to trigger a change in the perception of value in labour in companies and their organizations.

Anatomy of ideation/conception

The conception support system would be a computerized system designed to support, not execute, the performance of creative acts of ideation/conception. The development of such a system would have to begin with thorough research of the mode of performance, characteristics and limits of human ideation/conception, in order to determine the kind of support system that is desirable.

Figure 8.4 presents a specific example of the sequence of conception. A researcher working for a food product manufacturer was faced with the need to find a simple way of measuring the adsorptive capability of food product materials in the course of R&D of new food products. The figure shows the sequence of conception that culminated in the idea of applying fractal theory.

The line of thought of the researcher in question may be regarded as having proceeded in the direction of the horizontal arrows. The other two arrows at each step signify the directions that might have been taken by other researchers. It is also clear that each step involved high-order intellectual information processing in the form of the marshalling of a host of knowledge, careful examination of the same, and finally the construction of a hypothesis.

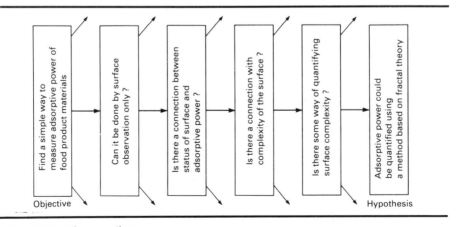

8.4 Anatomy of conception.

This underscores the complexity of the act of conception. The sequence in question, which constitutes but a small part of the entire act of creation, could not be produced through analogical inference or successive changes of perspective alone; it suggests the need for the application of a systematic method of conception.

Characteristics of ideation/conception

A systematic method of ideation/conception would amount to a kind of information processing. In the construction of such a method, particular attention would have to be paid to the following five characteristics of ideation/conception.

1 Handling of 'meaning-rich' information

'Meaning' is obviously a key word in the method of ideation/conception. Information laden with meaning is 'meaning-rich' information, as opposed to the numerical and other types of 'formalistic' information handled in large quantities by today's information systems. The processing and disposal of 'meaning-rich' information using the current information processing technology is far from satisfactory; the technology being inept at handling such information.

For creative activities in companies, 'meaning' would come down to knowledge of where and how to produce added value. As such, the ability to process and convert 'meaning-rich' information would become the key know-how for the creation of added value in tomorrow's companies.

2 Turnabout/adjustment of perspective/point of view

In today's information society, companies are awash in a flood of information about 'phenomena'; the developments unfolding within and around them.

One of the most crucial requirements in the method of ideation/conception would be an ability to distinguish the phenomenon or small group of phenomena which could generate valuable 'meaning' from the boundless mass of all other phenomena. Such phenomena would have to be distinguished at an early, fragmental stage. The target would not be phenomena and facts of demonstrated value recognizable to all, but more tentative, advance suggestions that could serve as the basis for the construction of hypotheses, such as a single experimental result.

To do so would call for an ability to adjust and turn around perspectives. The classic example is that of the shoe salesman out to find new markets who encounters a community of barefoot people. He may first conclude that there is absolutely no market there, but with a turnabout of perspective, would see a vast latent market.

3 Horizontal progression and vertical progression

Two basic types of conception may be identified: flexible conception that is not bound by fixed ideas, and conception that focuses on causality or depends on knowledge concerning the facts and logic.

In terms of the mode of progression, the former type may be termed 'horizontal' (diffuse) conception, and the latter type, 'vertical' (convergent) conception. The former may be regarded as analogical, and the latter, as logical. The conception support system would have to strike a balance between them.

4 Mutual interplay of intuition and logic

Human power of intuition is an extremely important part of ideation/conception. While its systematization may not be utterly impossible, humans will have to continue to be relied upon for intuitional conception for the foreseeable future, judging from the current level of cognitive science and knowledge information processing. As such, the question is how the conception support system (the role of which would consist mainly of logical and retrieval operations) could maintain a beneficial relationship of mutual interdependence with human intuition.

The construction of a model assisting comprehension of human intuition would therefore be needed and the results of research of neural networks and related technologies would have to be incorporated to this end.

5 Factual premises and value premises

The substance of creation in corporate activities is the creation of added value. However, it is intrinsically impossible for any company to create 'added value' in general. At the same time, it would be unrealistic for a single company to attempt to create all kinds of particular added value.

A company must create added value through a particular method that makes use of its own particular resources in a particular domain. The creation must also reflect the company's perception of its obligation to society as well as its philosophy/vision and CI.

All such factors constitute premises of value in ideation/conception. These premises differ greatly in kind from the premises of fact and phenomena that are the ordinary subjects of knowledge processing. As a result, the conception support system would have to accommodate not only factual premises, but also value premises.

Anatomy of conception

As part of this project, a test was conducted in order to obtain an image of the sequence of the transformation of meaning in conception. The test began with the posing of two research objectives of a technical nature. The subject researcher was asked to construct a hypothetical means for the attainment of the objective, noting the stages of conception in arriving at this means. The respective hypotheses and the stages of conception leading up to them are shown in Fig. 8.5.

In point of comprehensibility, the stages exhibit a diversity; in some cases, the outside observer can easily see how the researcher made the leap from one stage to another, but in other cases, this mode of transition is not apparent.

Overall, the case 1 sequence is fairly easy to understand, and the case 2 sequence, relatively opaque to the outside observer. As a result, most observers would presumably rate the case 2 conception as more interesting.

Perhaps the most noteworthy thing about the case 1 conception is the selection of space as the environment. Information about the use of space as an environment for activity is now fairly commonplace, but the same idea would have been viewed as highly innovative ten years ago.

The case 2 conception hinges on an unconventional perspective; where the ordinary thinker would have searched for a body-safe material that would remain undeformed and otherwise unchanged, the subject researcher hit upon

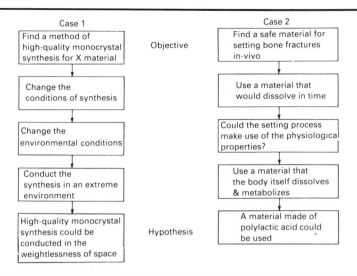

8.5 Anatomy of conception as explained by the researcher.

the idea of a soluble material. This idea of dissolution apparently led to the next stage of dissolution by the workings of the body itself. The proposal of polylactic acid as a material rested not so much on the power of conception as on specialized knowledge about organic materials for in-vivo use.

The conception support system would presumably provide fairly substantial assistance for conception along the lines of case 1. In the case 2 type, the crux would be eliciting the pivotal idea of dissolution; the proposal of polylactic acid as the material could be arrived at with a sufficiently extensive data base.

The conception support system and corporate management

The workings of human conception are as mysterious as they are complex. Psychology and cognitive science are still far from an explanation and even if research became of prime importance, illumination could be several decades to several centuries away.

Companies must begin developing conception support systems now if they are to be ready for the impending age of creation. In order to develop such a system tailored to its needs, each company would first have to acquire a firm grasp of the strengths and weaknesses of its personnel, the possibilities and limits of its technology, the actual status of its organizational mechanism and its functions, the status of its fields of business and customers and other matters that bear in some degree upon its overall management. This is to say that the conception support system can also be positioned as a strategic system for creative intensification in companies.

The first step on the road to the development of the conceptor would be a return to the basic question of how human conception works. The reflections presented above may be regarded as a kind of mental exercise that was motivated by this simple question. It is hoped, however, that similar attempts will be made by the whole spectrum of companies and specialists in all kinds of fields in the coming years.

RESEARCH OF THE PROCESS OF CREATION
various interpretations of the process of creation

Stages of problem-solving

Akira Onda	E K Von Fange	W J J Gordon	H R Buhl	Kikuya Ichikawa	Masakazu Nakayama
1) Detection of problem 2) Formulation of task 3) Performance of task (solution)	1) Study of orientation 2) Setting of standards of measurement 3) Development of method 4) Formation of optimal mechanism 5) Proposal of solution 6) Convincing others of the propriety of the solution	1) Posing of problem 2) Acclimation to the heterogeneous 3) Determination of problem 4) Formation of practical mechanism 5) Acclimation to the heterogeneous 6) Psychological state 7) Integration with the problem 8) Formation of point of view 9) Reply (research objective)	1) Posing of problem 2) Analysis of problem 3) Collection of information 4) Analysis of information 5) Synthesis of information 6) Evaluation 7) Presentation of information	1) Detection of problem 2) Posing of problem 3) Investigation of 'Vi' (proper perspective) 4) Determination of 'e' (essence/principle) 5) Search of 'Ao' (models/hints) 6) Application of 'C' (conditions) 7) Integration of 'C' & 'e', discovery of 'Ce' (idea)	1) Setting of objective (determination of problem) 2) Conception 3) Determination of method 4) Determination of procedure 5) Implementation of procedure 6) Evaluation

Source) Akira Onda, 'Research of Creativity Development'

RESEARCH OF THE PROCESS OF CREATION
various interpretations of the process of creation

Stages of problem-solving

J Dewey	C S Peirce	C E Gregory	Research process (Methods of Research)	Zenji Katagata	Jiro Kawakita
1) Recognition of problem situation 2) Posing of problem (clarification) 3) Hypothesis (formulation of plan for solution) 4) Inference (investigation of implications of hypothesis) 5) Test 6) Substantiated assertion	1) Abduction a) Observation of phenomenon b) Discovery of hypothesis c) Hypothetical thesis 2) Deduction a) Elucidation of hypothesis (analysis) b) Demonstration (deductive inference) 3) Induction a) Classification b) Test c) Decision	1) Setting of objective 2) Analysis of problem 3) Collection of data 4) Systematization of data 5) Induction 6) Formulation of plan 7) Advance check 8) Execution of plan 9) Evaluation	1) Selection of research topic 2) Collection of information (including documentation) 3) Formulation of hypothesis 4) Testing of hypothesis (planning and execution of experiments)	1) Posing of problem (deduction or presentation of problem) 2) Analysis of problem (analysis of problem features and objectives, setting of objectives, analysis of materials) 3) Solution of problem (selection and execution of means of solution)	1) Posing of problem 2) Collection of information 3) Organization, classification, storage 4) Summarization of information 5) Consolidation of information 6) Processing of by-products 7) Assessment of information 8) Decision 9) Structural planning 10) Procedural planning 11) Execution 12) Evaluation of result

9

Management for creation

Evolution of management

Management for creation

Management for creation is the implantation of a corporate environment conducive to creation and implementation of managerial know-how for creation.

Creation intensification in companies would be an acceleration of creative
output in the forms of new technology, products, systems and business. This
would have to be done by constructing a mechanism spanning the spheres of
strategy, organization, personnel and information to ensure that management
resources (personnel, material, funds and information) are allocated to corporate
activities (R&D, product development, system development, and business development) in the manner required for creation intensification, see Fig. 9.1.

If properly implanted, this environment would enable the most effective
(creative) use of the monthly, biannual and yearly input of personnel and financial
resources for R&D and planning, thus leading to an expanded creative output and
an ability for creative response to consumers.

In the age of creation, the power of a company would be measured in
terms of its ability to adapt creatively to changes in its environment and to make
creative proposals to its consumers.

The leading companies in the age of creation would be those which demonstrate a superior ability to anticipate still-latent needs and to make creative proposals for them that fully satisfy their consumers.

It should be noted that 'strategy' here is used not in the broad sense of
creative adaption to environmental changes, but in the narrower sense of the subjects and timing of allocation of managerial resources.

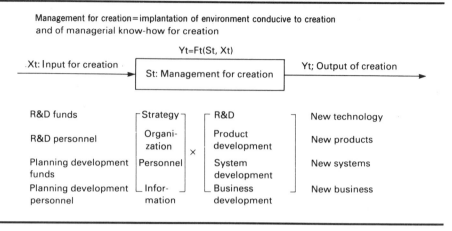

Management for creation = implantation of environment conducive to creation and of managerial know-how for creation

9.1 Management for creation.

Evolution of management

Corporate management must, of course, change with the times. Only companies capable of executing management adapted to the times will be able to subsist, grow and advance. Conversely, those with a management out of step with the times will suffer a loss of growth, decline and eventual failure. In this sense, the principle of survival of the fittest applies to corporate entities as well as to living beings, and is the prime force behind socioeconomic dynamism and advancement.

Figure 9.2 presents the evolution of management from the agricultural age to the age of creation. In the age of agriculture, which began around 3000 BC, management had to be adapted to agriculture. The priority in management was co-operative work in cultivation, i.e. getting the members of the community to perform the operations of tilling, sowing, watering, weeding and harvesting together as effectively and efficiently as possible in step with the cycle of seasons. Management know-how in this age could be defined as the ability to effect the optimal schemes of co-work, i.e. to induce the optimal co-work merit.

In feudal Japan, the categories of such management know-how included the system of head and branch houses, 'kumi' (units of co-operative cultivation and self-government), 'ko' (units of religious activities and of mutual aid), a scheme for ostracism of undesirable members from the community, 'matsuri' (community festivals) and sense of duty to one's lord and fellows. This body of know-how supported the pursuit of the optimal co-work merit.

When the age of industry was ushered in by the industrial revolution in the 18th century, management had to be adapted to industry. The categories of management know-how were divisions of labour, specialization, standardization, scale expansion and co-ordination of the efforts of several tens or several hundreds of workers, in pursuit of the optimal economy of scale, i.e. scale merit. Management stressed efficiency in its attempt to reduce costs as far as possible through the 'experience curve' effect.

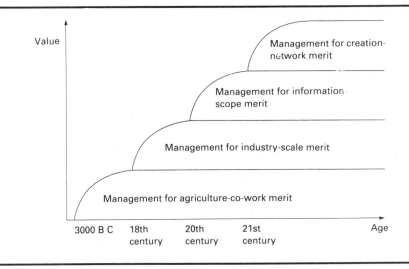

9.2 Evolution of management.

In the age of information, which began in the late 20th century, management has to orient itself to information.

Management has attempted to expand the scope of business by widening its circle of customers, domains of technology and territories of business based on the intensified collection, organization and editing of information in groups. Management know-how in this age could be defined as the ability to induce the optimal economy of scope, i.e. scope merit, through clarification and delegation of group responsibilities and authority.

A key priority is the generation of a synergy through the expansion of business domains.

In the age of creation arriving in the 21st century, management would have to be adapted to creation. Management would work to construct a loose network of specialists to support the method of creation (hypothesis construction, dissimilation, concept creation and chain of empathy) needed for output assisting the consumer's pursuit of self-fulfilment. Management know-how would consist of the means of inducing the optimal effect from this network, i.e. the optimal 'network merit'.

Trinity of the creation-intense entity

In the age of creation, the existence of a company would lack meaning unless its management were geared for creation.

Without management for creation, its goods and services would lack appeal in the eyes of consumers, and it would be unable to provide its employees with the opportunity for what would give them the greatest pleasure, feeling of self-fulfilment and incentive; creation. As such, it would be devoid of attractiveness as a place of employment.

Such companies could be expected to experience declining sales and profits and increasing difficulties in recruiting talented personnel, and to gradually head toward failure. In the age of creation, companies would have to evolve into creation-intense trinities, see Fig. 9.3.

This trinity would consist of: a) a supply of new goods and services through the exercise of creativity and self-actualization of its employees, b) satisfaction of customer needs in the non-material aspect with these new goods and services, and c) an organization enjoying a high level of prestige for its creation of value that is consequently able to attract first-rate personnel.

In the eyes of management, employees would rank first as a priority, followed by customers and the organization.

First and foremost, employees of the creative-intense company would be called upon to use not their hands and feet or their eyes and ears, but their heads. In this sense, the employees must be thinkers.

In the information-intense company, the corresponding trinity consists of satisfaction of the customer's informational needs, a high information literacy among the employees and a high output in the form of information value and profit from the organization, see Fig. 9.4. The top priority is accorded to the first element (satisfaction of customer informational needs), followed in order by employees and the organization. Figuratively speaking, employees are hired for their eyes and ears, not their hands and feet.

The corresponding trinity in the industrial company, Fig. 9.5, was a high organizational output in the form of material value and sales, satisfaction of the customer's material needs and great supply of labour by the employees. The top priority was accorded to the organization. The employees were workers in the physical sense, hired for their hands and feet.

To apply this metaphor of corporate evolution to countries, it could be said that such countries as the Soviet Union, Eastern European countries, and China were more adapted to the times (at least in purely economic terms) during the age of industry than today. This is because the socialist system of centrally

9.3 Trinity of the creation-intense corporate entity.

9.4 Trinity of the information-intense corporate entity.

9.5 Trinity of the industrial-intense corporate entity.

planned economies, concentration of power in a central bureaucracy, decision-making by a privileged elite and tight control of information was effective for expansion of the organizational (national) output. All that had to be satisfied were the material wants of the people as customers, and all the people as employees were called upon to do was supply their labour.

Like others, however, these countries are also moving out of the age of industry and into that of information. Under such a socialist system, NRI believe, it is impossible to achieve the trinity arrangement demanded by the age of information.

By nature, a socialist country cannot tolerate a satisfaction of the informational needs of its customers, an increase in the information literacy of its employees, and an increase in the information value and profit of its organization. In fact, the leaders of various socialist countries appear to be awakening to this reality. In other words, they seem to have come to a realization that, in the age of information, it is more effective for the 'operation' to be based on a free market process than on a centrally planned economy, a decentralized delegation of authority than on a centralized bureaucracy, a democratic process than on decision-making by a privileged few and free access to information than on restriction of such access.

Marx's times were the age of industry. The system of state communism that was Marx's ideal was effective in the aforementioned sense during that age and demonstrated a measure of such effectiveness in the 1950s and 1960s.

Nevertheless, the effectiveness of this system has declined in the transition to the age of information, jeopardizing the subsistence of governments applying it. Viewed in this light, the forceful promotion of the 'perestroika' (socio-economic reform) and 'glasnost' (freer access to information) campaigns in the Soviet Union are means of an evolution from state communism to a system better adapted to the age of information.

With the transition to the age of creation, the same countries will, like others, presumably have to remake the socioeconomic system for support of the exercise of individual creativity.

Management for creation

Method of and management for creation

Part III, Chapter 8 presented an account of creation methodology. As noted in the previous section, management for creation is the implantation of the environment and mechanisms required to support this methodology and make it work. Figure 9.6 illustrates the relationship among ages, methods and management.

The method of creation concerns mainly individual and group creation. Management for creation provides the atmosphere needed for the effective operation of this method and elevates individual and group creation to the level of corporate creation, i.e. leads them to success as corporate undertakings.

In the age of information, there is a corresponding method of information which is supported by management for information. There were counterparts in the ages of industry and agriculture, i.e. methods of industry/agriculture supported by the appropriate management.

So, each age is characterized by its own method and type of management supporting that method. In the general pattern, the employee adopting the method suited to the age will move up within the organization, as will the manager managing in a manner suited to the age.

The aspects of corporate management may be divided into the following four major categories, see also Fig. 9.7.

- Strategy in the limited sense, i.e. the subjects and timing of a concentrated input of managerial resources.

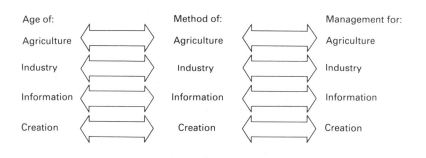

9.6 Relationship among ages, methods and management.

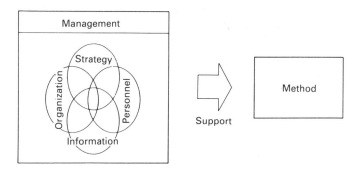

9.7 Management and strategy.

- Arrangement of the most important managerial resource of personnel. The major consideration here is organization; the organization of personnel placement in accordance with the division of functions.
- The construction of a system for personnel recruitment, placement, transfer, evaluation, treatment, education, etc.
- The use of information/communication. The concern here is the setup for conferences, reports, flow of slips, information systems, etc.

At the same time, these four aspects are mutually interdependent. The key is inducing dynamic advancement in them while maintaining a mutual conformance among them.

More specifically, a dynamic innovation must take place in each, in step with the changing times and methods.

As noted in the previous section, the method of creation consists of four stages: a) hypothesis construction, b) dissimilation, c) concept creation, and d) chain of empathy, see Fig. 9.8. Management for creation would optimize the operation of each of these stages in each of the aspects of strategy, organization, personnel and information.

Since a certain kind of know-how would be required for the stage and aspect in question, NRI proposes 16 categories of management know-how. In

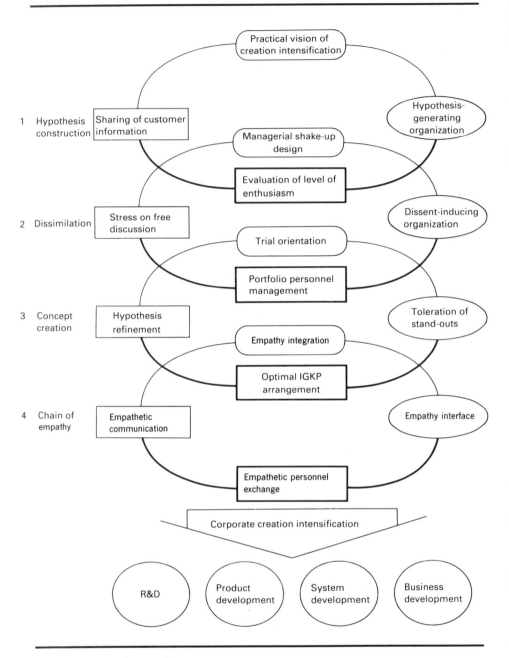

9.8 Management for creation.

addition, each of these categories comprises three subcategories, yielding a total of 48 types of management know-how.

These types of know-how were formulated on the basis of the results of the case study outlined in Part II.

Because there is an interrelation among the four stages of method and the four aspects of management, it would be vital to maintain a corresponding linkage among the 16 categories of management know-how.

The remaining part of this section presents an account of the management of creation – and requisite management know-how in the aspects of strategy, organization, personnel and information. Table 9.I outlines this.

Table 9.I Creation management know-how

	1 Strategy	2 Organization	3 Personnel	4 Information
1 Hypothesis construction	Practical vision of creation intensification	Hypothesis-generating organization	Enthusiasm-oriented management	Sharing of customer information
	1 Formulation of vision of the creation-intense company 2 Construction and sharing by all employees 3 Individual freedom of suggestion	1 Employee as president 2 Direct proposal to units studying ideas from a companywide, long-term perspective 3 Encouragement of sideline development	1 Stress on level of enthusiasm in hiring 2 Self-transfer 3 Leadership opportunity for younger employees	1 Expanded interface of contact with customer 2 Relationship management 3 Understanding of customer sensibility
2 Dissimilation	Managerial shake-up design	Dissent-inducing organization	Portfolio personnel management	Stress on free discussion
	1 Long-term scenario 2 Design of shake-up 3 Flexible budgetary management	1 Intellectual partnership 2 Dynamic organizational change 3 Deliberate fusion of the heterogeneous	1 Heterogeneous grouping 2 Rhythmic work cycle 3 Grooming of transdisciplinary personnel	1 Brainstorming 2 Intellectual network 3 Conception support system
3 Concept creation	Trial orientation	Toleration of stand-outs	Optimal IGKP arrangement	Hypothesis refinement
	1 Next-generation orientation 2 Stress on trial activities 3 Toleration of failure	1 Flat organization 2 Non-intervention 3 Respect for 'maverick' views	1 IGs on periphery 2 Transfer of IKs 3 Attention to idea co-ordination	1 Constructive defiance 2 Return to basics 3 Listening to customers
4 Chain of empathy	Empathy integration	Empathy interface	Empathetic personnel exchange	Empathetic communication
	1 Commitment at the top 2 Communication as an investment 3 Re-creation	1 Empathetic project team 2 Alternate separation and fusion of the principles of 'creation' and 'efficiency' 3 Customer as the partner	1 Individual reward and commendation 2 Circulation of success 3 Double-loop exchange	1 Communication as event 2 Free access to specialists inside or outside the company 3 Customer education

Creativisionary strategy

The vital element in management for creation in the aspect of strategy is 'creativision'.

Its substance is the formulation of a corporate vision: a portrait of the company as it should evolve during the five-year period beginning five years in the future, that is shared by all employees, and of measures to attain this vision.

It is important for all employees to share the same dream and values in order to nourish creation from the individual level to that of group creation, and further to that of corporate creation, in which a company-wide synergy is induced. Since they would have a stake in it, all employees would, on their own initiative, exercise their creative powers to the fullest in an attempt to make the dream a reality.

The four categories of management know-how in this aspect corresponding to the four stages of creation are noted in Fig. 9.9. The following is an account of each.

Practical vision of creation intensification

Hypothesis construction calls for the construction and sharing by all employees of a practical vision of creation intensification.

Employees cannot be expected to 'put out' for hypotheses that have been forced upon them from above. In such cases, it would be impossible to maintain a high energy level in the frontal lobe of the brain, which is said to be the seat of drive for self-actualization/fulfilment. At the same time, an organizational synergy could not obtain effective results if each individual were allowed to go off in pursuit of his own hypothesis, however unrelated to those of the others.

Management must therefore ensure that the hypothesis is constructed by the individuals themselves based on their own dreams and aspirations for their life work, and also that it is in conformance with the direction in which the entire organization must proceed.

The stratagem is to find the intersection between the hypotheses and dreams which would motivate the individuals to work to the best of their ability of their own accord and the direction in which the organization must head. This intersection must then be articulated as a clear vision that can be acted upon, aims at creation and can be held in common by all employees.

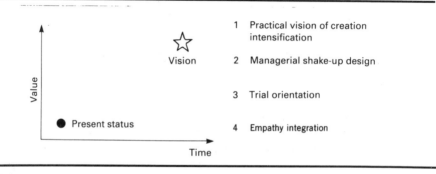

9.9 Creativisionary strategy.

A long-term vision is generally regarded as consisting of a corporate vision, management philosophy, pattern of action, domain targets and quantified targets. Of these five components, corporate vision is the most important.

This practical vision of creation intensification contains three sub-categories of know-how.

1 Formulation of a vision of the creation-intense company

Management must make it clear that the company's role is in line with the fundamental reason for the existence of corporate enterprises; the planning of new business and creation of new value. In so doing, it must identify the company's target fields and the types of creative activities in each during the period five to ten years in the future. It can also be noted that employees tend to be most enthusiastic about their work when they see themselves as forerunners creating a new business.

Some variation of the word creation is, in fact, contained in the long-term visions of many companies. Cases in point include Kanebo 'creator and supplier of beauty, health, and value in living', Mitsubishi Petrochemical 'the creative chemical company' and Fujita Tourist 'creation of amenities and impressions'.

2 Construction and sharing of the vision by all employees

Long-term visions should be constructed every five or ten years through a process of in-depth discussion involving the top, middle and bottom layers of the organization and lasting about six months. The vision should be perceived as having been fashioned by all employees together and should be held in common by all. The formation of a consensus in the process of construction is liable to be more significant than the actual substance of the vision. The construction could be approached by the institution of a special committee about six months before a scheduled change at the top. The membership of this committee, which would be chaired by the person who is to succeed to the post of president six months later, would consist of representatives of the board of directors, departmental and sectional heads, and young employees. These three groups would engage in extensive joint discussion and deliberation. The committee could also conduct in-house interviews and questionnaire surveys that would involve all employees in the construction process. Once constructed, the vision should be thoroughly explained to all employees and announced to the public. Announcement to the public would boost awareness of the vision inside the company and could lead to the generation of ideas to facilitate its promotion.

Such action was taken in the case of Toyo Sash, which instituted a 'committee for distribution reform' headed by its president, Kenjiro Shioda. This committee constructed a vision (next-day delivery, anywhere in the country) which was readily comprehensible to all employees. And the penetration of this vision at all levels of the organization led to a successful reform of the company's distribution.

3 Individual freedom of suggestion

Management must build a mechanism furnishing individual employees with the opportunity for suggestion and implementation of their own ideas within the context of the practical vision of creation intensification. The person making the proposal would ideally be given the chance to lead a project built around it upon its approval at the top. This would require a certain degree of flexibility in organizational and budgetary arrangements. Management know-how of this type was a factor in the successful development of Sony's Handycam 55 and it is also exemplified by Honda's scheme for individual suggestion using yellow slips of paper, and Texas Instrument's idea proposal system.

Managerial 'shake-up' design

The management know-how required at the second stage of creation (dissimilation) in the aspect of strategy is the design of managerial shake-up.

Effective dissimilation hinges on diversity and flexibility; the aim is the avoidance of flat uniformity that would result from assimilation. This diversity and flexibility could be maintained by periodic shake-up, the extent of which has been arranged in advance.

It is advisable for each hypothesis to be exposed to dissent in the form of counter and alternative hypotheses formulated from various viewpoints in various fields. As a result, the requirement at this stage is not only adjustment and fuller articulation of the hypothesis by its original proposer, but also a wide range of dissent on the part of the other members of the group.

An effective means to this end would be 'managerial shake-up design'; shake-up with a built-in dissimilation effect.

The three subcategories of know-how in this category are as follows:

1 Formulation of a long-term scenario and search for the optimal combination of functions and personnel

The long-term scenario should view the outlook for the course of development three to five or even ten years into the future. As a first step, detailed plans should be made for the first year. Naturally, the long-term scenario would conform with the long-term vision.

Consideration of development from a long-term perspective is conducive to discussion of essentials as opposed to minutiae. It could also forestall the diminution of the hypothesis and the shrinkage of the range of counter-hypotheses that could result from assertions about what is technically possible.

NEC's vision, 'C&C' ('computers and communications') includes a general scenario of the company's R&D to the year 2000.

2 Design of shake-up

'Shake-up' could be deliberately induced by putting the organization through a continuous cycle of centralization (arrangement in terms of function) and decentralization (arrangement in terms of business) with a period of three to five years per phase. The same effect could be obtained by recombination of personnel, entailing the reassignment of 20–30% of all employees each year to keep the organization fresh. Particularly important is the movement of personnel among the development-oriented divisions (R&D, product development, system development, business development) and between these divisions and the efficiency-oriented divisions (production, distribution, marketing and control). Komatsu, for example, revamps the organization of its laboratory substantially every five years or so.

3 Flexible budgetary management

By nature, developmental projects are prone to unanticipated occurrences. To cope with such occurrences, the management of the budget must be flexible. It should allow a high degree of freedom in the use of funds within a general budgetary framework on the authority of the developmental manager or other party on the site of the development. It is also recommended to budget a special allowance that could be carried around by those in charge of the development.

Trial orientation

The category of know-how in the third stage of creation (concept creation) in the aspect of strategy is a trial orientation.

The creation of an entirely new value requires some kind of leap from or discontinuity with the present. For this reason, management must be willing to try and test hypotheses and counterhypotheses as intensively as possible. A rigorous process of experiment, trial, observation and discussion could be expected to generate viable new concepts with a certain frequency.

Successful creation entails movement; it cannot take place in stasis. The three subcategories of this know-how are as follows.

1 Next-generation orientation

The target is a next-generation concept that represents a jump from prevailing concepts, that is closer to the essence. The development must constantly stay on the leading edge and pursue a value that is not available from any other sources. This attitude can be glimpsed in Honda's decision to venture into the field of Formula 1 race cars.

2 Stress on trial activities

Top and middle-level management should constantly incite their subordinates to give new ideas and approaches a try. Younger personnel in particular should be encouraged to attempt approaches that differ from those taken by their superiors. The importance of trial may be illustrated by the results of an experiment conducted on barracudas.

A water tank was prepared with a removable glass partition. The testers put several barracudas into the left side of the tank, and then dropped food into the right side. For a while, the barracudas continued to bump their heads against the partition in a vain attempt to get at the food, but eventually stopped swimming toward the right side. At this point, the glass partition was removed, but the barracudas still made no move toward the right side. An additional barracuda was then introduced into the left side, and immediately swam over to snatch the food in the right side. Similarly in the course of their existence, organizations build up a store of experience, some of which concerns past attempts that failed. This experience can block new attempts along the same line and new approaches to the same problem. Since the environment is constantly changing, there is no guarantee that attempts which failed yesterday will not succeed today. This is why instilling an attitude of constant challenge and trial is so important.

3 Toleration of failure

Failure resulting from a challenging, bold attempt must be tolerated and used as a springboard to success.

Members of an organization that does not tolerate failure will not take the risks that accompany challenge. If management tries to increase the probability of success, it will produce an organization that confines itself to development most likely to succeed. Such development can only result in minor creation, not the landmark creation in question here.

The project success rate at 3M, for example, is only about 10%, and management is not out to boost it. While this rate suggests that nine out of every ten of its project leaders will experience failure, it also indicates the presence of an atmosphere conducive to challenge and free of fear of failure. Personnel participating in developmental projects at 3M are assured that failure will not have any adverse consequences for their position or treatment. If any, it is the personnel reluctant to participate in such projects who are viewed with concern by management.

Empathy integration

In the fourth stage of creation (chain of sympathy), the category of know-how in the aspect of strategy is 'empathy integration.' Management must see that the concept created in the previous stage takes definite shape as developmental output which is then produced and supplied to customers.

This 'materialization' of the concept must be promoted by inducing an empathy toward it on the part of developers. The chain of empathy forged among developers must then be broadened from the creation-oriented divisions (those engaged in the generation and materialization of the concept) to the efficiency-oriented divisions (production, distribution, marketing, control), and finally to the vendors and customers.

This stage is one of problem-solving through the co-operative efforts of various types of specialists, an area in which Japanese companies tend to excel. By contrast, the stages of hypothesis construction through to concept creation are stages of problem discovery, which tend to be the weak point of Japanese companies.

In inducing the required empathy in the aspect of strategy, it is important for management to aim for integration of the concerned divisions. This is because a localized empathy could not power a companywide effort and also would only have a limited influence on customers.

On this point, it can be noted that the 'network merit' (economy of network) increases dramatically along with an increase in the number of network participants. Viewing network participants as nodes and the network merit as equivalent to the number of internodal arcs, the degree of network merit can be found by solution of the following formula:

Merit (# of arcs) = (# of nodes) × (# of nodes − 1) / 2

Applying this formula, the merit would be minimal, 1 for a network with two nodes (participants), but would rise to 3 for one with three nodes, 6 for one with four nodes, and 10 for one with 5 nodes, see Fig. 9.10.

Empathy therefore proliferates in a geometrical progression; it can snowball when the product of creation has a great potential and is backed by high-energy integration activities.

The three subcategories of empathy integration know-how are as follows.

1   Firm commitment at the top

In most cases, projects forcefully promoted at the top meet with success. A company is at its most powerful when all the energies of its employees are directed to a single objective under the leadership of the top-level management. New ideas are bound to encounter opposition in various divisions, and particularly those that are efficiency-oriented' new ideas cause disruption which hurts efficiency. A staunch commitment to the new idea at the top-level of management is vital to overcome such opposition. This know-how is illustrated in the case of Toyo Sash by the president's decision to head the committee for distribution reform himself, and in the case of Seven-Eleven Japan by president Suzuki's firm commitment to system development.

2   Treatment of communication costs as an investment

The chain of empathy cannot be forged without sufficient communication. However, a sufficient current of communication cannot be generated if the cost entailed is handled as a mere expense that should be pared as far as possible in the interests of rationalization. Instead, it should be regarded as a crucial investment producing a benefit commensurate with its level and with a view to long-term benefits, like programmes of employee education.

Communication investment could be expected to reinforce the ties linking employees to each other and with vendors and customers, promote the sharing of information, and boost the speed of information dissemination.

3   Re-creation

A company only merits continued subsistence if it is able to produce new value continually. The expansion and reproduction of creation should therefore be at the heart of the corporate mission.

Instilling an ability for re-creation requires a systematic feedback of the particulars of successful creation to all divisions in order to promote a sharing of the know-how that was instrumental in it. This process also serves to build up an atmosphere congenial to creation in the company.

In sum, the key is setting in motion a cycle of creation by recycling the know-how of successful creation. Such a mechanism is apparent in Sony, where

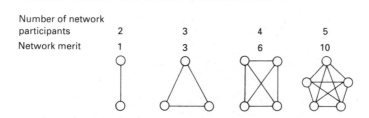

| Number of network participants | 2 | 3 | 4 | 5 |
| Network merit | 1 | 3 | 6 | 10 |

9.10 Network merit.

the creation cycle proceeded in succession from the transistor radio to the Walkman and the compact 8 mm video camera (Handycam 55).

Differences among the ages of industry, information and creation in the aspect of management of strategy

As noted in Fig. 9.11, the key word for management of strategy in the age of creation is creativision. The counterpart was quantitative expansion in the age of industry and is expansion of scope in the age of information.

In the age of creation, management would have to promote the construction of a target vision to be realized by the company five to ten years in the future that coincides with the dreams and career aspirations of its employees, who can consequently share it. It would also have to formulate a flexible strategic scenario for realization that would additionally serve as a guideline for the exercise of creativity by the employees in their daily work. This section described four categories of know-how needed for such management and corresponding with the four stages of creation, i.e. a) a practical vision of creation intensification, b) managerial shake-up design, c) a trial orientation, and d) empathy integration.

CREATION THROUGH VARIABLE THOUGHT
a researcher's view of conception

Researcher   Heisuke Hironaka

Subject   Researchers, educators

Basic perspective   Practical perspective

Substance: A mathematician, Heisuke Hironaka's own research experience led him to propose 'variable thought' as a key factor in creation. This term refers to the treatment of thought itself as a variable in the mathematical sense through the discarding of all fixed ideas and preconceptions in all aspects. Hironaka sees this status as leading to creation.

Hironaka also draws a distinction between needs and wants. He defines need as existing in a certain place and time, dictated by external circumstances and based on past experience, knowledge, and analysis of the present, and want as essentially removed from place and time, dictated by the individual's perceived inner sentiments or aspirations for the future. He consequently interprets the 'necessity' in Edison's famous aphorism, 'Necessity is the mother of invention', as referring more to wants than needs.

Ranking alongside Hideki Yukawa and Koji Fushimi as one of Japan's most prominent creative thinkers, Hironaka's theory of creation carries an authority that derives from the fact that it has grown out of his own experience.

Source) Heisuke Hironaka, 'Creation Through Variable Thought – A Handbook for Conception in Planning, Education and Technology'

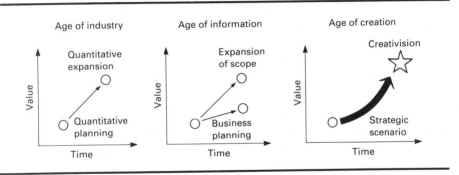

9.11 Management of strategy.

In the age of industry, the target of business was quantitative expansion. Planning consequently stressed quantitative targets for sales, output and input, and efficiency depended on inducing a good 'experience-curve' effect. Improvement activities such as TQC (total quality control) campaigns were effective means to these ends.

In the age of information, the target is expansion of scope. Emphasis is laid upon expanded inroads into new domains in business planning, and PPM (product portfolio management) is an effective means to this end.

Organization conducive to individual creation

The management of creation in the organizational aspect must strive for an organization conducive to individual creation.

In the final analysis, creation begins with individuals. The organization conducive to this would enable the individual to exercise his creativity to the fullest while linking him with other individuals in the organization in a loose network.

The total output of power in a tug of war pitting ten individuals against ten others is generally less than ten times that in one pitting a single individual against another. For some reason, each member usually cannot or does not exercise his full power in the former case. The situation is one of minus synergy, the whole being less than the sum of the parts.

The organization conducive to individual creation would, on the other hand, be one of positive synergy, the whole being greater than the sum of the parts. Such an organization would use a high network merit to generate a spiral of positive synergy, a group creation that is greater than the sum of individual creation and a corporate creation that is greater than the sum of group creation.

The four categories of required know-how corresponding with the four stages of creation are indicated in Fig. 9.12.

Hypothesis-generating organization

The category of know-how in the first stage of creation (hypothesis construction)

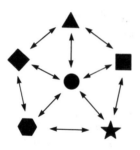

1 Hypothesis-generating organization

2 Dissent-inducing organization

3 Toleration of stand-outs

4 Sympathy interface

9.12 Organization conducive to industrial creation.

in the organizational aspect (Table 9.I) is the formation of a hypothesis-generating organization. The three subcategories of know-how are as follows:

1 Employee as president

In most cases, the person with the greatest awareness of the company's situation and the most ability to construct hypotheses is the president. Nevertheless, no president, however competent, can construct all hypotheses for all action required by the company singlehandedly; various hypotheses must be constructed for various business and roles by the individuals performing them. This requires an organization in which all of the members constantly stay abreast of customer needs and dissatisfaction and form ideas and hypotheses in response to them, almost as if each were president or owner of the business in question.

This orientation is visible in Yamato Parcel, whose president, Masao Okura, is aiming for an organization of 'management by employees', in which management could be equated with the aggregate of employees, each working to the best of their ability of their own accord. He likens the mentality of this organization to that of the owner-operator of a neighbourhood sushi bar, who takes a personal interest in everything from the laying in of stock (fish) to production (preparing orders) and sales ('one more sir?').

It is also the aspiration of Yoshiro Maruta, president of Kao, who has remarked: 'As a human being, even the newest recruit is on the same footing as the president; there can be no relationship of subordination in that respect. This kind of perspective makes it possible to elicit ideas from all employees and to make a bigger contribution to society'.

2 Direct proposal to units studying ideas from a companywide, long-term perspective

New ideas can of course be born in conventional organizations. In many cases, however, such ideas entail a change or replacement of the existing flow of work in that organization. If viewed only from a short-term perspective, they are therefore likely to be frowned upon by the proposer's immediate superior. This underscores the importance of a system through which employees can freely propose ideas directly to units which will consider them from a medium-to-long-term, companywide perspective.

Such systems are in place in Honda and Texas Instruments, where employees can make suggestions directly to the staff of the director of the research division or to a study group composed of senior researchers.

3 Encouragement of sideline development

It would also be effective to allow each employee to spend 10–15% of his time on his own 'sideline hypothesis construction' work on a 'pet project' matching his perception of his life work. Such work is known as 'under-the-table' projects at Toshiba and 'skunk work' at 3M and Corning Glass Works. The work in question should not be subject to any excessive restrictions; its conduct should be left to the employee, who should be able to change the orientation or subject as he sees fit, as far as possible. The articulation of any ideas emerging from this work should also be left to the employee up to a certain point. This kind of arrangement can serve as the wellspring of ideas for the construction of a rich diversity of hypotheses.

Dissent-inducing organization

The category of know-how required in the second stage of creation (dissimilation) in the organizational aspect is the formation of a dissent-inducing organization.

In such an organization, a single hypothesis will spontaneously evoke dissenting opinions and counterhypotheses, which will themselves evoke further dissent and hypotheses in a kind of self-proliferation. Such an organization can result from a deliberate fusion of divisions with fundamentally different perspectives.

The three subcategories of know-how are as follows:

1 Instilling the idea of an intellectual partnership

All employees must realize that they are on equal footing with each other as far as proposal of ideas is concerned, and that ideas will be given the same consideration whether the source is the president or a freshman. Free expression of opinion is encouraged, regardless of position and organizational boundaries.

Constructive dissent is not going to surface in an organization with rigid hierarchies and high interdivisional walls. If the president is always right, the level of creation will rise no further than that of the president's creativity.

2 Dynamic organizational change

As noted in connection with managerial shake-up design, the organization should be revamped substantially every three to five years in order to assure that it remains a fertile soil for dissent.

The resulting destruction of complacency and collision of personnel with mutually different perspectives provides a climate in which dissent can flourish.

3 Deliberate fusion of the heterogeneous

Project teams or in-house ventures should deliberately be composed of members who do not see eye-to-eye. The proposer of the idea or hypothesis should be appointed as leader of the group. The membership should bring together a diverse range of personnel, and could even include specialists from outside the party. Such a mix is conducive to the upsurge of dissent needed for creation.

Toleration of stand-outs

The category of know-how required for the third stage of creation (concept creation) in the aspect of organizational management is toleration of organizational stand-outs. Such an organization would give free rein to the energies of its younger employees and allow mavericks to follow through with their ideas, in the recognition that such a policy often leads to creation. The three prerequisites for such a policy are as follows:

1   A flat organization; one with small management
A flat organization would provide opportunity for employees aged around 30, when creative powers are thought to be at their peak, to head developmental projects. The development of Sony's Handycam 55, for example, was placed in the hands of a 29-year-old employee, Katsuya Nakagawa.

2   Non-intervention by management in the workings of the project
Along with the responsibility for the development, the developers should also be given the authority to make decisions about personnel, budgetary and other matters directly related to the work, without interference by outside parties. This point was brought home to Yutaka Kume, president of Nissan, when he was stopped from commenting on the Cima design by the head designer, who told him that anything he said would only adversely affect the aesthetics.

3   Respect for 'maverick' points of view
Creation comes from divergence, from sidestreams as opposed to mainstreams. The seeds of creation are often contained in views which encounter the most opposition. Such views should not immediately be uprooted, but left to sprout while being carefully monitored. When such views surface, it is important to take time to investigate them patiently and objectively to see whether or not they contain something of value.

Empathy interface

The category of know-how required in the fourth stage of creation (chain of empathy) in the organizational aspect is the formation of an interface for empathy with the creation. There are several interfaces in question here: those needed to recruit members for the developmental team, those between the development-oriented divisions (those involved in the generation and materialization of the concept) and efficiency-oriented divisions (production, distribution, sales, control, etc), and those between the company and its vendors and customers. The three subcategories of know-how are as follows.

1   Formation of an empathetic project team
The first requirement is formation of a project team consisting of members empathetic with the subject of development through a companywide campaign of recruitment. The chances and magnitude of success will be greatest if the members of the team are participating of their own accord, out of such empathy.

   If possible, the team should start out with five to ten members. As noted in connection with the tug-of-war, it is likely to be difficult to induce a full synergy if the team is composed of more than ten members. In addition, the development should be propelled not on the basis of the knowledge of the formal members alone, but also on that of discussion with employees who are not members, and even specialists outside the company, both inside and outside Japan. In this way, the promotion of the project could draw upon knowledge assembled from not only Japan, but from around the world.

2   Alternate separation and fusion of the principles of creation and efficiency

Viewed in spatial and temporal terms, the principle of creation seeks originality and diversity, and that of efficiency, continuity and uniformity.

The key here is a periodic cycle of concentration (arrangement in terms of type of function) and decentralization (arrangement in terms of type of business) of creation and efficiency-oriented divisions at intervals of three to five years. Both concentration and decentralization have their own respective advantages and disadvantages, but either is likely to result in stagnation and complacency if left in place for more than five years. Interdivisional walls are likely to grow higher, and the disadvantages to outweigh the advantages. This effect could be achieved not only by reorganization, but also by physical relocation.

A change of location opens up new avenues of information and changes perspectives. The relocation, for example, of an R&D division that had been housed in the same quarters as the production division to new quarters in closer contact with customers could change the orientation in development from technological seeds to market needs.

In the case of such physical separation it would be vital for divisions to remain in close touch through conferences and exchange of personnel.

3   Customers function as partners in the project

It is important to construct interfaces that enable the major target users or customers to function as partners in the project. The range of this partnership should not be confined to sales; employees of the manufacturing, distribution, control and developmental divisions as well should actively be encouraged to make and deepen contact with the customers, thereby erecting a framework for empathy.

Differences between the ages of industry, information and creation in the aspect of organizational management

The word characterizing organizational management was the pyramid in the age of industry, the paperweight in the age of information, and would be the network in the age of creation, Fig. 9.13.

Geared for individual creation, the network organization would be virtually flat, i.e. devoid of hierarchy. Almost no work would require more than three stamps of approval; virtually all work documents would be complete with the stamp of the person preparing them, the person in charge of the work group, and a single superior. Interdivisional walls would be virtually non-existent, enabling a dynamic interaction between R&D, production and marketing. There would also be a healthy exchange of personnel across divisional boundaries, and full communication among the directors, who would work together in a room without partitions. In addition, the organization would be greatly revised every three to five years.

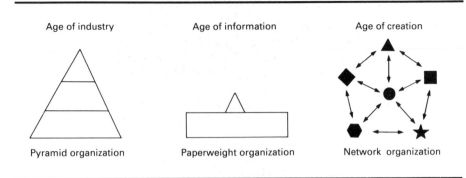

9.13 Organizational management.

The prime units of the organization would consist of about seven employees each. The views expressed by individual employees would be duly considered for reflection in management of the organization.

Hypothesis and dissent would occur spontaneously, and 'maverick' ideas would not be immediately discarded.

In-house ventures would be started up as the occasion demands, pooling employees sympathetic to the subject, regardless of their regular post. The organization would also form many tie-ups with those in other companies and make extensive use of information networks outside the company. Honda, Sony, and AT&T's Bell Laboratory can be cited as harbouring organizations approaching this vision.

In a pyramid organization, advancement is driven by the twin axles of innovation at the top and efforts of improvement through TQC activities at the bottom; the main function of middle management is co-ordination or regulation of the two. The organization is one of multilayer hierarchy with high walls and little personnel exchange between divisions. There is also little interaction between R&D, production, and the front-line business; the top is expected to bind these three strands together. The prime units of the organization contain about 50 employees each, and stress is laid on co-operation and an efficient division of labour. In effect, the control-oriented divisions (labour, personnel, accounting, general affairs) are the only ones with a say in management. Reorganization is infrequent; the organization may not be altered significantly for seven or more years. There are no provisions for in-house ventures. Even the operation of group-level activities shows a strong awareness of parent-subsidiary relationships, the subsidiary being placed under various restrictions in the aspect of personnel, fundraising and budgetary matters. This organization is common in heavy industries.

The paperweight organization stands intermediate to the pyramid and the network organizations. As compared with the pyramid, it has a smaller middle management and lower interdivisional walls. There is consequently some inter-action and personnel exchange among R&D, production and marketing. The prime units of the organization consist of about 20–30 employees each, and individual opinions may be reflected in the organization to a certain degree. However, opinions arriving from the profit centres (business/marketing divisions) carry the greatest weight. There may be two or three in-house ventures, none of which, however, is resoundingly successful. On the group level, subsidiaries are allowed a measure of autonomy. In some cases, the relationship between parent and subsidiary has come to resemble one of siblings. The paperweight organization is common among 'high-tech' manufacturers, distributors and information service suppliers.

Figure 9.14 outlines some of the leading pitfalls that can occur within organisations.

PHYSIOLOGICAL BASIS OF CREATIVITY
genius but one remove from mediocrity?

Researcher Shuichi Kato

Subject Researchers

Basic perspective Cerebral physiology

Substance: A relatively small proportion of research on creativity proceeds from the perspective of physiology and peripheral fields. Shunichi Kato's research begins with a classification and organization of the research of this type conducted to date.

Kato takes up power of mental imagery, heredity, temperament, personality, level of consciousness, and other factors as deeply involved with creativity. He also comments on the conditions required for the emergence of creative mental images, the relationship with mental disease, the traits of personality contributing to creativity, and the possibility of active exercise of creativity under conscious control. Although his ultimate objective appears to be the elucidation of the mechanism of the creative process in terms of cerebral physiology, he has not yet reached convincing conclusions in this aspect.

Source) Shunichi Kato, 'The Cerebral Basis of Creativity'

Creation-rewarding personnel management

The kind of personnel management required for creation is that which rewards personnel for creation, Fig. 9.15.

Since it is the personnel who must create, the key in management is making personnel more creative. To a great extent, personnel activity is shaped by the evaluation of that activity. Personnel may be expected to act in a manner that will gain a high evaluation from their superiors, peers or subordinates. Creation-rewarding management refers to the institution and operation of a system that accords a high evaluation and generous treatment to the personnel behind creation and motivates them to demonstrate their creativity to the fullest.

People tend to become more conservative in outlook as they age, Fig. 9.16. As time passes, the past becomes longer than the future, and people tend to look back more than they look ahead. Judgements too, tend to be grounded in an attempt to preserve the past. The eagerness to take up new challenges and take in

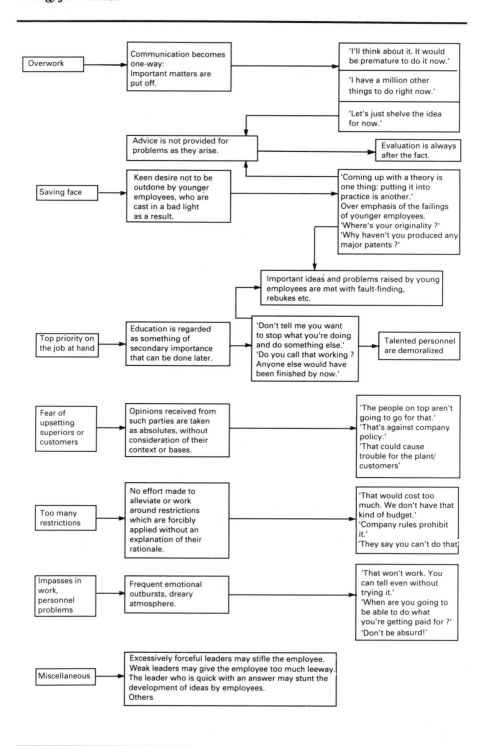

Source: Zenenon Abe 'What is Cultivation of Creativity?'

9.14 Leader pitfalls and killer phases.

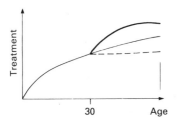

1 Stress on enthusiasm

2 Portfolio personnel management

3 Optimal IGKP arrangement

4 Sympathetic personnel exchange

9.15 Creation-rewarding personnel management.

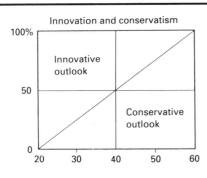
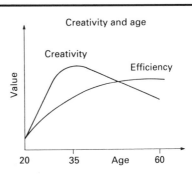

9.16 Comparison of innovation/conservatism and creativity and age.

new developments declines; imitation and habit are more reassuring than creation. In a life spanning 80 years, the point of transition from an innovative to a conservative outlook and from creation to imitation could be put at around the fortieth year.

A questionnaire survey concerning creative R&D implemented in February 1984 with research managers and researchers in Japan's leading private companies, national research institutes and universities found that 94% of the respondents regarded the late 30s as the years in which creative R&D capabilities are at their peak. While unfortunate, it appears that creative powers generally begin to ebb around the age of 40. Efficiency, on the other hand, is thought to rise with age.

In creation-rewarding personnel management, personnel would be accorded ratings and treatment commensurate with the degree of creativity exercised during their 30s, when the creative powers are presumably at their height. All personnel would be given an equal opportunity for creation and treated in accordance with their creative performance. By avoiding a blind equation of similar results that ignores differences in degree of creativity, such management would motivate demonstration of creativity.

Enthusiasm-oriented management

The category of know-how required in the stage of hypothesis construction in the personnel aspect is enthusiasm-oriented management. The subcategories are evaluation of enthusiasm in hiring, personnel 'self-transfer', and provision of leadership opportunities for younger employees in development.

Modifying one's personality is said to be even more difficult than changing one's field of expertise. The latter takes root generally in the university years, but the former is largely determined in childhood and solidified in adolescence.

1   Stress on level of enthusiasm in hiring

Creation requires a kind of enthusiasm, a drive to take up a new challenge actively, physiologically manifested in the form of a high energy level in the frontal lobe of the brain. There is a strong possibility that this enthusiasm is nourished during childhood, and reinforced by praise received for successful efforts exhibiting it.

It would therefore be more realistic to hire personnel perceived as in possession of this enthusiasm than to attempt to cultivate it through in-house programmes. To this end, in some companies, prospective recruits are personally interviewed by the president, director of planning, and head of the research division to evaluate their level of enthusiasm. One such company is Nippongene.

2   Self transfer

The chances of success in development could be increased by conducting it in the form of a project or in-house venture that is a voluntary association headed by the proposer of the kernel idea. Generally, people 'put out' the most for something they like doing in the first place. In this sense, creation depends more on enthusiasm than on an expenditure of time or effort. An association of individuals sharing an enthusiasm for the idea will further stimulate and sustain the enthusiasm of each. For this reason, provisions should be made for companywide recruitment of members for development in the form of projects and in-house ventures, to which interested employees could, in effect, perform their own transfer.

3   Leadership opportunity for younger employees

Transfer by order from above may be an effective means of boosting efficiency, but is not likely to boost creative output. In addition, a lower limit should not be imposed on the age of the project leader; young employees should be given the chance to head projects. Sony actively encourages young employees to lead its projects of product development. The Handycam 55 resulted from one such project.

Kao believes that researchers should yield to their juniors once they reach 40 years. It is building a research organization consisting mainly of personnel in their 20s and 30s.

Honda regards the 30s as the pinnacle years of creativity in research. Over the past ten years, it has made a point of placing young researchers in charge of developmental projects and encouraging them to give free rein to their creative powers.

The survey of Japanese and US companies conducted as a part of this study found that stress was placed on level of enthusiasm in hiring in 61% of the Japanese respondents and 11% of the US respondents. The corresponding figures for provisions for 'self-transfer' were 1% and 78%, and for extensive appointment of young employees to positions of responsibility, 20% and 45%.

Portfolio personnel management

The category of know-how in the second stage (dissimilation) in the aspect of personnel is portfolio personnel management.

The substance is achieving combinations of personnel with mutually different specialties and perspectives that are marked by a vitality and proper level of tension and which are periodically recombined with a view to maintaining these traits. The three subcategories are as follows.

1 Heterogeneous grouping

The desired dissimilative effect in developmental projects and in-house ventures can be induced by deliberately providing them with a heterogeneous membership. In short, members should be drawn not only from the developmental division but also from the production and marketing divisions. This approach makes for a richer diversity of ideas and is liable to keep the ideas tied to the realities of the business.

2 Rhythmic work cycle

Stagnation tends to set in if personnel are kept in the same unit or site for a long period of time. The stimulation of dissent and of new points of view through new combinations of personnel weakens as personnel get accustomed to those combinations. As such, recombination through reassignment or relocation should be conducted every three to five years in order to resharpen this stimulation. This recombination should not take place too frequently, however; if the cycle is only one or two years, for example, the new combinations may not have the time to jell into the foundation needed for landmark creation.

3 Grooming of transdisciplinary personnel

This approach differs from that of a multidisciplinary scheme, which is the formation of teams composed of personnel with mutually different backgrounds in the hope of generating something new from the resulting mutual stimulation. A transdisciplinary scheme would foster the development of individuals with more than one field of expertise in order to catalyze a sustained creation on a deeper level.

Transdisciplinary personnel would each be versed in two or more specialized areas, i.e. would each be 'pi-type' as opposed to 'T-type' personnel. This dissimilation on the individual level would form the basis for dissimilation on the group level, and would call for two or more areas of specialization on the part of the individual. Such internal experience of dissimilation would enable individuals to accept dissimilation on the group (organizational) level and to enjoy the tension accompanying the cycle of organizational concentration and decentralization.

A scheme of this type was noted in the case of the US control equipment manufacturer (A Co), which generally requires experience of several different divisions for promotion to the post of divisional manager. Nissan as well has begun to apply a similar requirement for its divisional managers.

Optimal IGKP arrangement

In the third stage (concept creation), the category of know-how in personnel management is the optimal arrangement of IGs (idea generators), IKs (idea killers), and IPs (idea promoters).

As was noted in the R&D case study, the key for successful concept creation is an IGKP arrangement in which IGs are in a position of strength relative to IKs. The three subcategories of know-how are as follows.

1 Positioning of IGs on the periphery

Creation emerges from dissent; ideas which conflict with or are otherwise different from the prevailing ideas. To nourish such ideas, it would be effective to separate the IG group from the regular developmental corps (perhaps even physically) in order to distance it from IKs. This is part of the rationale for the formation of special project teams and establishment of ventures inside or even outside the company. It may be difficult for the group to free itself from prevailing concepts if it is too close to or involved with the regular organization.

The case of organization 'B' in the survey of neurocomputer research exemplifies a situation tantamount to failure resulting from the positioning of the IG group too close to the regular organization. IBM's personal computer development may be cited as a case of success achieved through application of this know-how. The product was developed in the space of a year by a 12 member team working in Florida, away from the environment of IBM's general-purpose computer development.

2 Prevention or transfer of potential IKs

Generally speaking, an employee with specialized knowledge of only a single field is liable to become a potent IK after the age of 40. One prospective means of preventing the growth of IKs would therefore be the cultivation of transdisciplinary personnel by requiring employees to acquire experience of at least two different areas before they reach that age.

The growth of IKs could also be prevented by transferring developmental personnel to a field other than that of their expertise once they reach the age of 40. If they stay ensconced in their field of expertise, such personnel are likely to function as IKs, 'I tried the same approach many years ago, and it didn't work'. However, the same personnel could become IPs outside their field of expertise, 'Sounds interesting; why don't you give it a try?'.

This is part of the reason that Kao and Honda relieve researchers from their research duties once they reach age 40.

3 Attention to idea co-ordination

The optimal IGKP arrangement will vary depending on the circumstances, and is, in any case, hardly self-evident; one could never be sure that a given arrangement is the optimal one. The optimal arrangement must therefore be viewed as an ideal that can only be approached through a willingness to try various arrangements. The critical factors in this process are the awareness, objectivity and insight regarding IGKPs at the top and among other managers with the authority to make personnel changes.

Empathetic personnel exchange

The category of know-how in the fourth stage (chain of empathy) in the personnel aspect is 'empathetic' personnel exchange, consisting of the subcategories of individual reward and commendation, circulation of the experience of success, and double-loop exchange, Fig. 9.17.

1 Individual reward and commendation

The individuals behind creative concepts should be rewarded and honoured in the presence of others both inside and outside the company in order to heighten interest in the developmental results based on this concept. By according such treatment to them as individuals instead of as members of a group, management could expect to boost the level of individual creation. While group-level reward and commendation are also important, a creative atmosphere could be more effectively prepared by singling out individuals. This recognition by top-level management would act to accelerate the spread of empathy with the work, and so facilitate the allocation of resources (particularly personnel) for further development, production and sales. It would also make good publicity in the target market.

2 Circulation of success

The experience of success must be used to trigger the next round of creation. This means sharing the taste of success by such activities as announcement within the research organization, coverage in the company newsletter, presentation at learned societies and release to the press.

Hitachi's Central Laboratory promotes this circulation of the experience of success by featuring the achievements of individual researchers in 'Hitachi Forum', a publication carrying news of its research work. Such articles are complete with photos of the researchers in question. At Corning Glass Works, Xerox and Texas Instruments, researchers who have made a great contribution to the company in the form of some creative discovery or invention are designated 'research fellows' and accorded treatment on a par with that received by directors. This system provides research personnel with a powerful incentive for creative achievement.

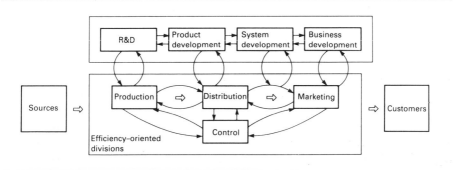

9.17 Double-loop exchange.

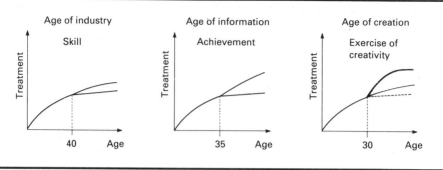

9.18 Personnel management.

3 Double-loop exchange

Numerous problems and organizational barriers are encountered in the process of putting a concept into a concrete form and getting it manufactured, marketed and purchased by customers. To muster the energies required for problem-solving calls for the elimination or lowering of the organizational barriers. One of the most effective means of breaking down barriers is mutual exchange of personnel between divisions in order to deepen mutual understanding of positions and perspectives, Fig. 9.17.

Differences among the ages of industry, information and creation in the aspect of personnel management

The key item of personnel evaluation was skill in the age of industry, is achievement in the age of information, and would be exercise of creativity in the age of creation, Fig 9.18.

In the age of industry, management attempted to realize the optimal division of labour, degree of specialization, scale of production and standardization. In the aspect of personnel management, an effective means of supporting this effort was treatment according to seniority. Routine work could be smoothly performed under the direction of a senior employee. And since efficiency generally rises with age, there was a good conformance between the level of productivity and that of treatment.

As a result, personnel were evaluated on the basis of their skill, which however, tended to be measured in terms of the number of years with the company. Promotions consequently depended largely upon seniority, and transfers were made by orders from above.

Personnel management based on evaluation of skill is not adapted to the age of information, in which the operational method is the sequence of information collection, organization, editing and dissemination. The work is not routine, but highly diverse. Gaps in achievement cannot be reduced to differences of age; to a great extent, they depend on the degree of information literacy, i.e. sensitivity to value in information.

As a result, personnel are evaluated on the basis of their achievement. With the proper level of achievement, younger employees may be promoted ahead of their seniors. A gap in treatment generally begins to open around age 35, when achievers can expect promotion to the post of section head. Not all transfers stem from the orders of superiors; in some cases, they are made upon notification by the employee in question.

In the age of creation, employees would be evaluated on the basis of their exercise of creativity. Individual creativity is not spent with a single demonstration, but is an abiding potential of its possessor. The organization should be geared to induce exercise of individual creativity on a continuous basis. For these reasons, management should evaluate personnel from a long-term perspective and accord deserving personnel, regardless of their age, a position and salary that will spur an even greater demonstration of creativity in the future. In addition, the evaluation should not simply look at the result (success or failure), but also consider the boldness and creativity of the endeavour, in order to produce an atmosphere of challenge.

In such an organization, 'equality' is equality of opportunity, not result. Personnel are not going to attempt to exercise creativity if all results are treated equally regardless of differences of creativity.

Creation-oriented information management

Management for creation must also manage information in a manner conducive to creation.

Individual creation results not only from individual thought; in many cases, it is born out of discussion with other individuals. The clash and reconciliation of hypotheses, dissent and counterhypotheses can lead to the creation of concepts. To stimulate creativity, management should therefore work to achieve a dynamic interplay between, and give-and-take in, hypotheses. Creation-oriented information management would support this effort in the aspect of information. Of particular importance are provisions for the sharing of information and for ample communication (exchange of thoughts and hypotheses). This, in turn, would demand a removal of barriers to the flow of information both inside and outside the company.

The four categories of know-how required for such management are noted in Fig. 9.19.

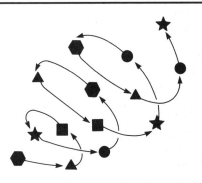

1   Sharing of customer information

2   Stress on free discussion

3   Hypothesis refinement

4   Sympathetic communication

9.19 Creation-oriented information management.

Sharing of customer information

The category of know-how in the first stage of creation (hypothesis construction) in the information aspect is the sharing of customer information. The three subcategories of know-how are as follows.

1 Expanded interface of contact with customers

Customers constitute the pool of needs which must be addressed by corporate activities (R&D, product development, system development, business development). In this sense, latent hypotheses are contained in the desires and complaints expressed by customers. Genuine hypothesis construction in corporate activities must rest on the discovery of what the customer is truly seeking.

It is consequently vital for customer information to be held in common by all employees. Hypothesis construction begins when all employees can hear the customer's desires and complaints and begin thinking about how to respond to them.

An organization in which only personnel attached to the marketing and service divisions come into direct contact with customers cannot acquire the right kind of customer information. The circle of contact with customers should be broadened to include personnel engaged in R&D, product development, system development and business development. Furthermore, those engaged in design, manufacture, distribution and control should also make an active effort to meet and talk with customers.

In line with its policy of free access to information and direct information channels, Kao has constructed a network to relay information directly to the units requiring it. Employees have the same access to customer information as the president. The research, production, marketing and business divisions share all their customer information with each other.

In the CIM business development by the US electronics instrumentation manufacturer (D Co), the work began with in-depth interviews with 20 prospective customers conducted by a team mixing R&D personnel with production personnel.

2 Relationship management

As a company expands, a single customer comes to form relationships with various divisions and units. The customer is liable to be left unsatisfied, and omissions to occur in response as a company, if each division and unit continues to deal with the customer independently of the others. All customer relationships should therefore be managed in a co-ordinated manner through unified management and effective use of customer information.

In Japan, this type of relationship management was first adopted by Sumitomo Bank, in 1979. It has since spread to other financial institutions and to companies in the distribution and manufacturing industries.

3 Understanding of customer sensibility

It would be insufficient to view customer needs only in quantitative terms, e.g. level of sales, level of profit and purchasing lots. More important is an understanding of their needs in the qualitative realm of desires and dissatisfaction that borders on insight into their sensibility. In its product development, Sony makes an exhaustive investigation of the prospective scenes of use of the subject by its prospective purchasers. One of the key factors in the development of the Handycam 55 was the concept of a compact camera that could be easily carried by young women on international trips; a scene that emerged from such an investigation.

Stress on free discussion

The category of know-how in the second stage (dissimilation) in the aspect of information is a stress on free discussion across vertical and horizontal boundaries within the organization, and even across corporate boundaries, for a dynamic interplay of hypotheses and counterhypotheses. The three subcategories of know-how are as follows:

1 Brainstorming

There should be an extensive resort to brainstorming sessions, where discussion must be positioned as a vehicle for idea generation. Participants must realize that the primary purpose is to produce good ideas, not necessarily a consensus. Honda has its directors work in a single partitionless room in order to stimulate the flow of ideas among them. The aforementioned US electronic instrumentation manufacturer forbade the members of its CIM developmental team to make remarks to the effect, 'That is not my area'.

2 Intellectual network

A 'human network' could also be constructed and put to extensive use in order to add impetus to the exchange of hypotheses and counterhypotheses. Dedicated to the furtherance of a communication of ideas regardless of their source, this network would bridge horizontal and vertical divisions within the organization and also encompass organizations and individuals outside the company. Such a network was built for neurocomputer development in the case of organization 'A', which encouraged free discussion between its members and other parties both inside and outside the company.

3 Conception support system

As was noted in Part III, Chapter 8, the process of ideation and conception could be facilitated by the development of a 'conceptor' (conception support system) as the successor to today's computer. Management should take vigorous steps to promote the development and application of this tool.

Concept refinement

In the third stage (concept creation), the category of know-how in the aspect of information management is concept refinement.

Concept refinement is the process of eliminating extraneous elements from the mass of hypotheses and counterhypotheses that culminates in the moment of inspiration; the birth of the essential concept. The three subcategories of know-how are as follows.

1 Constructive defiance of adverse circumstances

In Meitec's case, the development of business hinged upon the turnabout in attitude from the negative, 'all we have are personnel and expertise', to the positive, 'at least we have personnel and expertise'.

In Yamato Transport's case, pessimism about the prospects of turning a profit in the home delivery business was brushed aside with exhortations to think about how to make it profitable. Those pointing out the lack of density (consignments per unit of area) required for viability were told to find a way to boost it. The organization eventually hit upon the concept of unmatched service, 'next-day delivery anywhere in the country' and 'just phone for pick-up', that paved the way to success.

2 Return to basics

The substance is a commitment to the essence of the concept and the reinforcement and harnessing of technical strength to maintain this commitment. Its basis is the FINDS perspective described in the product development case study.

The cases in point include the R&D of restriction enzymes at Nippongene, the combination of high performance and compactness in Sony's Handycam 55, Asahi's successful effort to revolutionize perceptions of flavour in beer, Attack's pairing of fortified cleaning power and compactness, the 'earthenware aesthetics' of the Cima design, and the use of high-sensitivity film in the disposable Utsurundesu. None of these products resulted from a mere matching of technological seeds with market needs; each shows an unswerving commitment to an idea of excellence that approaches a manifestation of the corporate philosophy.

3 Listening to the customers

Listening to customers is the starting point of concept refinement in the stage of concept creation, just as it is the starting point of hypothesis construction and dissimilation. It is also the terminus of the chain of empathy.

The concept of 'body plus bite' behind Asahi Super Dry was only arrived at after extensive surveys of consumer preferences and flavour. The flight reservation system developed by the US airline company (C Co) was refined in accordance with the results of in-depth surveys of its users; travel agencies and the personnel staffing its own reservation counters. In developing its CIM business, the US electronics instrumentation manufacturer (D Co) posted customer comments on a bulletin board to make sure they were reflected in the work.

Empathetic communication

The category of information management know-how in the fourth stage (chain of empathy) is empathetic communication, consisting of the subcategories of communication events, free access to specialists and user education.

1 Communication as event

The circle of empathy with the concept can be widened through the staging of events attracting the participation of top-level management, the personnel in the division in question and its related units, and the customers, e.g. technology development events sponsored by the R&D division and product development events sponsored by the product development division.

By bringing personnel in various posts and customers together, these events would serve as venues for the spread of empathy with the concept across horizontal and vertical boundaries. The very atmosphere would be one of shared enthusiasm and interest.

2 Free access to specialists, whether inside or outside the company

Many problems are encountered in the process of putting a concept into concrete form and developing products, systems and business from it. The participation and advice of specialists both inside and outside the company are indispensable for the solution of many such problems. Personnel not on the project team should be able to offer their opinions on the work. Conversely, the members of the project team should feel free to seek the opinions of non-members. Provisions should also be made for a free give-and-take of information with personnel not employed by the company. The environment should be open enough to absorb ideas arriving from outside the company.

3 Customer education

To win the empathy of customers (or users) toward them, the supplier must first deepen customer understanding of the new technology, products, systems, or business. Suppliers can no longer view their job as finished with the injection of quality goods and services into the market. Mere advertizing and publicity will not be sufficient; the need is for programmes to actively educate customers to the merits and mode of use of the goods and services. The importance of such programmes rises along with the creativity of the base concepts.

At Toyo Sash, the resources expended to promote the use of systems outweigh those expended to develop them. Seven-Eleven Japan's organization includes a corps of consultants called 'operation field counsellors' who make the rounds of stores to provide instruction in the use of systems.

Differences among the ages of industry, information and creation in the aspect of information management

The thrust of information management was centralized processing in the age of industry, is a hybrid of centralized and decentralized processing in the age of information, and would be creation-oriented management (information sharing and communication, i.e. exchange of ideas and hypotheses) in the age of creation, Fig. 9.20.

In the age of industry, information management was based on centralized processing. Decisions and tasks were handed down from the top, and work was monitored through centralized processing of information on it, mainly of the numerical type. All information was therefore concentrated at the top; the only sharing of information was with middle managers, who were supplied with certain data concerning their own unit. The execution of the daily routine was more important than communication. This kind of information management was well-suited to the pyramid organizations of this age. It is still found today on the sites of production in heavy industries.

In the age of information, information management is based on a hybrid of centralized and decentralized processing. Decisions and tasks are formulated in groups, and the varieties of information, much of which must be handled on the

BRAINSTORMING

four guidelines for creation

Researcher   A F Osborn

Subject   Developers

Basic perspective   Pragmatic

Substance: Brainstorming is a method of generating an abundance of ideas that is commonly applied in companies and other organizations. It was reportedly devised by A F Osborn, who used it to prepare an idea checklist during his years as president of an advertizing firm. Osborn cites the following as four basic guidelines for conducting brainstorming sessions.

- Ban of criticism – members should refrain from criticizing ideas while the session is in progress.
- Free flight – ideation should be completely unrestricted; members should freely raise any ideas without fear of criticism or other adverse consequences.
- Quantity – the session should produce as many ideas as possible, since the chances of hitting upon good ideas would generally increase along with quantity.
- Combination and improvement – members should try to link their ideas with, and improve upon those of others.

Osborn discovered that a chain reaction of ideation could be ignited and that many goods ideas could be generated if criticism was postponed and quantity was given precedence over quality. This method has remained essentially unchanged since it was first proposed in the 1950s. In widespread use in business, research, and education, it must be termed a truly creative method of idea creation.

Source) A F Osborn, 'Applied Imagination', 3rd edition

site of work, include not only numerical but also textual and graphic information. Decentralized processing is therefore conducted in parallel with centralized processing, as the situation demands. Access to information is more open than in the age of industry, and there is a healthy flow of communication. Such hybrid systems are spreading in the business divisions of manufacturers and in distribution, banking, transportation, real estate and other segments of the service sector.

In the age of creation, information management would have to be oriented toward creation, and would depend on information sharing and communication. Great emphasis would be placed on proposal and execution of tasks by the individual employees themselves in this age. However, this approach would not be viable if the tasks selected by individuals strayed too far from each other and those of the organization as a whole. For this reason, it would be vital for the top, middle and bottom layers to share information and ideas concerning customers and technological seeds, as far as possible. In this way, hypotheses and counterhypotheses would spring from the same fertile ground.

This kind of information management is found in only a partial form in a limited circle of companies, such as Kao and Honda.

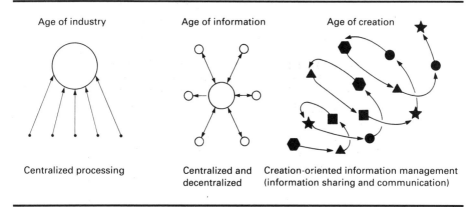

Age of industry

Centralized processing

Age of information

Centralized and
decentralized

Age of creation

Creation-oriented information management
(information sharing and communication)

9.20 Information management.

Management for coexistence

In the age of creation, management would have to be oriented toward creation. Inducing creativity on the part of the organization would require a type of management differing fundamentally from that oriented strictly toward efficiency, i.e. management during the age of industry. The 16 categories of know-how, presented in the previous section and in Table 9.I, can be regarded as tools for making this change. At the same time, however, the 1990s may be positioned as a time of transition to the age of creation. Not all corporate activities conducted during the 1990s could rest wholly upon a pursuit of creativity; pursuit of efficiency would still be the major orientation in many aspects.

The relative importance of creativity, efficiency, and consequently the type of management know-how required, would vary depending on the situation of the company and the identity of the division.

Management would therefore have to work to achieve the optimal coexistence of creativity and efficiency in the corporate orientation by the proper application of two sets of know-how differing 90 degrees from each other in orientation, Fig. 9.21.

The stress, however, would be on creativity in R&D and development of products, systems and business, and on efficiency in production, distribution, marketing and control. Management for coexistence would induce the fullest demonstration of both functions of these groups, despite their mutually different orientations, while steering them as a unified whole as the company. In the age of industry, it was sufficient to apply the same efficiency-oriented management for all divisions. In the transition to the age of creation, management would have to provide for the cohesion and unity of an organization in which the relative importance of creativity and efficiency tends to vary from division to division.

Management for coexistence would also tolerate or even encourage diversity, multiplicity, change and dynamism on both the individual and group levels, and therefore contribute to the overall management for creation.

MAPPING OF RESEARCH OF CREATIVITY

The figure below is a map of the researchers surveyed in the course of this book. The positions of each were plotted with reference to two co-ordinate axes: 1) a vertical axis indicating research subject (organization/individual), and 2) a horizontal axis indicating research approach (personality/technique or method).

It can be seen that the Japanese researchers tend to focus on creation by organizations or groups, and Western researchers, on enhancement of individual creativity. The overall trend appears to be a drift toward the domain of corporate creation described in this book (positioned in the upper right corner).

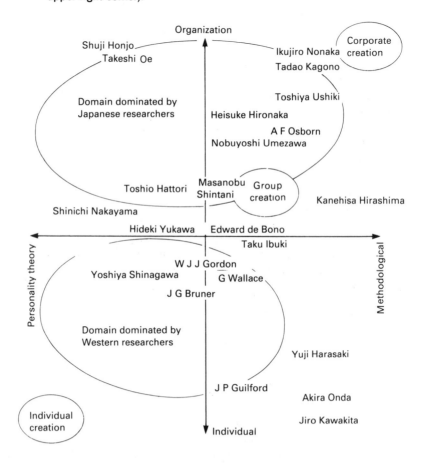

Source) NRI

Comparison of leading Japanese and US companies

Implementation of management know-how for creation

As a part of this project, a survey was conducted in November 1989 with leading Japanese and US companies in order to ascertain the current status of management for creation in them. The survey took the form of questionnaires mailed to the directors in charge of business planning at the Japanese companies ranking among the top 1,000 for corporate earnings in 1988, and to the vice-presidents in charge of business planning at the 1,000 US companies named in Fortune's 1988 lists of the top 500 companies in the manufacturing and service sectors. The questionnaire retrieval rate was 22% for the Japanese companies and 8% for the US companies.

The respondents were asked to indicate the current locus of stress at their company in each of 33 categories of management know-how. Each category presented the respondent with a choice of one of three subcategories. The questionnaire was prepared on the assumption that the third subcategory (the one farthest to the right in Table 9.II and 9.III) contained management know-how for creation. This assumption was basically corroborated by the results of the comparison of companies succeeding in creation and those failing in imitation, which will be described below.

The overall average degree of implementation of management know-how for creation was about the same (27%) in the case of both the Japanese and US respondents, Fig. 9.22. In other words, on average, about one out of every four respondents in both countries implemented a given subcategory of creation-oriented management know-how, and the average respondent in both implemented about nine of the 33 subcategories.

However, there was a gap between the two groups in respect of the average degree of implementation in each aspect of management. As compared with that for the US respondents, the average degree of implementation for the Japanese respondents was higher in the aspects of strategy and information and lower in

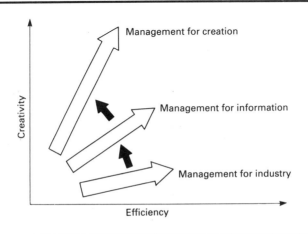

9.21 Management for coexistence.

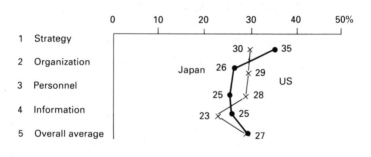

9.22 Implementation of management know-how for creation.

Table 9.II Implementation of management know-how for creation (Japan)*

Categories of management know-how	Subcategories of management know-how		Management for creation
Strategy			
1 Objective	Quantitative expansion 24%	Expansion scope 29%	Long-term vision 47%
2 Planning	Quantitative planning 8%	Business planning 69%	Strategic scenario 23%
3 Overall stress	Production 14%	Products 44%	Customers and employees 42%
4 Stress in investment	Production 34%	Information systems 27%	R&D education 39%
5 Stress in activities	TQC 27%	Information collection 43%	Trial activities 24%
Organization			
6 Organizational layers	Multi (more than 7) 7%	Moderate (4–6) 66%	Flat (3 or less) 26%
7 Organizational walls	High (little exchange between groups) 30%	Low (some exchange between groups) 54%	Non-existent (extensive exchange; directors all in partitionless room) 16%
8 Degree of integration of R&D, production and marketing	Low 13%	Medium 69%	High 16%
9 Size of prime units	Large (50 employees+) 15%	Medium (around 30 employees) 54%	Small (around 7 employees) 30%
10 Priority	Cost centre 14%	Profit centre 57%	R&D and planning 27%
11 Reorganization	Every 7+ years 4%	Every 5 years 30%	Every 3 years 63%
12 In-house ventures	None 47%	2–3 46%	5 or more 7%
13 Group-level relationship	Parent-subsidiary 54%	Siblings 21%	Tie up 19%
Personnel			
14 Hiring procedure	Written test 2%	Written test and interview 73%	Interview 27%
15 Evaluative stress in hiring	Academic 12%	Specialized knowledge 25%	Enthusiasm 61%

Categories of management know-how	Subcategories of management know-how		Management for creation
16 Transfer	On order from superiors 30%	Hybrid (on order and self transfer) 69%	Self-transfer 1%
17 Appointment to positions of leadership	On basis of seniority 19%	Some appointment of younger employees 60%	Much appointment of younger employees 20%
18 Main basis of evaluation	Skill, capability 48%	Achievement 50%	Innovation challenging outlook 2%
19 Subject of evaluation	Overall organization 5%	Groups 9%	Individuals 86%
20 Term of evaluation	Once every half year 43%	Once every year 51%	Once every 2-3 years 5%
21 Reward	Bonus 11%	Promotion 40%	Commendation 46%
22 Mode of address	Title 82%	'Mr' 18%	Nickname/first name 0%
23 Working hours	Strict regular hours 65%	Partial flex time system 32%	Complete flex time system 3%
24 Training for management	Lectures 28%	Case study of other companies 31%	In-house case study 40%
25 Office space layout	Stress on efficiency 77%	Stress on information 15%	Stress on comfort 7%
Information			
26 Proposal of tasks/themes	From the top 30%	By groups 48%	By individuals 20%
27 Sideline research	Prohibited 30%	Tolerated 52%	Encouraged 7%
28 Discussion	Of minor importance 12%	Encouraged 67%	Of major importance 21%
29 Type of information stressed	Technological seeds information 15%	Product information 19%	Customer information 65%
30 Stress of in-house information management	Operational information 44%	Control information 27%	Strategic information 29%
31 Information processing	Centralized process 24%	Centralized and distributed process 65%	Distributed process 11%
32 Information base	Numerical data 68%	Text data 22%	Knowledge data 9%
33 Scope of information sharing	Departmentwide 30%	Divisionwide 33%	Companywide 37%

*Responses from companies who were uncertain varied from 0 to 12% within each category. Source: 'Strategy for Creation – Questionnaire for Japanese and US companies', NRI, November 1989.

the aspects of organization and personnel. The Japanese respondents indicated that, in the aspect of strategy, they were vigorously investing in R&D and education, and that, in the aspect of information, the management was highly customer-oriented. The implementation by US respondents, on the other hand, was centred in the aspects of organization and personnel. Many of these respondents had already incorporated flat organizations and systems of 'self-transfer' by the individual employee.

The totalized findings of the questionnaire are presented in Table 9.II and 9.III.

Table 9.III Implementation of management know-how for creation (US)*

Categories of management know-how	Subcategories of management know-how		Management for creation
Strategy			
1 Objective	Quantitative expansion 36%	Expansion scope 18%	Long-term vision 46%
2 Planning	Quantitative planning 31%	Business planning 28%	Strategic scenario 40%
3 Overall stress	Production 28%	Products 19%	Customers and employees 51%
4 Stress in investment	Production 69%	Information systems 20%	R&D education 9%
5 Stress in activities	TQC 70%	Information collection 26%	Trial activities 4%
Organization			
6 Organizational layers	Multi (more than 7) 7%	Moderate (4–6) 44%	Flat (3 or less) 49%
7 Organizational walls	High (little exchange between groups) 36%	Low (some exchange between groups) 50%	Non-existent (extensive exchange; directors all in partitionless room) 14%
8 Degree of integration of R&D, production and marketing	Low 16%	Medium 62%	High 21%
9 Size of prime units	Large (50 employees+) 42%	Medium (around 30 employees) 24%	Small (around 7 employees) 33%
10 Priority	Cost centre 40%	Profit centre 48%	R&D and planning 3%
11 Reorganization	Every 7+ years 15%	Every 5 years 16%	Every 3 years 68%
12 In-house ventures	None 14%	2–3 66%	5 or more 20%
13 Group-level relationship	Parent-subsidiary 59%	Siblings 9%	Tie up 21%
Personnel			
14 Hiring procedure	Written test 39%	Written test and interview 56%	Interview 5%
15 Evaluative stress in hiring	Academic 15%	Specialized knowledge 73%	Enthusiasm 11%
16 Transfer	On order from superiors 5%	Hybrid (on order and self transfer) 3%	Self-transfer 77%
17 Appointment to positions of leadership	On basis of seniority 10%	Some appointment of younger employees 43%	Much appointment of younger employees 45%
18 Main basis of evaluation	Skill, capability 11%	Achievement 84%	Innovation challenging outlook 4%
19 Subject of evaluation	Overall organisation 44%	Groups 29%	Individuals 22%
20 Term of evaluation	Once every half year 6%	Once every year 63%	Once every 2–3 years 31%
21 Reward	Bonus 75%	Promotion 14%	Commendation 8%
22 Mode of address	Title 2%	'Mr' 10%	Nickname/first name 89%
23 Working hours	Strict regular hours 45%	Partial flex time system 42%	Complete flex time system 13%

Categories of management know-how	Subcategories of management know-how		Management for creation
24 Training for management	Lectures 53%	Case study of other companies 26%	In-house case study 13%
25 Office space layout	Stress on efficiency 61%	Stress on information 15%	Stress on comfort 23%
Information			
26 Proposal of tasks/themes	From the top 29%	By groups 61%	By individuals 8%
27 Sideline research	Prohibited 21%	Tolerated 55%	Encouraged 19%
28 Discussion	Of minor importance 3%	Encouraged 71%	Of major importance 25%
29 Type of information stressed	Technological seeds information 18%	Product information 41%	Customer information 39%
30 Stress of in-house information management	Operational information 60%	Control information 18%	Strategic information 20%
31 Information processing	Centralized process 19%	Centralized and distributed process 69%	Distributed process 12%
32 Information base	Numerical data 68%	Text data 9%	Knowledge data 21%
33 Scope of information sharing	Departmentwide 29%	Divisionwide 31%	Companywide 38%

*Responses from companies who were uncertain varied from 0 to 9%. Source: 'Strategy for Creation – Questionnaire for Japanese and US companies', NRI, November 1989.

Of the 33 subcategories of management know-how for creation, the five most commonly implemented among the Japanese respondents are as follows (Fig. 9.23) (figures in parentheses indicate degree of implementation): a) evaluation on individual basis (86%), b) stress on customer information (65%), c) reorganization about once every three years (63%), d) stress on enthusiasm in hiring (61%), and e) long-term vision (47%). The corresponding top five subcategories for the US respondents are as follows: a) use of nicknames/first names (89%), b) self-transfer (upon notification) (77%), c) reorganization about once every three years (68%), d) overall stress on customers and employees (51%), and e) flat organization (no more than three layers of approval) (49%), Fig. 9.26.

There is a great gap between the Japanese and US degrees of implementation for certain subcategories. Those in which the former is significantly higher than the latter are as follows: a) stress on enthusiasm in hiring (61% vs 11%), b) reward including commendation (46% vs 8%), c) stress on R&D and education in investment (39% vs 9%), d) use of in-house case studies in manager training programmes (40% vs 13%), and e) stress on customer information (65% vs 26%).

Those subcategories in which the degree of implementation for the US respondents is significantly higher than that for the Japanese respondents are as

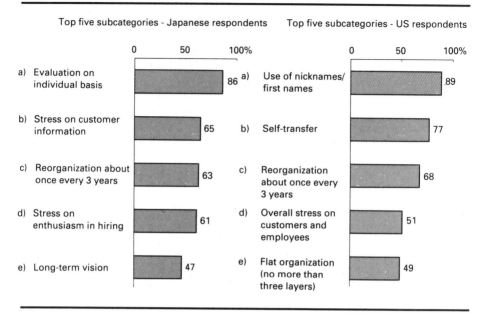

Top five subcategories - Japanese respondents   Top five subcategories - US respondents

Japanese	%		US	%
a) Evaluation on individual basis	86	a)	Use of nicknames/first names	89
b) Stress on customer information	65	b)	Self-transfer	77
c) Reorganization about once every 3 years	63	c)	Reorganization about once every 3 years	68
d) Stress on enthusiasm in hiring	61	d)	Overall stress on customers and employees	51
e) Long-term vision	47	e)	Flat organization (no more than three layers)	49

9.23 Implementation of management know-how for creation among leading Japanese and US companies, (figures indicate degree of implementation as percentage).

follows: a) use of nicknames/first names (89% vs 0%), b) self-transfer (77% vs 1%), c) evaluation once every 2–3 years (31% vs 5%), d) appointment of younger employees to leading positions (45% vs 20%), and e) flat organization (49% vs 26%).

This pattern of gaps can be glimpsed behind the calls for provisions for systems of self-transfer and for more extensive leadership opportunity for younger personnel in Japan and for the emergence of evaluation of enthusiasm, commendation, and heavier investment on R&D and education as major priorities in the US. In essence, companies in both countries are trying to bolster areas of weakness relative to the other.

Comparison of companies succeeding in creation and companies failing in imitation

The responding companies were also placed into one of four categories of type in each aspect of corporate activity (R&D, product development, system development and business development) in terms of the degree of originality and success in it. As shown in Fig. 9.24, the four types are: a) companies succeeding in creation, b) companies failing in creation, c) companies succeeding in imitation, and d) companies failing in imitation. The rating of the degree of originality and success in each aspect was made by the respondents (directors of business planning) themselves.

The composition of the total number of respondents in each country and each aspect in these terms is shown in Fig. 9.25.

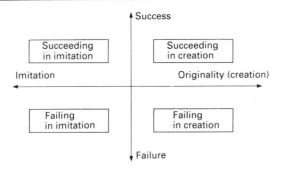

9.24 Definition of companies succeeding in creation.

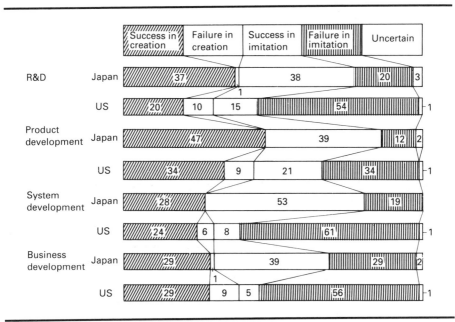

Source: 'Strategy for Creation – Questionnaire for Japanese and US companies' NRI, November 1989

9.25 Composition of total number of respondents in terms of type (success/failure/ creation/imitation).

While it may be a result of overestimation of their own achievements, the share of the total occupied by companies succeeding in creation or in imitation is higher for the Japanese respondents than for the US respondents in every aspect.

The graphs in Fig. 9.26 were formed by plotting the average degree of implementation of creation-oriented know-how for those Japanese and US companies succeeding in creation and failing in imitation in each of the four aspects of management (strategy, organization, personnel and information). There is a separate graph for each category of corporate activity (R&D, product development, system development, business development).

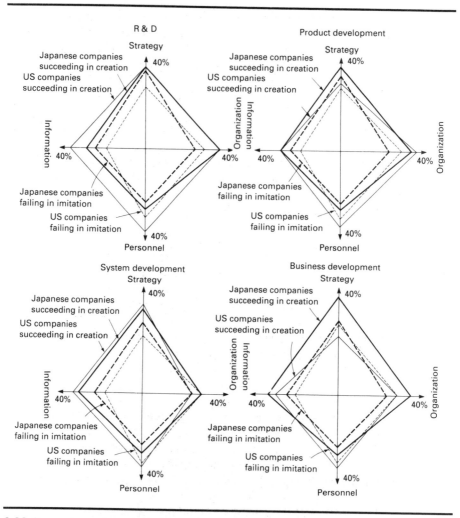

9.26 Comparison of companies succeeding in creation, failing in imitation.

This degree of implementation rises as the plot distance from the centre increases. A bigger diamond shape therefore indicates a higher degree of advancement as far as implementation of management for creation is concerned. In each category of activity, the degree of implementation for companies succeeding in creation is higher than that for companies failing in imitation in virtually every aspect in both Japan and the US.

In the category of R&D, the gap between the Japanese companies succeeding in creation and those failing in imitation is widest in the aspect of organization. Many of the companies succeeding in creation have flat organizations and provide for close integration of R&D, production and business. Among the US respondents, the corresponding gap is widest in the aspect of information. The US companies succeeding in creation tend to promote a companywide sharing of information and to stress strategic information over routine or control information in-house.

In the category of product development, the gap between the two types of Japanese companies is again widest in the aspect of the organization, where the know-how in question includes flat organizations, integration of R&D, production and marketing and leadership opportunities for younger employees. That between the two types of US companies is widest in the aspect of information (companywide sharing) and that of personnel (stress on enthusiasm in hiring).

In the category of system development, the gap between the two types of Japanese companies is widest in the aspect of information (stress on customer information and companywide sharing). That between the two types of US companies is widest in the aspects of information (companywide sharing, knowledge data bases, stress on strategic information in-house) and strategy (stress on customers and employees).

In the category of business development, the gap between the two types of Japanese companies is widest in the aspects of the organization (integration of R&D, production and marketing), personnel (leadership opportunities for younger employees), and information (stress on strategic information in-house). The gap between the two types of US companies is widest in the aspect of information (stress on customer information, knowledge data bases).

This pattern of gaps suggests that success in creation stemmed from use of know-how for creation in the organizational and personnel aspects, such as flat organizations, ample leadership opportunity for younger employees and integration of R&D, production and marketing, for the Japanese respondents, and from the corresponding know-how in the aspect of information, such as companywide sharing, stress on customer information and construction of knowledge data bases, for the US respondents.

Figure 9.27 plots the average degree of implementation of know-how for creation for the two types of companies, both Japanese and US, in the category of product development. The plots are made with reference to a vertical axis indicating the degree in the aspect of information management and a horizontal axis indicating that in the combined aspect of organizational and personnel management.

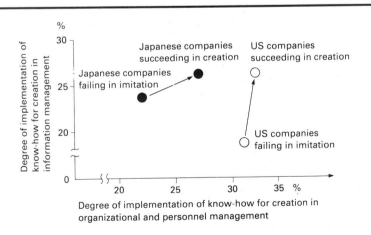

9.27 Keys for success in creation in product development.

For both the Japanese and US companies succeeding in creation, the plots are in the area of 30% in both aspects. However, there is a sizeable Japan–US gap in the case of the plots for companies failing in imitation. The weakness is in the aspect of organizational and personnel management for the Japanese companies and in the aspect of information management for the US companies. Similar plots were derived in the categories of research and development, system development and business development.

The implication is that Japanese companies failing in imitation could boost their chances for success in creation by implementing know-how for creation in the aspects of the organization and personnel, and that their US counterparts could do the same by implementing such know-how in the aspect of information.

Toward 'creagement'

In the age of creation, management would have to be a fine-tuned system oriented toward creation. The 1990s, however, may be positioned as a period of transition to the age of creation. The substance of this transition is a reorientation of management in the aspects of strategy, organization, personnel and information, which has been oriented around the principles of the ages of industry and information, around the principles of creation. This means that management for the 1990s would have to be a management for transition.

NRI call this management for transition (evolution into a creation-intense company) 'creagement', a coinage from the words creation and management, Fig. 9.28.

Creagement is the preparation of schemes and setups that would stimulate full exercise of creativity on the group and corporate levels by motivating individuals to fully actualize their creative potential, by inducing the generation of ideas and sympathy toward them, and by achieving optimal arrangements of personnel and systems to that end.

In this project, the result of the case study and questionnaire survey with Japanese and US companies were used to elicit a different category of know-how for creagement at each of the four stages of creation (hypothesis construction, dissimilation, concept creation, and chain of empathy) in each of the four aspects of management (strategy, organization, personnel, and information). Furthermore, each category of know-how contained three subcategories. Consequently, a total of 16 categories and 48 subcategories of creagement know-how was proposed. The respective groups of four categories and 12 subcategories in each aspect were termed 'creativisionary strategy', 'organization conducive to individual creation', 'creation-rewarding personnel management', and 'creation-oriented information management'.

These 16 categories and 48 subcategories of creagement know-how may be regarded as guiding concepts for management in the promotion of creation intensification. At the same time, however, they could also function as yardsticks for the measurement of the degree of creation intensification.

To date, many companies have formulated visions for revitalization or diversification. With the approach of the age of creation, companies would have to begin formulating visions for creation intensification, detailing their strategies for achieving creation-intense organizational and personnel setups. The 16 categories and 48 subcategories of creagement know-how should be used as points of departure in this effort and as gauges of progress in it in the auditing of creation intensification by management.

NRI are convinced that the practice of creagement will constitute both a necessary and sufficient precondition for corporate subsistence, growth, and advancement in the 21st century; the age of creation.

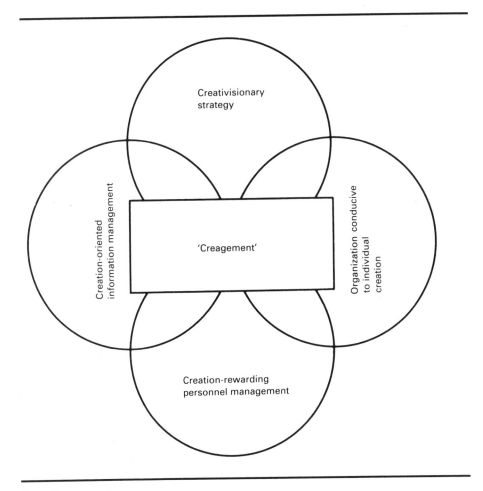

9.28 Creagement.

Appendix

Megatheme Projection Committee

The membership of the Megatheme Projection Committee which implemented this project is as follows.

Chairman

       Teruyasu Murakami

Project leader

       Takashi Nishiwaki

Core members

       Naoki Ikezawa
       Toshihiko Kubokawa
       Keiichi Kusano
       Tetsuo Shibauchi
       Toru Yokoyama
       Shunroku Yoshida

Other members

       Koji Adachi
       Koichi Baba
       Masataka Fujii
       Manabu Fukuchi
       Hiroshi Fukui
       Ryoichi Hara
       Toru Hatano

Shigeki Higashiyama
Katsuhiro Koike
Yukinobu Masaoka
Yuji Mizuno
Masahiro Muroi
Haruo Sato
Masahiro Toriyama
Kentarou Tsuchihashi
Takayoshi Yodokawa
Makoto Yokozawa

Secretariat

       Tadayuki Aikawa
       Shiro Komi
       Takako Ozawa

Superintendent

       Kaita Gion

International co-ordination

       Keith Clarke
       Denise Coupe

Index

Abe, Z 170
advanced technology, industrialization
  of 55-6
advertising 70, 71, 73, 74, 76, 88-9
age
  and creativity 70, 71, 90, 122, 165-
    6, 169, 171-2 *passim*, 173-4,
    176, 190, 192-3
agricultural societies 25, 30-5 *passim*,
    148-9, 152-3
airline companies 103-4, 106, 109,
    180
aluminium sash industry 96-8, 105-6,
    108, 133, 157, 161, 181
Animage 122
animation industry 121-3, 127, 128
art, industrialization of 55-6
artware 56
Asada (president, Toyo Sash) 105
Asahi Super Dry (Asahi Breweries)
    71-5, 88, 90, 180
Attack (Kao Co, compact detergent)
    75-7, 88, 89-90, 164, 172, 178,
    180

beer industry 71-5, 88, 90, 180

brainstorming 136-7, 155, 179, 182
brand-name items 68
Bruner, I S 184
Bruner, J G 184
budgetary management 159
Buhl, H R 146
business development
  case studies 113-27
  companies succeeding/failing in
    creation/imitation 190-4
  creativity in 110-3
  method of and management for cre-
    ation in 114-5, 116-7, 118-23,
    124-5, 118-28
  as subject of creation 19-20, 26,
    42-3
  system development and 93-5, 100,
    105-7
business planning 35

cameras
  disposable 77-9, 89-90, 180
  video 69-71, 88, 89, 90, 135, 157,
    161, 166, 172, 178-9, 180
car industry 79-83, 88, 89, 90, 166,
    173, 180

centralized processing 181-3
cerebral physiology 169
chain of empathy 132, 133, 135, 137, 153-5
  creativisionary strategy and 161, 194-5
  information management and 180-1, 194-5
  organizational management and 166-7, 194-5
  personnel management and 174-5, 194-5
  in product development 73-4, 90
  in R&D 52-3, 57-60 *passim*
  in system development 109
channel-type creation 66-7, 69, 71, 116
Cima (Nissan Motor) 79-83, 88, 89, 90, 166, 180
cognitive psychology 94, 105
company philosophies 65, 67, 69, 77, 82, 88, 90, 105, 106, 107, 112, 144-5, 157, 180
computer integrated manufacturing (CIM) 15, 83, 90, 123-5, 127, 128, 178, 179, 180
computer reservation systems (CRS) 103-4, 106, 109, 180
concentrated (logical) thought 94, 95
concept creation 132, 133, 137, 153-5
  in business development 115, 127
  creativisionary strategy and 159-60, 194-5
  information management and 179-80, 194-5
  organizational management and 165-6, 194-5
  personnel management and 173-4, 194-5
  in product development 78, 178
  in R&D 53, 57-60 *passim*
concept refinement 155, 177, 179-80
conception support systems
  anatomy of ideation/conception 142-5
  concept of 140-2

corporate management and 145, 155, 179
  harbingers of 139-40
  need for 31-2, 137-9
conceptors *see* conception support systems
construction industry
  new fields in 3-11, 13-14
consumption patterns 25, 27, 32, 72, 78
convenience stores 98-100, 106, 108, 109, 135, 161, 181
corporate creation 132, Ch 9
corporate difference (CDI) 118
corporate functions
  creation intensification and 19-20
  externalization of 34-6, 174
  see also under names of individual corporate functions, e.g. research and development
corporate growth
  product life cycles and 23
corporate philosophies *see* company philosophies
creagement 194-5
creation, companies succeeding/failing in 193-7
creation industry
  employment in 38, 40
  growth of 34-7, 42
  structure of 37-9
creation societies 30-34, 38, 42, 43, 133, 138, 152-3, 162-3, 167-8, 175-6, 181-3, 194-5
creativisionary strategy 45-6, 147-8, 152-5, 156-63, 186, 185-90, 192, 194-5
culture, company *see* company philosophies
customer education *see* user education
customer information, sharing of 155, 178-9, 192

De Bono, E 184
decentralized processing 181-3
demand, domestic 17-18, 69
demand, surplus 67-8

Dentsu 139-40
designers, freedom of, in Nissan
    Motor 79-83, 166
detergent industry 75-7, 88, 89-90,
    164, 174, 178, 180
Dewey, J 146
diffuse (empirical) thought 94, 95
discussion
    in business development 120, 128
    intellectual activity and 137, 140
    management for creation and 155,
        157-8, 166, 170, 179, 187
    in product development 73-4, 81,
        84
    in R&D 58-63 *passim*
disposable cameras 77-79, 89-90,
    180
dissent-inducing organization 155,
    165
dissimilation 132, 133, 136-7 153-5
    creativisionary strategy and 158-9,
        194
    information management and 179,
        194
    organizational management and
        165, 194
    personnel management and 173-4,
        194
    in R&D 53, 57-60 *passim*
    in system development 107-108
distribution industry/systems 67, 68,
    76, 92, 96-100, 105-106, 108,
    109, 115-17, 127, 128, 157-8,
    161, 164-5, 180, 181
diversification
    Misawa Home 119-20
Do House Co 100-103, 105-106, 108
Do-sans 100-103, 108
double-loop exchange 175

earthenware aesthetics 80, 88, 89,
    180
economic growth 17, 67-8, 111
education, creativity in 87
empathetic communication 155, 178,
    180-1

empathetic personnel exchange 155,
    174-5
empathy integration 155, 160-1
empathy interface 155, 166-7
employees, management by 117, 164-
    5
employment
    in creation industry 38, 40
enthusiasm-oriented management
    155, 171-2, 185, 190, 193
essence, commitment to 88, 159, 180
evolution of management 147-52
exports, expansion of 16-17, 19, 55,
    68
externalization of corporate functions
    34-6, 174
    see also under names of individual
        corporate functions, e.g. research
        and development

factory automation (FA) 83, 85, 90,
    123, 127
failure, toleration of 117, 122, 127,
    160, 177
fields, next-generation 3-16, 159-60
FINDS (development of what is truly
    needed) 66-7, 69, 74, 77, 82, 88,
    112, 180
flexible manufacturing systems (FMS)
    15
food industry
    new fields in 3-12
four-stage model of creation 52-4,
    57-61, 132-5, 136-7, 153-5
    creativisionary strategy and 156-62,
        195
    information management and 177-
        81, 195
    organizational management and
        163-7, 195
    personnel management and 171-7,
        195
franchises 98-100 *passim*
Fuji Photo Film 77-79, 89-90, 180
Fujitsu 143

Gennai 142

Gordon, W J J 64, 146, 184
governments
    and creativity 42, 44
Gregory, C E 146
group creation 132, 136, 184
    see also corporate creation
Guilford, J P 94, 184

Handycam 55 (Sony 8mm video cam-
    era) 69-71, 88, 89, 90, 135, 158,
    161, 166, 172, 178, 180
Harasaki, Y 184
Hattori, T 184
herbicides 85-7, 90
high-technology industries 55
Higuchi (president, Asahi Breweries)
    73-5
Hirashima, K 184
Hironaka, H 162, 184
Honjo, S 126, 184
hours of work 27-8, 82, 186
hybrid teams 71, 72, 78, 83-4, 90-1,
    105, 124, 127, 128, 155, 165,
    171, 172, 178
hypothesis construction 132-3, 136,
    153-5
    creativisionary strategy and 156-8,
        195
    information management and 178-
        9, 195
    organizational management and
        163-7, 195
    personnel management and 171-2,
        195
    in R&D 52-3, 57-60 *passim*
hypothesis-generating organization
    155, 163-7
hypothesis refinement *see* concept
    refinement

Ibuki, T 184
Ichikawa, K 146
idea co-ordination (IC) 50-4, 57-63,
    155, 174-5
idea engineering 31-2
idea generators (IG) 50-4, 55, 57-63,
    87, 105-107, 124, 127, 128, 155,
    174

idea killers (IK) 50-4, 55, 57-63, 87,
    97-98, 105-107, 108, 124, 125,
    155, 170, 174
idea promoters (IP) 50-4, 57-63, 82,
    87, 90, 105-107, 108, 125, 127, 174
idea proposal systems 102-1, 157,
    164-5
IGKP model 50-4, 55, 57-63, 82, 87,
    90, 97-98, 105-108, 124-8 *pas-
    sim*, 131-2, 154, 155, 170, 174
imitation, companies succeeding/fail-
    ing in 190-4
industrial societies 25-6, 30-5 *pas-
    sim*, 133, 138, 148-53 *passim*,
    162, 167-8, 175-7, 181-2
industrial structure, next-generation
    3-16, 159
information-dependent product devel-
    opment 67-8
information industry 35, 36-7
information intensification
    and consumption patterns 27
    and creation intensification 30-31, 42
        42
    improved productivity through 26
    and information industry 35, 36-7
    and information societies 30-35
        passim, 133, 138, 148-53 *pas-
        sim*, 162, 167-8, 175-7, 181-2
    and product life-cycles 24-5
information management 92-3, 153-
    5, 161-2, 164-5, 177-82, 185-
    90, 191, 193-5
information processing and disposal
    92-3
information societies 30-5 *passim*,
    133, 138, 148-53 *passim*, 162,
    167-8, 175-7, 181-2
information transmission and
    exchange 92-3
intellectual activity 136-45
intelligenceware 56
internationalization
    and creation intensification 16-22
intuition, role of 144

Japanese characteristics 54-5
Japanese companies

management for creation in 185-95
see also under names of individual companies, e.g. Sony
Japanese-style massiveness 80, 82, 89

Kagono, T 184
Kao Co 75-6, 88, 89-90, 164, 172, 178, 180
Katagata, Z 146
Kato, S 169
Kawakita, J 134, 146, 184
Kazuyuki, A 57
key technology, reinforcement of 89-90
KJ method 104, 134, 136-7, 138
know-how, management *see* management know-how
knowledge data bases 140
Kon, I 95
KPS method 95
Kume, Y 81-2, 166

machine vision 83-4, 89, 90
machinery manufacturing 124-5
management for creation Ch 9
    method of creation and 152-5
    see also business development; product development; research and development; system development
management know-how
    categories of 153-85, 194
    implementation of, for creation 183-94
managerial shake-up design 155, 158-9
manufacturing industries
    new fields in 14-5
market surveys
    beer 180
    computer integrated manufacturing 123-4, 128
    computer reservation systems 180
    food products 100-103, 105-106, 108
    parcel shipment 127
marketing personnel
    as market sensors 125, 127

Maslow, A H 25, 27
mass-oriented product development 67-8
material affluence 25, 27-8, 150-1
mature industrialization
    and creation intensification 22-6, 42
meaning-rich information 143
measurement of creativity 32, 43-5.
Meitec (*formerly* Nagoya Technology Centre) 113-15, 127, 128, 133, 179-80
mergers and acquisitions 110-11, 117-18
method of creation, in corporate activities Ch 8
    and management for creation 152-5
    see also business development; four-stage model of creation; product development; research and development; system development
middle management 45, 159, 168
Misaka, Y 81
Misawa Homes 117-21, 127, 128
mixed teams *see* hybrid teams
Murai (president, Asahi Breweries) 73-4

Nakagawa, K 70, 166
Nakayama, M 146
Nakayama, S 101, 184
needs-type creation 66-7, 69, 84, 87, 88, 99, 105, 107, 111-13, 123-5, 150-1, 177, 178-9
network organizations 161, 167-8, 179
neurocomputers 51-2, 56-61, 97, 174, 178
Nissan Motor 79-83, 88, 89, 90, 166, 174, 180
NM method 138
Nomura Research Institute Ltd (NRI) 30, 36, 65, 93, 112, 132, 153, 194
    Strategy for Creation questionnaire (Nov 1989) 3-16, 166-7, 185-95

Nonaka, I 184
non-material affluence 25, 27-9, 150

Oe, T 126, 184
Okura, (president, Yamato Parcel)
    117, 127, 164
Onda, A 87, 146, 184
operation field counsellors (OFC)
    109, 181
organizational management *see* personnel resources
Oriental thought 87
origami 87
Osborn, A F 182, 184

paperweight organizations 167-8
parcel shipment 115-17, 127, 128,
    164-5, 180
Pierce, C S 146
personal difference (PDI) 126
personality, individual
    and creativity 17-18, 105, 126,
    131-2, 135-6, 169, 184
personnel resources
    management of 153-5, 186-7, 169-77, 185-90, 192-5
    organization of 20-22, 55, 61-2,
    71, 74, 97, 105, 147-8, 153-5,
    159, 163-9, 185-90, 191-5
philosophies, company *see* company philosophies
Polanyi, M 184
portfolio personnel management 155,
    173-4
POS systems 15, 24, 68, 92, 99-100,
    102
prefabricated housing 117-21, 127,
    128
price inflation, forecast 17
problem-solving, stages of 146
product development
    case studies 69-88
    companies succeeding/failing in
    creation/imitation 190-3
    creativity in 65-9
    method of and management for creation in 70-71, 73-5, 76-7, 78-9,
    81-4, 87-91

method of and management for creation in 70-71, 73-5, 76-7, 78-9,
    81-4, 87-91
    as subject of creation 19-20, 26, 42-3
product differentiation 70, 77-8
    see also brand-name items
product life cycles 22-5, 41, 66-7
profits
    product life cycles and 22-3
property rights, intellectual 37-9
pyramid organizations 167-8

quality
    in business development 117
    in product development 70. 74, 79

recruitment, personnel 118, 120, 150,
    153, 155, 166, 171, 185, 186,
    190, 193
research and development
    case studies (neural networks) 56-61
    companies succeeding/failing in
    creation/imitation 190-3
    creativity in 49-56
    externalization of 35-6, 57-8, 60,
    63, 87
    Japan's weaknesses in 54-6
    method of and management for creation in 61-3
    as subject of creation 19-20, 26,
    42-4
research of creativity, mapping of 184

scenes of use 70, 71, 77, 88-9, 108
    see also advertising
seeds-type creation 66, 69, 84, 90,
    111-112
Sekiguchi (president, Meitec) 113-15,
    127, 128
self-fulfilment, need for 27-9, 32-3,
    69, 149-50, 156
self-transfer 172, 185-90
service industries
    new fields in 14
Seven-Eleven Japan 98-100, 106, 108,
    109, 135, 161, 181
Shinagawa, Y 184

Shintani, M 184
shortages of goods *see* demand, sur-
    plus
SI model 94
sideline development 165
SINIC theory 95
socialist economies 150-2
Sony 69-71, 88, 89, 90, 135, 158,
    161, 166, 172, 178-9, 180
Sozo creation 46
specialists, access to 181
stand-outs, toleration of 155, 166
steel industry
    new fields in 3-13
strategic information systems (SIS) 96,
    103-105
suggestions, employees' *see* idea pro-
    posal systems
supply, surplus 68
Suzuki (president, Seven-Eleven
    Japan) 99, 161
synetics 64
system development
    and business development 93-5,
        100, 105-106
    case studies 96-105
    companies succeeding/failing in
        creation/imitation 190-3
    creativity in 91-5
    method of and management for cre-
        ation in 97-8, 99-100, 102-103,
        104-9
    as subject of creation 19-20, 26,
        42-3
system image 91-2

tension, atmosphere of 114, 115, 120,
    128, 133, 137
think module (TM) 95
Toffler, A 30
Tokuma, Y 121, 128
Tokuma Shoten Publishing 121-3,
    127, 128
top-level management, commitment
    of 73-4, 97, 104, 105-107, 155,
    159, 161
    see also chain of sympathy
TOPICS system 96-8

Toyo Sash 96-8, 105-106, 108, 109,
    133, 157, 161, 181
TRAIN system 96-8
transdisciplinary personnel 84, 97-8,
    108, 155, 173-4
trial orientation 155, 158-9
trinities
    of creation-intense corporate
        activities 151-4

Umezawa, N 184
United Kingdom
    R&D creativity in 52
United States
    business development in 123-7,
        127, 178, 179, 180
    management for creation in 185-95
    product development in 83-4, 85-
        7, 89
    R&D creativity in 42, 52, 57-61,
        172, 173, 178, 179
    share of new business in manufac-
        turing sector 14
    system development in 103-105,
        106, 109, 180
universities
    and creativity 42, 44, 60, 63
user education 85, 86, 98, 99, 109,
    155, 181
Ushiki, T 184
Utsurundesu (Fuji Photo Film) 77-9,
    89-90, 180

value added 147, 152, 161
value systems 25, 27-9, 41-2
variable thought 162
video cameras 69-71, 88, 89, 90, 135,
    157, 161, 166, 172, 178-9, 180
Von Fange, E K 146
Von Neumann computers 56

Wakabayashi, N 81-4 *passim*
Wallace, G 184
word/image association 141-2

Yamato Transport 115-117, 127, 128,
    164-5, 180
young employees *see* age
Yukawa, H 184